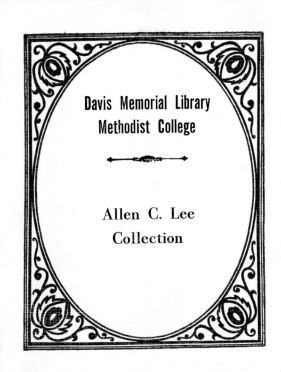

FRANK MASON NORTH

FRANK MASON NORTH

His Social and Ecumenical Mission

Creighton Lacy

ABINGDON PRESS
Nashville • New York

FRANK MASON NORTH: HIS SOCIAL AND ECUMENICAL MISSION

Copyright © 1967 by Abingdon Press

Library of Congress Catalog Card Number: 67-14983

SET UP, PRINTED, AND BOUND BY THE
PARTHENON PRESS, AT NASHVILLE,
TENNESSEE, UNITED STATES OF AMERICA

*In grateful tribute
to my parents,
Carleton and Harriet Lacy,
partners in the
Christian World Mission
of Frank Mason North*

The Life of Trust

Jesus, the calm that fills my breast
No other heart than Thine can give;
This peace unstirred, this joy of rest
None but Thy loved ones can receive.

My weary soul has found a charm
That turns to blessedness my woe;
Within the shelter of Thine arm,
I rest secure from storm and foe.

In desert wastes I feel no dread,
Fearless I walk the trackless sea;
I care not where my way is led,
Since all my life is life with Thee.

O Christ, through changeful years my Guide,
My Comforter in sorrow's night,
My Friend, when friendless,—still abide
My Lord, my Counselor, my Light.

My time, my powers I give to Thee;
My inmost soul 'tis Thine to move;
I wait for Thy eternity,
I wait in peace, in praise, in love.

Magnolia, Massachusetts
1884

FOREWORD

In a sense I owe my life to Frank Mason North. My father, born and raised in a missionary family in China, returned in 1914, after higher education in America, to the land of his birth. As corresponding secretary of the Board of Foreign Missions of the Methodist Episcopal Church, Frank Mason North was his executive officer. Four years later my father brought to New York his bride, a Congregationalist secretary of the Young Women's Christian Association in China, for examination by the personnel committee. Asked what she thought of the Methodist *Discipline,* she replied candidly that she had never read it. With quiet dignity but unmistakable authority Dr. North commented: "I guess any wife that Carleton Lacy chooses must be all right." There was no further questioning.

Still later, following the birth of a son and a brief term of teaching in central China (cut short by a health furlough), that same missionary couple was loaned by the Methodist Board of Foreign Missions to serve the American Bible Society, whose future general secretary was Frank Mason North's son, Eric McCoy North. For a decade and a half Eric North in New York and Carleton Lacy in Shanghai collaborated to create the China Bible House by integrating the Chinese work of the American Bible Society, the British and Foreign Bible Society, and the National Bible Society of Scotland. During a furlough year in 1928-29 the Lacys were often in the Eric North home in Madison, New Jersey, and though I cannot honestly recall meeting Frank Mason North, by then retired but living in the same town, I am sure that I must have done so. Certainly that friendship between our families lay in the background of my long-standing desire to make this study.

In the forefront of that resolution, however, stands a remarkable

9

conjunction of interests. North's two decades in the New York City Church Extension and Missionary Society represent supremely the social gospel in practice, not a shallow humanism or even humanitarianism, but the redemptive love of Jesus Christ applied to the city. Actively for twelve years, and even into his retirement, Frank Mason North presided over the foreign missionary enterprise of the Methodist Episcopal Church. Meanwhile, as one of the founders of the Federal Council of Churches, as its executive chairman from 1912 to 1916 and its president from 1916 to 1920, he laid unshakable foundations for the ecumenical movement in America. In each of these periods his poems expressed his faith—and enabled millions of Christians around the world to sing forth theirs.

Involved from birth in the world mission of the church, trained in Christian social ethics, committed to the ecumenical dimensions of Christian service, I could hardly have avoided the shadow—or, more correctly, the radiance—of Frank Mason North. When Eric North consented to give me access to his father's papers and to assist in any way possible with this study, the prospect was irresistible, though its execution has been long delayed. Back in his senior year in college, in a satirical recitation on chapel orations (see chapter 2) , Frank Mason North set down guidelines for any biography:

In speaking the history of some body, particular stress must be laid on the fact that the individual was born and that he died. These two events may seem to us of trifling importance, but they doubtless had considerable influence on his career. It must also be stated, whether his parents were poor but honest—and whether "he early exhibited those characteristics etc—". At the same time it is strictly necessary not to express any individual opinion in regard to the subject of your sketch. That would be presumptuous. Your own judgment, you know, may be weak—so adopt the critical opinions of other writers—only it is best that they should agree with each other. A man, six dates, and two facts will make a first class biographical oration.

It has been impossible to observe all these strictures—and North himself would never have tried! He was a methodical man who, despite the preservation of a number of youthful writings, con-

10

signed few of his innermost thoughts to paper. Aside from literary
expressions, there are more clues in his files to the youth and
personality of his father than of himself. His available correspondence deals strictly with business. So occupied was he in writing
articles and speeches and sermons that he published no books.

Yet for such materials as are accessible this writer is indebted
beyond measure to the subject's son, Eric M. North; to the
archives of the National Council of the Churches of Christ in the
U.S.A., the Methodist Board of Missions, and the New York City
Society; and to the libraries of Drew University and the Methodist
Board of Missions. More significantly I acknowledge with bound-
less gratitude the personal recollections and interpretations of
Eric North, Bishop Herbert Welch, Arthur B. Moss, Samuel M.
Cavert, Bishop Frederick B. Newell, Lynn Harold Hough, Leland
P. Cary, Henry C. Whyman, the late Harry F. Ward and Frank
T. Cartwright, and others whose lives were touched more briefly
but as brightly by Frank Mason North. The errors in this tribute
are not their fault, but these persons helped make an imposing
hero human.

Creighton Lacy

Duke University

CONTENTS

Texts of Hymns and Poems
by Frank Mason North

Looking Seaward

Bear swift my thoughts, O Ocean wide,
On currents deep to harbors far;
Like light-winged ships they skim thy shifting tide
And shake defiant sails against thy fiercest roar.

With eager keels they speed away
In search of lands no eye has seen;
In storm and calm their untried course they lay
And boldly turn their prows where man has never been.

For out beyond horizons dim,
Beyond that far uncertain line
Where meet the sea and sky in circling rim,
There may be mines of gold in continents Divine.

This little harbor, locked in land,
This narrow strip of rugged shore
Mark not the limit of my soul's demand,
Intent the vast, unmeasured regions to explore.

The sweep of man's unaided sight
Discovers not the truths most rare;
Not on this side that line of curving light
Are found the broadest seas and lands, or days most fair.

Ah! blessed God,—out on the sea
I send my thoughts in ardent quest
For riches rare, in realms known but to Thee;
Guide Thou my ships to lands of peace and harbors blest.

Magnolia, Massachusetts
1884

1

"The Mysteries of Life Begin"

The love of God which lived in Thee
Was nurtured at thy mother's knee;
Thy kinship with the world of men
Was deepened, stirred, and strengthened then.

A psychoanalyst might have some peculiar explanation
of the little boy in northern New York who delighted to climb
roofs. On one occasion the youngster mounted a ladder to peer
into a bird's nest, then hid behind the chimney when the store-
keeper came out to investigate. The second time his presence was
discovered, he was ordered off with a whip. Another time Charles
North climbed onto his own roof and down the chimney into his
mother's third-story room—a miniature and presumably sooty
Santa Claus. Twice he came near drowning in the nearby river he
deeply loved.

His family and neighbors may well have concluded he was
predestined for something! Charles Carter North had been born,
the eldest son (fifth child) of Benjamin (1793-1833), and Hannah
Carter North (1791-1879), in Walton, New York, on February
19, 1819. (His first "American" ancestor, Thomas North, had
settled in Dorchester, Massachusetts, in 1670.) Within a few
months Benjamin's family moved to Jefferson County. There,
during a "revival of religion," they joined the Presbyterian
Church, and Charles was baptized. A vigorous, cheerful leader
in sports, the boy (according to his wife's later report) was "too
fond of mischief and play to become a very brilliant student, so
that when obliged to enter upon the active duties of life, and

17

feeling his deficiencies, he endeavored to make up for misspent opportunities by improving every spare moment."

That responsibility came early. By the time he was fifteen, his father had died, and Charles undertook to help his mother in the support of the other children. Four years later a relative arranged for his employment in Alabama, and Charles—still an adventurous teen-ager—set out by sea. The voyage from New York to Mobile took seventeen days. "Very seasick, but upon the whole have enjoyed myself well," he reported. Arriving on a Friday (November 2, 1838), he presented his letters of recommendation *and* his church certificate on Saturday, joined the church and Sunday school and wrote home on Sunday. "I think there is a broad field for usefulness" in the Sunday school, he observed, and before long was teaching a class of boys.

Of his work he said very little. "Oh! Ma! our store is one of the most beautiful in Mobile and some pretend to say that it has not got its equal. *My* desk is completely out of sight." He boasted at securing his board (and room?) for $25-$30 when others he knew were paying $35-$50. After three months he reported proudly, "All I've spent unnecessarily since coming has been from 2 to 3 dollars." Apparently he sent money home regularly for his mother's rent but felt hurt when she made a special request. Later he apologized for his pique and urged his mother to let him know of major needs so that he might anticipate the payments.

Mobile must have been pictured in those days as a wicked city. In his very first letter home Charles North had explained his prompt attendance at church as follows: "You perceive that I am determined to employ the one safeguard against the many—very many vices of this place." Two weeks later he added:

In regard to [Mobile's] wickedness [my expectations] have been realized, but in regard to its good society, its religious and literary associations, they have been more than realized. . . . I feel no disposition to neglect my Christian duties, or deny my Lord and Master; on the contrary, according to a resolution which I made before leaving New York, have come out and boldly declared (on suitable occasions) that my determination is to serve God and pursue righteousness, even while surrounded by a multitude who seek to do Evil continually.

18

For example (from a subsequent letter), "On Christmas night the bewitching egg-nogg was presented to my lips, but I refused." North was determined to take advantage of cultural opportunities and to further his education. Despite the temptations of Mobile, he wrote his family that "it will be a fine place for this little intellect to expand in." He gave up Latin studies for science, English classics, and grammar. A phrenology lecturer, he reported, had felt his head and concluded that this young man possessed "ambition and perseverance prodigious," plus excellent literary talents. His only implementation of this talent seems to have been "occasional" verse, on the death of a friend and on a birthday cake. After more than a year in the South Charles joined his "brother pat-riots" in the local militia and described them thus: "We looked like loafers, felt like loafers, and marched like loafers—besides having loafer officers." All in all, "my health is fine; my prospects for heaven and earth are brightening."

Whether from homesickness or filial concern, the young clerk maintained a steady correspondence with his family. In one letter he would admonish his brother to learn to write better; in several he expressed concern for his sister's spiritual welfare: "Tell me in your next how your soul prospers, we really are too temporal." Even to his mother he appealed: "Mother, Religion is prospering in *my* soul. . . . Will you tell me in your next how you and sisters and brother are getting on in the divine life." A year later he remarked that he would not miss his family so keenly if he were assured they would all go to heaven.

Charles North, just turned twenty, did not stop with pious contemplation about the state of his soul. He devoted his energy to humanitarian needs at their worst. In October, 1839, fires laid waste a third of the city of Mobile, and Charles spared no effort to help. The preceding month he had been ill with yellow fever, presumably contracted as a result of his selfless service during the epidemic. In fact, he quoted his landlady as saying that "my mother ought to be thankful that I'm alive, for I've been in every Irish hovel and negro hut in this part of the city."

That was another thing about which he wrote little but must have felt much—the race question. In answer to his mother's caution soon after his arrival in the South he replied: "I really

19

am prudent! I shall neither write or speak on a certain subject altho' my opinions are the same." Two years later, describing a friend and business associate, North wrote: "He liberated some years since a large number of his negroes and sent them to *Liberia.* This act will give you an idea of his firmness as a Christian."

In addition to his youth and his restlessness—or perhaps because of both—a further anxiety gnawed at the boy's heart. He had left a girl behind, a girl whose affections he did not doubt but whose parents had forbidden any communication. "Tell her [Elizabeth Mason]," he wrote thirteen months after his departure from home, "that she is daily fervently remembered before a throne of grace, that I am faithful and true, and that I calculate as much as ever—yea, more—upon a union with her. . . . Ask her if she has not yet *negotiated* for a correspondence between us."

A short time earlier Charles had retorted in adolescent indignation to his sister's report that Elizabeth was getting fat:

You need not try to scare me off from the track or swerver [*sic*] my resolutions by such doleful, woeful sort of representation about her accumulated flesh! . . . Her constancy amid opposition has ever been great! And because she had involuntarily increased in flesh, is this an apology for my sneaking off? My honor is at stake, laying aside any affection for her.

And he follows with another expression of concern for his sister's religion!

It is hard to understand why the Mason family should have objected so strongly to Charles Carter North, except as an indigent orphan. Thomas Mason (1787-1843) was book agent for the Methodist Episcopal Church. He had been assistant editor and general steward in the Methodist Book Concern from 1819 to 1824, when his "constitutional term" expired, and apparently resumed the post in 1833. At least the *Journal* of the General Conference of 1840 reports that "Thomas Mason was elected principal Book Agent at New-York, and George Lane assistant Agent." [1] Furthermore, since the "officiary of the Missionary Society was closely tied in with that of the Methodist Book

[1] *Journal,* General Conference of the Methodist Episcopal Church, 1840, p. 119.

Concern," [2] Mason seems to have served (from 1819 to 1825 at least) as corresponding secretary of the Missionary Society, almost a century before his grandson occupied a similar position, and *The History of American Methodism*[3] lists Mason as one of the founders of the Missionary Society in 1819, along with Nathan Bangs, Freeborn Garrettson, Joshua Soule, and five others.

His wife, Mary W. Morgan Mason, had founded or aided the Methodist Home for the Aged in the Bronx, the Woman's Hospital, the Colored Orphan Asylum, the Five Points Mission, the first Methodist Sunday school in New York. She was also the first directress of the Female Missionary Society of New York, an auxiliary to the Missionary and Bible Society. That organization provided hospitality for returning missionaries from Africa and aided Indian converts of John Stewart and J. B. Finley. The noted missionary from the northwest, Jason Lee, delivered an address at the twentieth annual meeting. When the family moved to Troy in 1828, Mrs. Mason organized a Female Branch Missionary Society and later the first Juvenile Missionary Society.

On New Year's Day, 1840, Charles North confessed again his loneliness and despair. "I ardently and devotedly love *one* whom I am debarred all intercourse with. . . . I know that she is unchanging—but parental authority still keeps us apart." Six months later, faithful to both love and honor, he wrote: "I do not send my love to E.—for I wish none to charge me with being underhanded." Whatever the objection on the part of the Masons, it was ironically lifted by a change of circumstances. In October, 1841, North (whose other pertinent letters are missing) commented to his family: "Poor Lib Mason, how heavy her task must be to take charge of that school and bear the brunt of her father's disgrace."

The precise nature of the scandal remains veiled in mystery— or lost in history. On September 30, 1840, the *Christian Advocate and Journal* proclaimed on its masthead, as usual: "Published by T. Mason and G. Lane for the Methodist Episcopal Church."

[2] Wade Crawford Barclay, *Early American Methodism, 1769-1844*, I (New York: Board of Missions and Church Extension, 1949), 287.
[3] (Nashville: Abingdon Press, 1964), I, 590; cf. Barclay, *Early American Methodism*, p. 206.

A week later it read: "Published by G. Lane for the Methodist Episcopal Church." The present author and others have assumed that some kind of embezzlement or "financial defalcation" had taken place. But tucked away in both the above issues, its twelve lines easily overlooked, appeared this item, quoted in its entirety:

Agency of the Book Concern—The connection of Thomas Mason with the above agency has been dissolved. The Concern will be conducted in future by George Lane, as sole agent; and all persons having business therewith will please address themselves to him only.

To allay any apprehension concerning the financial affairs of the Concern which the above announcement might occasion, we are authorized to say, that Mr. Mason's business transactions as agent have been performed with fidelity. The Book Committee have had the necessary investigations made, and this fact has been fully ascertained.[4]

This notice—if fully truthful—would seem to exclude any kind of fiscal fraud, but no other clues have been discovered. On May 19, 1841, the New York Annual Conference answered its traditional Question 9, "Who have been expelled from the connection this year?" with two names: Thomas Mason, David Plumb.[5] No public explanation was ever given, no discussion in the *Minutes,* no Conference obituary when he died three years later. As one unsuccessful investigator remarked, "Both church and family simply drew a curtain."

Meanwhile North's fortunes in Mobile improved. He changed jobs, first to a bank at $1,500 a year, and wrote optimistically about "better pecuniary circumstances . . . to give you a more comfortable support. . . . I am happy temporally and spiritually." But in January, 1841, the bank closed down five positions and fired young North. Charles headed up the Tombigbee River to Columbus, Mississippi, where he bought a store (at "North's Corner") with a small stock of goods and set up partnership with a Mr. D. C. Lowber in Mobile, each to have exclusive local handling of wholesale and retail groceries. He also purchased cotton and hides and corn from Mobile. With the business came "a negro

---

[4] *Christian Advocate and Journal,* September 30 and October 7, 1840.
[5] *Minutes,* New York Annual Conference, 1841, p. 139.

man to work around the store, etc. He is a fine fellow, and to add dignity to the concern—he is married."

During this period North maintained an increasingly active role in the church. In Mobile he had started an Infant School (kindergarten) and a Juvenile Missionary Society. He had recently been elected librarian of the Sabbath School, receiving nineteen of the twenty votes cast. In Columbus he continued Sunday-school teaching and prepared addresses, a dialogue, and children's recitations for an anniversary program. Here, however, he found that most of the first families were Methodist and seems to have labeled his business "Methodist Temperance Store." ("My terms are cash, and no Mississippi money is passable.") (In 1904 a resident of Columbus located an elderly citizen, Dr. W. L. Lipscomb, who "has a pleasant recollection of Mr. North, says he was a faithful church worker and was the first to build up a good lively Sabbath School here." [6])

Very soon North began serving as a Methodist exhorter and accepted a license. For two weeks he accompanied a circuit rider on his rounds, staying in log cabins and adding his witness. In answer to his mother's somewhat anxious inquiries, he replied: "Yes, mother, stood up in the pulpit, took my text and spoke from it, the first time about half hour, the next time an hour. . . . No, mother, God does not call me to preach, but to attend to my business, which I shall do till he directs me otherwise." Between his arrival at Columbus, Mississippi, in March, 1841, and Christmas of that year, a second and third Methodist Churches were started, with a total of a thousand members, white and black. Furthermore, "temperance has shed her gracious rays abroad here," so that several liquor shops closed, between two and three thousand signed the abstinence pledge, and unsold liquor had to be shipped back north.

Shortly after arriving at Columbus, Charles had written home, "The best of all is, God is my friend." Undoubtedly one major reason for this conviction was the fact that letters were finally coming from Elizabeth Mason, even before "her father's disgrace." Now that his business was prospering, Charles resolved to go home

[6] J. M. Shumpert, letter to F. M. North, April 6, 1904 (in North files).

and claim his bride. "Though I am pleased with the openness and frankness and warm-heartedness of Southerners, yet I prefer the dignity, the chastness [sic], the justice and lasting friendship of the Northerners."

For a while it looked as if his plans were to be thwarted once more. In April, 1842, the partner in Mobile failed, but North succeeded in buying him out without serious loss. Less than three weeks later he reported: "I have just received notice that the boat on which about $1800 of my goods were on [sic] is sunk—but thank the Lord I was prudent enought [sic] to Insure." By summer, however, he was able to leave the business and return home to New York, for the first time since he left as a nineteen-year-old "greenhorn" four years before.

Charles Carter North (1819-90) and Elizabeth Mason (1820-92) were married on August 24, 1842. From this point on her letters often reveal more than his about this young couple and their life on the southern frontier. They sailed to Mobile in October and then pressed on to Columbus, part of the journey on foot, staying in homes of Negroes. Not all city-bred daughters have to put into practice their mothers' dedication to missionary austerities. While Elizabeth added feminine touches to a bare house, Charles worked outside, getting "his lips [sunburned] so bad that he could not laugh, nor even kiss!"

Realism readily shatters illusion, even if it strengthens love. Two months after their arrival in Mississippi Elizabeth wrote of her husband's religious activities: "It is really amusing to hear him dignified with clerical honors, for I am sure no man living ever looked less ministerial." "Exceedingly unbecoming and loaferish," she called him in the same letter, and so absentminded that she found him "diligently engaged in scrubbing his nails with his tooth brush!" But he had been living the bachelor life for four years, and she was fresh from the elegant East. Yet nearly two years after the wedding, Charles could write honestly: "The married life to me is no romance—it is a happy reality."

Ever since 1840—perhaps much earlier—Charles North had expressed his ambition to be an independent farmer or a country gentleman. He had written from Mobile, "I do not like this country, only for making money." Still talking of farming in

24

Illinois, he tried to convince his mother (not his wife) that he would have greater independence, freer time for mind and body, "freedom to worship God! I can worship God at the plough handle—I can fall on my knees at the end of a furrough and commune with my God."

A stronger pressure was to pry him out of the South. In 1845 the church in Columbus voted 169 to 3 to follow the new separatist Methodist Episcopal Church, South. The three dissenting ballots were cast by Charles and Elizabeth North and Charles's sister, who was staying with them. With one small child and another due shortly, they started home, overland, taking with them "Black Harry," a freed slave. Back in New York, with practically all their financial resources left behind, the Norths began a new life, not as Illinois farmers, but as a merchant family in the great metropolis.

Charles North had a remarkable knack for picking up the pieces of commercial ventures and constructing an even firmer edifice. To put it mildly, business flourished. So did his contributions to the church. In New York, as in Mobile and Columbus, the Norths remained constant in church attendance and philanthropic work. Charles not only found time for Sunday "exhortations" in Sing Sing Prison but frequently helped former convicts find a place in society. He was one of the founders of Drew University, a charter member and first secretary of its Board of Trustees, and also a trustee of Wesleyan University from 1864 to 1882 (chairman, 1871-78). As a member of the Methodist Board of Education, he helped plan the observance of American Methodism's centenary in 1866, served as first (unsalaried) secretary of the Board from 1866 to 1868, and initiated collections for the Methodist Student Loan Fund.

It has often been said that Charles Carter North was the founder of Children's Day. When, at his death, George R. Crooks published a eulogy under that title, Frank Mason North hastened to correct the story.[7] Charles North, he pointed out, had served on a subcommittee of six, had been chosen to speak before the General Committee, and wrote the official recommendation to

[7] F. M. North, letter to George R. Crooks, January 2, 1891 (Drew Library archives).

the General Conference. However, he had dictated a statement in June of 1888 to this effect: "Your officers and teachers are accustomed to call me the 'father of Children's Day.' This is not strictly true. There were several fathers of whom I am but one. I have been so-called for my greater activity in promoting the scheme." Then, with typical family modesty, the son asked for a public denial of "*exclusive* honors in which he had only a share." "My regret now is this—" Frank Mason North explained, "that by the very effort to do his memory honor—the general public will surmise that he has claimed a position which now his long-time friend [Crooks?] has shown was not justly made—and will suspect the existence of a difference concerning the facts as between yourself and him."

Elizabeth North followed in her mother's footsteps and kept pace with her husband. "Devoted to her family" (as her son often declared), she mothered eight children of her own and countless more through the American Female Guardian Society and the Home for the Friendless, which she served as president of the Board of Managers for many years. That organization undertook such diverse civic functions as providing matrons at city prisons, getting truancy officers appointed, establishing industrial schools, and opening a permanent hostel on East 30th Street.

In the One Hundredth Annual Report of the Society, presented in 1934, the spirit of the organization was summarized thus: "Here was not only rescue from evil, but preparation for good, not alone cure but prevention; here was more than correction, here was guidance; more than escape from ignorance, here was inducement to knowledge; it meant more than restraint, it planned for character." Elizabeth North presided over this Society from 1874 to 1892. Sometimes one or more of her children sat through these Board meetings, absorbing a bit of this philosophy, observing what the Centennial report called "the presence and power of personality at work."

For intermittent months before his death in 1890 Charles Carter North spent his time as a patient in a sanatarium in Clifton Springs, New York. A woman who knew him there recalled much later how joyfully the children used to gather around Mr. North on the porch, or how (despite Parkinson's disease) he would lead a parade across the grounds, with the nearest youngster hanging to his coattails. "We all were lifted, strengthened and cheered by the courage and kindness with which he played with the children in his last illness." His body lies buried in Sleepy Hollow Cemetery, Tarrytown, New York. In the family record is a statement to the effect that "the last few months of his life he gave evidence of being a new creature in Christ Jesus."

It would be difficult to describe or define such an observation. Charles Carter North was undoubtedly a remarkable man. As a businessman, he handled both commercial and philanthropic affairs with efficiency. As a churchman, he not only participated actively in Sunday school and congregational life but actually initiated new programs and outreach for the Methodist Episcopal Church. As a Christian layman, he never hesitated to make his personal witness, whether on the Mississippi frontier or at Sing Sing on the Hudson. His scrupulous sense of honor and of moral purity was Victorian virtue at its best. His energetic concern for yellow fever victims in the hovels of Mobile or for prostitutes and prisoners in the courtrooms of Manhattan represented Christian compassion at *its* best. As a stern but loving father, he mourned not only his children who died in childhood, but his eldest son, a distinguished clergyman, killed in a tragic accident the year before his own death.

His third and most famous son was very much like his father. Arlo Ayres Brown, for many years president of Drew University and a close family friend, commented: "I have long wondered what made this son of well-to-do parents a social prophet." Obviously he did not know the story of Charles Carter North. Of his own commitment Frank Mason North once wrote: "Out of a merchant's home, where he learned that honorable losses were less to be feared than doubtful profits, came another whose unconscious training then determines the principles of action now." [8] Less than three weeks after he died (December 17, 1935),

[8] "Preparation of Ministers for Social Work: The Preparation in Life," *Methodist Review*, September, 1911, p. 673.

his widow wrote to his long-time friend and colleague, Worth M. Tippy: "His interest in social service was, first of all, an inheritance." So was his executive talent; so was his devotion to the church. But inheritance, too, is a gift from God. Frank Mason North received a goodly heritage.

Chastened

How softly tread the spectres of our sorrow
 About our sunniest way!
How gently rest the shadows of to-morrow
 Upon our path to-day!

Beneath the laugh of pleasures evanescent
 The heart remembers pain
And catches from the hilltops of the present
 The sound of coming rain.

Yet not the skies in which no clouds are drifting
 Reveal the beauty rare
Of those whose veiléd smiles are ever shifting
 Their half-lights everywhere.

We turn unblessed from faces fresh with beauty,
 Unsoftened yet by fears,
To those whose lines are chased by pain and duty
 And know the touch of tears.

The heart whose chords the gentle hand of sadness
 Has touched in minor strain
Is filled with gracious joys and knows a gladness
 All others seek in vain.

How poor a life where pathos tells no story,
Whose pathways reach no shrine,
Which, free from suffering, misses too the glory
Of sympathies Divine!

Some day our souls may face the sun unclouded
And bear its wonders near;
'Tis well awhile to gaze on visions shrouded
In earthly atmosphere.

1885

2

"O Morning Land"

Where lies our path? We seek to know,
To measure life, to find
The hidden springs of truth whence flow
The joys of heart and mind.

The residential moves of Charles and Elizabeth North might almost represent a graph of changing New York. During the third quarter of the nineteenth century they lived in a dozen different places, not counting their country home of Ashridge. North and south, east and west, uptown and downtown, they migrated as business and society and income and even the city itself shifted. Second Street, Manhattanville (143rd Street), 186 East 15th Street, 220 West 30th Street, Scarborough, 25th Street near Seventh Avenue, 61 Madison Avenue, 361 West 19th Street, 229 East 57th Street, 7 West 129th Street, 1961 Madison Avenue, *et cetera, et cetera.*

Frank Mason North was born at #12 Second Street on December 3, 1850. There were three older children and four younger. Mary Elizabeth (born in Columbus, Mississippi, in 1843) died of "consumption," as did one younger sister. Charles Randolph (1845-89) was struck and killed by a train at Mott Haven, Long Island, while serving as corresponding secretary of the New York City Church Extension and Missionary Society. Gabriel Adolphus (1848-66) died at sea of "consumption." Lila (1854-1920) conducted a private school and later taught Greek at Goucher College. Only younger brother Ernest (1858-1945), besides Mason, lived to be over eighty, a dealer in rare books and long

31

an employee of Charles Scribner's Sons. His twin brother Albert had died in 1886. Though he could not remember living there as a baby, Frank Mason North once took a camera to Second Street to photograph his birthplace. Immediately a man rushed out to protest, offering him money not to take a picture, lest it be used for political muckraking or legal action against the owner. Time had altered the neighborhood in many ways, but North assured the man that he had only a sentimental interest.

When he was old enough, Mason attended Dr. McElligott's School—and played prisoner's base in nearby Madison Square. He joined the Methodist Episcopal Church at the age of eight, "after a religious experience always vivid in his memory." As he himself described it nearly seventy years later, "I made for my boy-self experiment of repentance for sin of which I felt personal guilt, and of faith in Jesus Christ as Saviour." [1] Once in a while his mother would take him to board meetings of the American Female Guardian Society, where Mason would dangle his legs and spell out the inscription over the folding doors: "God setteth the solitary in families." "I used to read it," he recalled at the age of 81, "and remember my own delightful home." Little did he imagine that he would one day serve on the Board of Counsellors of this welfare society and Home for the Friendless.

Throughout his life, Frank Mason North belonged to innumerable clubs and discussion groups of various kinds, practically all of them for intellectual stimulation and fellowship, not sheer recreation. Even in adolescence he took part in Phi Sigma, a high school society, and in his valedictory there urged his classmates to go forth to business or professional pursuits "as men and Christians . . . true to ourselves, humanity and our Maker." He also indulged in extremely fanciful literary productions in co-authorship with a friend, B. I. Gilman. One of these followed the pattern of *Canterbury Tales;* several interludes and at least one dramatic episode by North are still extant. Apparently their composition followed the technique described in one of these sketches: "Throwing the reins loose upon the neck of my imagination, I let it run."

---

[1] "Why I Am a Methodist," *The Forum*, July, 1926, p. 71.

A similar but apparently independent essay describes in romantic detail a scene in Spain, "From the Study of Don Vascone." Beginning with the sights and sounds and moods of dawn, the youthful author remarks: "The student and the man of literary taste can—notwithstanding the contrary opinion of men—sometimes see beauties and subjects of admiration elsewhere than in his books." But he promptly turns his attention to the library around him, where are found "the speculative theories of philosophers—the diplomacies and political economy of statesmen—the vagaries of poets, the theology of divines—the researches of travelers—the creations [he first wrote "fancies" and changed it] of novelists—in truth many subjects are represented in these books from the sublime to the ridiculous,—and from the most profound to the lightest." North also wrote (in June of 1868, on the threshold of college) "A Dream" of how Hope led him in dazzling light out from the sad and dark and gloomy forest in which he wandered.

That fall Mason North went up to Wesleyan University, Middletown, Connecticut (#984),[2] where his brother Charles had been graduated (#854) the year before. During his academic career he won prizes in Greek and Latin, in mental and moral philosophy, and in natural philosophy. He achieved top scholastic honors and Phi Beta Kappa. Meanwhile he served as president of the Missionary Lyceum, leader of the Chapel Choir, and music director of Class Day. An assortment of academic papers, carefully labeled and hoarded, indicates something of his breadth of interest but very little about his depth of feeling. In politics he wrote about republicanism in France, Louis Napoleon, and the Webster-Haynes Debate on public lands, "the heresy of State Rights," and slavery. A speech entitled "Ought the Right of Suffrage in a Republic to be limited by an Educational Provision?" (October 7, 1869) bears a notation, "early in sophomore year"—as if recognizing (perhaps as late as 1934, when other notes were added) the "sophomoric" character of some of his views. In this address he made reference to "ignorant foreigners" and to immigrants "ignorant of the first principles of government,

[2] Each student at Wesleyan University was assigned a number, in order of matriculation, long before the days of IBM cards.

and unacquainted with men and measures." In sober earnestness, with none of his occasional irony, North reached the conclusion that "the country needs statesmen, not pot-house [sic] politicians," and that government in a republic ought to be "not by the ignorant and prejudiced, but by the intelligent and educated." To arrive at this aristocratic verdict he accepted the pedagogical view derived perhaps from his emphasis on the Greek classics, that "as men become more educated, they become less vicious and degraded . . . [displaying] an increase of virtue and a more vigorous defense of right."

In oratory North followed the impressive style which he ascribed to Daniel Webster: "Its distinguishing characteristics are grandeur and dignity. It is like his physique, imposing; like his intellect deep and broad." But young North possessed also an undercurrent of satirical wit which bubbled up frequently among friends, rarely in public. Somewhat austere and formidable in his later years, he could disguise a prank more readily than most people. It was a Wesleyan tradition to have students deliver chapel orations. Occasionally, under the stress of public performance, North would forget his carefully prepared and memorized addresses. One morning he planned a speech with such a breakdown deliberately simulated. In the middle of a trite opening paragraph he exclaimed:

Well, there! I was sure I knew that thing! I commenced to commit it three weeks ago! It beats all creation how a man can spontaneously forget all he ever knew. Why, my mind is as innocent of ideas at this present moment as the palm of my hand is of hair. What a nuisance these chapel orations are, anyhow! They are a subjective and objective bore . . . false in theory—and particularly pernicious in practice.

From there he proceeded to launch into a brilliantly devastating analysis of chapel orations—all duly recorded ahead of time in his neat penmanship. He called such recitations "the action of gas on library deposits," ridiculed the "insane idea that an oration . . . must be written about something," and deplored arbitrary assignments of length "when a man's eloquence runs out with the six hundredth word, so that he is generally done—

though often unconscious of the fact—by the time he is half through."

Somewhere in the course of this *tour de force* the suspicious college president interrupted to inquire: "Mr. North, are you delivering your oration?" "President Cummings, I am," Mason replied—and continued to the end. That "end" was indeed expressive. Comparing these tedious speeches to a dog just clambering out of the water, North said: "You know how he begins to shake at his head, lets it wiggle down his body—and sends it off the end of his tail with a little jerk. Well, so these orations commence at the head with a wondrous shaking and spluttering, but the shake goes off at the tail with an indescribably insignificant wiggle." "I thought perhaps my real oration would come to me if I waited long enough," he concluded, still upholding the pretense, "but it has given me the slip—so I will not detain you any longer." It is reported to this day that the president was furious, not only with North, but with the speech advisor for permitting such a mockery of formal exercises. But the student orator himself labeled it many years later "my only really successful Chapel oration."

North's athletic record at Wesleyan was probably unique. Plagued with an abnormally rapid heartbeat from early youth, he was forbidden to participate in strenuous sports. Nevertheless, he played second base on the baseball team, with a substitute runner when he batted, and was chosen president of the club (i.e., team captain). Likewise in rowing, despite his apparent vigor he had to take the seat of coxswain but was elected president of the crew. When, at work in his father's office during his first year out of college, he felt the call to the Christian ministry, two top physicians warned him that he could not last a year on a fully active schedule because of this heart condition! Fifty years later he remarked to a group discussing life insurance that he had been turned down by a medical examination in his twenties.[3]

Three years after receiving his B.A. degree from Wesleyan in 1872, North was given an M.A. From 1899 until the end of his life he served on the Board of Trustees of Wesleyan University

[3] Loyd F. Worley, letter to the author, July 24, 1965.

and from 1907 on as a trustee of Drew University and Theological Seminary. Into these two educational institutions he poured a boundless quantity of time and energy, thought and prayer. In addition to the beloved "Students' Hymn," North proved his affection for the academic world by writing "O Morning Land of College Days" in 1891 and forty years later, for the centennial of his alma mater, "Wesleyan University, 1831-1931." Among his "occasional verses" was found the following, entitled "An Undergraduate":

'Twas but a by-scene of Commencement Day,
It had no place in scheme of graduation,
Yet men who saw and caught its meaning say
A truth was in it which will bear relation.

From chapel door moved out the long parade,
The great and wise and honored in procession,
Trustees and teachers, wits of every grade,
And men of law renowned in their profession.

A train of clergy, each with his D.D.
In proud possession, or in hope awaited,
And Learning's wards, and men of low degree,
And scholars who in fame are still belated.

Here were the callow preening for first flight,
And others, strong-winged, after years of flying,
The few whose pinions have out-worn the night,
The many who must be content with trying.

Here side by side were hoary age and youth,
And conquest arm-in-arm with crude ambition,
Misanthropy in touch with ardent truth,
Life yet unlived and life but a tradition.

On moved they all in column grave and slow
To share and grace the stately demonstration,
Just past a curtained window set full low,
A point of view for easy observation.

Wherein the pageant saw an etching rare
Of dimpling smiles subdued into sedateness,
While he—the two-years' rogue—so sweet and fair,
Just shook his curls and—kissed his hand to greatness.

Which would you be, you men of honored life,
And you whom fame, reluctant, ever misses,
Yourselves, the strong and struggling sons of strife,
Or just the child who laughed and threw the kisses?

This little ode to his son was composed in 1890 when its author was still among "a train of clergy, . . . with his D.D. . . . in hope awaited." His alma mater bestowed that honorary degree upon him in 1894, and in 1918 added an LL.D. Among the "men of honored life . . . whose pinions have out-worn the night," Frank Mason North remained the poet, grave and sedate, yet always aware of the child in the window.

After less than a year in his father's business office in New York City, North decided the world of commerce was not for him and he was not for it. Without any theological training—other than the classical education then provided in any respectable college!— North joined the New York Conference, was ordained to the Methodist ministry, and began serving his first parish in 1873. During the next fifteen years his pastoral appointments included two villages, two large towns, and two city charges: Florida (N. Y.), Amenia, Cold Spring, 109th Street (New York city mission), White Plains, and West Harlem. This variety gave to North a breadth of experience and a depth of sympathy which were to prove invaluable when he returned to New York to direct the City Society.

In May, 1874, Frank Mason North was married by Bishop Matthew Simpson to Fannie Laws Stewart of Philadelphia. She was an Episcopalian, more than three years older than he, converted to a vital Christian faith "while singing in Maryland in 1870." A son, Adolphus Stewart North (1875-1913), was born the next year, destined to join the loyal line of Wesleyan graduates (#2030). A second son, Mason Longacre North (1877-78), did not live to see his first birthday. Still more heart-breaking for the young minister, his wife died of tuberculosis on December 22, 1878. In the flowery style of the day the *Christian Advocate* reported: "Sickness came, long continued and wasting, involving resort to a Sanatarium, and separation from child, husband and friends. . . . She was the first to note the signs portending her

37

dissolution, and fixing her gaze steadily upon her husband, she quietly passed away." [4] North was desolate. A younger sister Lila cared for Adolphus for his first seven years, but Frank Mason North suffered almost unbearable loneliness. Undoubtedly he grew in wisdom and in spiritual stature, and in favor with his parishioners and his clerical colleagues. But there was little enthusiasm, little incentive, in his ministry.

In the summer of 1879 friends persuaded North to join them at Old Orchard, Maine. There he met Louise Josephine McCoy, of Lowell, Massachusetts. She was cultured and intelligent, a member of the first (1879) graduating class from Wellesley College. More important for a sad and somewhat withdrawn widower, she was attractive, lively, full of fun. They swam and played anagrams; then she departed for a year of study in Germany and travel in France and Italy.

Louise McCoy's mother was a staunch New England Congregationalist. She had no intention of letting her daughter marry a widowed Methodist preacher nine years older. In fact, she forbade her loyal daughter even to communicate with him, yet on each of Louise's birthdays a dozen roses arrived at Wellesley College, where she was teaching Greek following her return from Europe. After some years of silence her mother relented. Dean Lynn Harold Hough of Drew, a long-time family friend, expressed the opinion that Louise McCoy might have become president of Wellesley College but preferred marriage instead. She and North were married on December 23, 1885, in the first wedding to be conducted in the college chapel. President Alice Freeman (later Mrs. George Herbert Palmer) was one of the bridesmaids.

A few months before this second marriage, North had revealed his own scars in a little verse entitled "Chastened":

> How swiftly tread the spectres of our sorrow
>   About our sunniest way!
> How gently rest the shadows of tomorrow
>   Upon our path to-day!
> Beneath the laugh of pleasures evanescent
>   The heart remembers pain

[4] February 6, 1879.

And catches from the hilltops of the present
The sound of coming rain. . . .
The heart whose chords the gentle hand of sadness
Has touched in minor strain
Is filled with gracious joys and knows a gladness
All others seek in vain.

It was a happy marriage. Louise North never sought the limelight beside her husband. But her own talents and interests kept her busy at a thousand good works. Eric McCoy North was born on June 22, 1888. His mother kept up her "intellectual pursuits" after leaving the Wellesley faculty and later served as a trustee of her alma mater from 1894 to 1927 and as honorary trustee until her death in 1939. For her husband's magazine, *The Christian City*, she often wrote book reviews on such topics as *Prophecy and History in Relation to the Messiah, Epic of the Inner Life,* and discussions of the Oxyrynchus excavations and papyri Logia. Years later, after North's retirement, she taught Greek at Drew for three years. In 1926 she published *The Story of the New York Branch of the Woman's Foreign Missionary Society of the Methodist Episcopal Church,* an organization which she traced back to the Female Missionary Society of New York, founded by her husband's grandmother in 1819.

In their home the Norths were called Pāter and Māter (with the flat English pronunciation) by their children and grandchildren. Outsiders regarded North as dignified, reserved, even solemn. Indeed he often was, and a man of his stately build always appears more so. Photographs taken prior to 1905 show long bushy sideburns growing down to his jaw bone. His Memoir in the New York East Annual Conference *Journal* of 1936 speaks of "a native aristocracy that was not incompatible with a democracy of fellowship." [5] But underneath lay a rich and genuine sense of humor.

"I don't think he had any of what the modern mind would call hobbies," his son remarked, though he sometimes played casual golf or tennis with his family. Like many a city dweller, North enjoyed the seashore for relaxation and the mountains for physical

[5] P. 798.

and mental bracing. So the family spent weekends at Asbury Park in New Jersey, summers often at Twilight Park in the Catskills for golf and reading, a sailing vacation or two at Gloucester, quiet days in a farmhouse at West Pittsfield. North liked to bicycle and rode all the way in to Pittsfield for a doctor when his son, Eric, broke his arm. During the last twenty years of his life he took delight in a garden at his Madison, New Jersey, home and often joked about the summer when his total produce was one beet and some rhubarb.

Pāter and Māter to the children were Kalef and Turandot to each other, in a secret code based on Puccini's opera, *Turandot*. They even devised a combination of "Turan-Kalef" for a code address in trans-Atlantic cables. Dean Lynn Harold Hough, who visited often in North's home, recalled that "with anybody that he knew well he was always chortling." Seldom did a birthday or anniversary come round without a homespun poem to accompany a gift—or to promise a hitherto-forgotten present. North's son remembers that his father would occasionally disappear for a couple of hours on Christmas morning to compose appropriate verses.

Even during his pastorates North contributed columns and articles to a variety of religious publications. Often these dealt, loyally and affectionately, with the foibles of the church. For example, he shed some "Indirect Rays Upon Church Methods," apparently derived from a visit of Anglican churchmen to the United States. Noting that one of the Englishmen praised Methodist revivals, North commented: "The Methodist Church . . . has not only *believed* in revivals, but it *is* a revival." Some congregations, he remarked, give more for church music than to convert the heathen: "Oh, come, let us hear our quartette sing unto the Lord." Of the midweek prayer meeting: "It is perilous even to convert it into the pastor's lecture hour." Methodist faith, he declared, is in "present and full salvation." With all these virtues, North concluded, "the probability that during the present generation our beloved Church will suffer from the lack of laudation is comparatively slight. The indications are that her merit and achievements will not be cloaked by undue humility."

Through the period of personal sorrow and joy in the pastoral ministry Frank Mason North left his distinctive and transforming mark on each of the parishes he served. The deaths of his wife and infant son occurred during his three-year appointment at Cold-Spring-on-the-Hudson. Nevertheless, he managed to clear the church of a $20,000 debt between 1876 and 1879. His three years in West Harlem gave him a sympathetic understanding of the community which continued over the years, as he watched the parish change racially and economically and become one of the great centers of Negro Methodism. In 1887, believing that several pastors had declined the appointment, North accepted a transfer to the New York East Annual Conference in order to serve the College Church in Middletown, Connecticut.

During this final pastorate Frank Mason North began his participation in church gatherings, which were to occupy so large a portion of his later career. The First Ecumenical Methodist Conference had been held at City Road Chapel, London, in 1881. The Second, at Metropolitan Church, Washington, D.C., in October, 1891, was limited to five hundred delegates, but North attended as a reporter for *Christian Union*. Each of the next four decennial sessions found him present as an official representative of the Methodist Episcopal Church.

What seemed to impress the pastoral correspondent most was the "prime fact in the history of Methodism that there has never been a secession on grounds of doctrine." [6] True, he acknowledged, Wesley broke with Whitefield, but the latter represented "an absolute anomaly—a Calvinistic Methodism," which was too early and impermanent to count as a schism. More obvious were divisions which had taken place on grounds of race, territory, slavery, personal or factional conflicts, the episcopacy, or opposition to seminaries. One may question whether the issue of sacraments, which separated the "New Connections," was not doctrinal. In any case, noting the fact that "in all the ten days there has been no discussion of dogma, and no difference in theological opinion" among the followers of Wesley, North raised the clarion question: "What think these Methodists of Christian unity?" Regretting that there had been little recent progress toward

[6] Cf. *Christian Union*, October 10, 24, 31, 1891.

41

consolidation except in Canada, he hailed as the great day of the conference the passage of a resolution calling for closer union.

At an interdenominational Thanksgiving service in Middletown in 1891 North remarked that amid a growing appreciation for the rights of man, "when we look at Russia and Ireland and China—we cannot feel sure that all the battles have been fought and that the cause of human freedom will demand no more martyrs." For a man who would one day become corresponding secretary for foreign missions, he showed himself in the pastorate to be well informed on world affairs, but by no means free of bias. For example, in another Thanksgiving Day sermon he appears to offer his own prejudices as alternatives to the government's immigration policies:

We turn away from our doors with curses the advance guard of a race we ought to Christianize—drive to desperation by lying and cheating another race whom it is our policy to exterminate—while on our other border we open our arms to a third race as ignorant and unpromising and make them citizens at our earliest opportunity (November 29, 1883).

As the next chapter will make abundantly clear, North generally devoted his sermons and other public utterances to eternal truths rather than to contemporary events. For that reason it is all the more noteworthy that two of the most moving pulpit messages during his pastoral ministry came the day after President James A. Garfield was shot and the Sunday after he died more than two months later. The words of heartfelt personal and national sorrow carry greater poignancy because they touch so closely the mood of a similar tragedy eighty-two years later. Amid the country's grief and shame at the presidential assassination, North assured his shocked and mourning congregation: "Some will point to Communism as a cause here. There is no direct connection. Here seems to have been no conspiracy" (July 3, 1881). Then his notes (for he had had no time to write out a full sermon manuscript) direct: "(Dwell here upon the influence of Socialistic ideas in their tendency to cheapen the value of human life and to engender hatred of authority.)" And he went on to deplore the weakening of authority in the land and the "increase of immigration and the growth of Continental customs" represented in the assassin's background.

When the President finally died in late September, North was ready to broaden the responsibility—as other Americans did in 1963. After voicing the nation's shame for the "campaign of deceit and slander of less than a year ago," the young preacher expressed pride that the country could "lose its two purest and grandest Presidents by the hands of the assassin—and still move onward in its unfaltering march." He then gave thanks for the reforms (especially in the spoils system) which had been "inaugurated even during the short months of Mr. Garfield's administration . . . but also for the revelation that the life of the nation is not bound up in the life of any one man." Finally, speaking of the President himself, he added: "He died while the world loved him. Prolonged life could have brought no added proof of the world's affection" (September 25, 1881).

In preaching or writing or correspondence Frank Mason North seldom revealed his inner feeling or his personal experiences. For example, his sermons contain no hint of his first wife's death. Eight months earlier—*perhaps* after the death of his infant son—he preached on a text from Genesis 42:36: "All these things are against me." In that sermon he speaks of the ways in which opposition develops opportunity, or conflict develops strength and faith in God. "It is only in the lowest depths of our woe that we comprehend the wondrous reach of Divine Love" (April 28, 1878).

But one exception to the generalization above strikes through the crumbling sermon notes with fervent emotion—more powerful because so rare. When his brother, whom North later succeeded in the City Society, was killed by a train on Long Island, the pastor left his Connecticut parish for several weeks to get his brother's wife and seven children resettled in Montclair, New Jersey. The first sermon after his return dealt with Stephen's dying vision (Acts 7:55-56). In it North bared his soul by speaking of the "pain and grief and sudden terror . . . the lightning flash which in a moment scorched and shriveled and and blasted some of my dearest associations and fairest hopes of my life." And the message itself was a simple, honest, heartbroken

43

cry of faith: "I have no theory of visions to offer or discuss. You may reject what you cannot explain. What then have you left—of Bible or spirit or life? . . . Explain it, no! . . . But believe in Stephen's vision? Yes!" (May 12, 1889).

On one other occasion North lapsed into a reminiscent or introspective mood, but this time quiet humor instead of pathos mingled with his candor. He was preaching on "The Christian in Politics," the dangers of aloofness on the part of good men, the necessity for a single rather than dual conscience in public affairs. But then he recalled—with remarkable irrelevance for this dedicated man: "My childhood's creed. To believe in 3 things: The Methodist Church, Homoeopathy, and the Republican Party." But as he grew older and learned more about each of these, he discovered: (1) "There is quite as much piety outside the Methodist Church as there is in it." (2) "The old school of medicine like the old school of Calvinism can put a man under ground quite as quickly as the other." (3) "Even the Republican Party is not absolutely immaculate" (October 8, 1882). Here, then, was a man who could look at himself with wisdom and feeling and amusement, but who spent far *more* of his time looking at his Master and at his fellowmen—and trying to bring the two together.

Frank Mason North would have been happy to stay in Middletown. He loved the peaceful New England town and its cultural and intellectual attractions. With pardonable pride he considered Wesleyan "the oldest and greatest Methodist college" in the country—and never wavered in that conviction. But North was a "traveling elder" of the Methodist Church. Five years in the rolling hills of Connecticut were to be followed by twenty-three years in the canyons of New York, and two decades more of commuting from New Jersey. Not even the metropolis—which saddened and fascinated and challenged him—proved big enough for the compassionate heart of Frank Mason North. Beyond the city lay the world; beyond the Methodist Church the embryonic ecumenical movement waited to be born. North served them all, with the efficiency of a business executive, with the vision of a poet, and with devotion to a "social gospel" which was always and foremost personal.

44

My Lord, My Life

O Christ, my Lord, whose perfect life
Alone can make my life complete
With tears I bring that life to Thee,
And lay it at Thy feet.

The gifts of earth it has not lacked;
It knows the world's felicity;
Yet—Thee unknown—this golden wealth
Is direful poverty.

No human life was ever blessed
With human love more rich and rare;
But never finds my heart its peace,
Unless Thyself art there.

The grace of gentlest ministries,
The precious boon of love's caress,
Without Thy tender words and touch,
Leave only restlessness.

My life, 'mid richest joys so poor,
'Mid love's delights so incomplete,
I bring Thee, Lord, and humbly ask
To lay it at Thy feet.

Undated

3

"Of Winning Ministry"

They watched him with a strange surprise—
The sombre garb, the quiet word,
And in his hand the Book.

"Mere *desire* to do good should never be taken as a call to preach," North wrote in his fourth-year examination for admission to the New York Annual Conference in 1877. On the contrary, he declared, "the religious life means unqualified *submission* to God's will in all things," and the minister's chief duty is to preach the Word. This he did, with vigor and versatility, with conscience and consecration, for nineteen years in the pastorate and almost as frequently throughout his administrative career.

No one habit reveals the methodical mind of Frank Mason North more clearly than the systematic labeling and filing of hundreds of sermons and sermon notes. Each manuscript bore a Scripture lesson and a text, though not always a title. Each contained careful notations in the upper right-hand corner as to when and where it was preached. Often the notes would start out with a full verbatim text for the sermon, shift after several pages to an outline, and finally dwindle away to a few key words or phrases. Other preachers may be pardoned for wondering whether this represented North's homiletical technique—"priming the pump" and then letting the Holy Spirit pour forth—or whether he ran out of time on Saturday night. The "odds" (to use a term he would have denounced) are on the former interpretation.

Frank Mason North used comparatively few illustrations—and

indeed some of his friends who recall hearing him preach in much later years report that he was not a dramatic or colorful speaker! But references to such literary classics as *Pilgrim's Progress,* to figures of history such as William of Orange, Raphael, Morse, or the ancient Greeks, to the good works of John Howard, Florence Nightingale, John Wesley—all testified to the breadth of his reading. More important than detailed illustrations, however, were the simple, commonplace metaphors and the natural, expressive descriptions. In our preoccupation with evil in the world, for example, we are seeing the wrong side of the tapestry, "the loose ends and blotched figures." A Christian is like a diver under the ocean, drawing life-giving air through the breathing tube of prayer. Suffering ennobles life, as a stream produces power only when it is restricted and forced into narrow channels and heavy wheels. Over and over again North's love of nature shines through his language, as he points to the greater fruitfulness of a grafted branch, or asserts that faith in God lifts up all thoughts and values as a tree lifts a clinging vine. If in such parables he followed the Teacher of Galilee, in his pertinent use of modern science he showed himself almost a twentieth-century man in the late nineteenth century. He did not quote poetry often, but, when he did, his obvious favorites were Wordsworth, Shakespeare, and Milton.

Whether or not the sermon had a title, however lengthy the Scripture lesson might be, there was always a text, not necessarily from the same passage and usually limited to a single verse. In fact, it was by texts that Frank Mason North filed his past sermons, rather than by subject matter or date. By so doing he avoided repetition to a remarkable degree. In less than two decades of pastoral ministry, North preached at some time from all but four books of the New Testament (Titus, Philemon, II John, Jude) and all but fourteen books of the Old Testament. Of course the Gospels were most frequently cited: Luke (66 times), Matthew (58), John (37), Mark (26). What is surprising is that most of the Old Testament books omitted were prophets. One would have expected this later spokesman for the social gospel to neglect the narratives or the apocalyptic literature and focus heavily on appeals for justice and righteousness, morality and brotherhood.

48

Yet Isaiah appears but thirteen times, Jeremiah four, Amos only once, Hosea, Joel, Jonah, Micah, Habbakuk, and others not at all.

Although well-known verses were used with reassuring frequency in North's preaching, he had the homiletical knack—and the biblical knowledge—to vary these with unfamiliar texts and with unexpected twists. "Adders' poison is under their lips" (Ps. 140:3) condemned the devil in current literature—and by the devil North meant no mere allegory or symbolism; he meant black, soul-destroying sin and temptation. While other preachers would concentrate on Jesus' calming of the storm at sea, North took note of the fact that "there were also with him other little ships" (Mark 4:36). As the Lord asked Moses, "What is that in thine hand?" (Exod. 4:2), so he asks each of us to use the common implements at our disposal for his service. In a sermon on Jehu, who "drove furiously" (II Kings 9:20) North anticipated the automotive age in warning that "he drove not only with his hands but with his disposition." As "Elisha put his hands upon the king's hands" (II Kings 13:16) in drawing the bow, so does history move forward through a partnership between political authority and the man of God. Again North reprimands those worshipers of every generation who "offer burnt offerings unto the Lord my God of that which doth cost me nothing" (II Sam. 24:24). "What is your life?" (James 4:14). Or simply but undeniably, "There is much rubbish" (Neh. 4:10).

"Jesus is Jesus today—as He was 1800 years ago" (August 17, 1873). This proclamation in the first few months of North's ministry sums up the central message of his preaching. He believed in the Living Christ, one who "himself drew near, and went with them" (Luke 24:15) in days gone by—and does so still. Asserting his faith in "this same Jesus" as risen from the dead and ascended into heaven, the young pastor admitted (February, 1877) that "we are not quite able—perhaps—to comprehend the mode of it . . . not as Son of God, not as the Christ— least of all as some uncertain or vapory Essence." Despite occasional slurs at Adventists or premillennialists, he adds his conviction that there will be a Second Coming and that men will see once more, "however changed in condition or circumstance—

this Jesus." As for Methodist doctrines, North followed a typically cautious and open approach:

Our articles are singularly inexplicit concerning all eschatological questions. . . . The philosophy of humanity with its vision of the perfectability of the race, the conclusions of science touching the evolution of life and the world processes, the study of comparative religions, and not least the rapid advance of the race in modes of life and achievement—all conspire to place eschatological questions at a new angle of vision.[1]

While such a statement lays the groundwork for a "modernist" approach, the Connecticut pastor never answered his own rhetorical questions: Will the Second Coming be personal and visible? Will it precede or follow the millenial triumph? And in his interpretation of the passage, "He cometh to judge the earth," he seemed to imply a literal, corporeal fulfillment.

In the first year of his pastorate North took the familiar text from Mark 16:16: "He that believeth and is baptized shall be saved." But he did frank and courageous things with the verse even then. *Not* that baptism is essential to salvation, he declared, although he recognized the "general duty of baptism and the obligation upon us of using the sacrament whenever 'possible' " (August 24, 1873). Nor is belief mere exercise of mental faculties or acceptance of the facts of Christ's life. Rather it requires men to live by the truths of his gospel: "that He is the Son of God— that in human form He expiates the sins of men . . . that he rose from the dead . . . all the glorious truths that resurrection implies."

But over and over again appear two qualifications of this redemptive role of Christ—no, not qualifications, for this suggests restriction, whereas North was concerned with extension, with wider ramifications. The first extension, therefore, is a constant Wesleyan insistence on human response and responsibility. True belief, he concluded in the sermon quoted above, is dependent on us, "left to the decision of our own wills." We are never

---

[1] "Changes of Opinion Since the Apostolic Age with Reference to the Second Coming of Christ," to the New Haven District Ministerial Association, June 19, 1888.

coerced into the Kingdom. In the very first sermon discovered, dated a few months *before* North entered the ministry, he asserted that "salvation is conditional" on the believer as a free moral agent. It is equally erroneous, said the young businessman just out of college, to expect God to do everything or to expect God to do nothing. "The one appointed—true method—[is] the working together with God" (December, 1872).

The other extension of God's redeeming love reaches out to those who have never been told the good news. Admitting that we do not understand this "eternity of joy," North recognizes that "all have not heard the truth of the Gospel. God will not condemn them because they do not believe in truths they have never heard." Although he asserts, "Such exceptions need not be made in a Christian land," he softens even that judgment by declaring boldly, "I care not whether they are in the church or not" (August 24, 1873). The following year he reiterates the necessity for grace and faith, claiming that there can be no genuine knowledge of good and evil without Christ. "Can that poor degraded heathen—untaught and ungoverned—do good works? Can that man of prejudiced habits of thought and life do good works?" (February 15, 1874). Note that the nominal Christian may be included along with the nonbeliever.

This divine paradox, this continual tension between judgment and forgiveness, marks the affirmation of any thoughtful Christian. North concludes the first of two sermons on everlasting punishment with the ringing admonition: "Candid, unprejudiced minds can hardly fail to acknowledge that the Bible teaches a terrible retribution for the impenitent in a future world. . . . We disbelieve at our infinite peril" (February 10, 1878). Yet the very next Sunday, dealing with the problem of evil, he refuses to discuss original sin "since God requires of us only according to our light. . . . No man is punished until he has had the opportunity of salvation"—whether heathen, child, or philosopher!— and there is "always an equilibrium between opportunity and responsibility" (February 17, 1878).

Within this freedom of choice the pressures of "original sin"— or human nature—are alarmingly strong. Although Christ stands at the door knocking (Rev. 3:20), other appeals are more promptly heeded. "Harsh pride asks entrance—we let him in. Gaunt envy knocks stealthily but we hear and open. False hypocrisy comes—he is not kept waiting. Bitter anger—cruel hate—burning passion—eager lust—come clamoring for admittance—and we throw wide the door" (November 21, 1875). With fervid Methodist conviction North warned his congregation: "Every Christian may become a backslider" (December 6, 1885).

Though these and other central tenets of faith do not, for Frank Mason North, comprise a systematic theology, they can and must be summarized in a more systematic treatment of theology (chapter 13). Here, during the period of his pastoral ministry, we are concerned with the scope and variety of his preaching, at the first stage of his threefold career. The most striking impression is this: *one of the greatest exponents of the social gospel in the early twentieth century seldom if ever made direct social applications in his early preaching.* In fact, anyone aware of the great prophetic challenges from Frank Mason North will be amazed not only at the absence of such messages during his pastorate, but also by what seems at times a deliberate avoidance of homiletic opportunities. To be sure, North came close when he preached about love, which "builds hospitals and orphan asylums . . . bands together men and women in works of benevolence . . . pours oil into the wounds of humanity and binds up their broken hearts" (September 20, 1874). But although love can defeat envy, hatred, wrath, murder, theft, adultery, and selfishness, there was no mention of social change, no question about the *causes* of wounds and broken hearts. Five years later he declared: "We care for their bodies. We clothe and feed our children—we provide pleasant homes for our families—we look out for the material welfare of the community—but what are we doing for their souls?" (February 16, 1879). Of course this is a vital and valid concern for every true Christian. The noteworthy feature in the proclamations of Frank Mason North is simply the absence of the social balance for which he pleaded so eloquently at a later period.

Not until 1892, just before he left the peaceful college town, did he lift up the prophetic voice and the practical needs which so characterized his later preaching. "The struggle of the working man to better his condition has scant sympathy," he regretted, even though there were enough diamonds in Christian jewel boxes in New York City to feed and clothe every child of want there. "Is it to be questioned that—granting the churches' splendid charities—the needs of humanity in this world have been overlooked—that salvation in the world to come has seemed vastly more important than justice now?" (February 21, 1892).

It is not surprising that his new task in the metropolitan area demanded frequent preaching, usually on a social theme. That first year back in New York he spoke on "The Starving World" from the simple text: "Give ye them to eat" (Mark 6:37). With particular reference to the multitudes of different nationalities and to the "distribution problem" North shrewdly listed the choices in the biblical narrative: send them away, let them go to the villages, go and buy and give them to eat, or here are five loaves. "The crisis of New York is now," he asserted. "We cannot postpone it. We must meet it or die."

Over the next two decades it can be said of North, as he said of his Master in another pointed sermon: "He measured the city" (Rev. 21:16). The larger dimensions of this urban ministry will be reviewed in chapter 5. Preaching on "Christ and Society" at Nostrand Avenue Church, Brooklyn, he defended this new emphasis indirectly:

There are two classes of folk who deprecate the strong inclination some ministers show to busying themselves about human welfare: the one those excellent people who regard him as a spiritual guidepost to point an occasional wanderer a way out of the world of earth into the world of heaven; the other those observant men of the world who cannot understand what possible interest in or equipment for human affairs a man who prays, believes in Christ, and preaches the Gospel can have (June 3, 1893).

How does one explain the previous neglect of prophetic preaching on the part of this spokesman and statesman of the social gospel? The bits of writing from his college days, the isolated clues to social involvement during his pastorates, the outstanding series on "Socialism and Christianity" described in the following chapter—all these would refute any theory of abrupt conversion to social concerns when he moved to "the unchristian city." Undoubtedly he studied more deeply into urban problems, in connection with his brother's brief tenure in the City Society and in preparation for his own new appointment there. This in itself would be insufficient to account for any sudden shift in preaching emphasis.

Certainly, too, exposure to the sin and suffering of the great metropolis weighed heavily on Frank Mason North. His administrative responsibility in the New York City Missionary Society brought him into far more intimate contact with poverty and injustice, with vice and indifference, than any single parish would provide. But unless one denies the social consciousness and social conscience inherited from and nurtured by his parents, one must find another explanation for his earlier silence. One can surmise, therefore, that North began his ministry with a genuine reservation about the place and purpose of the pulpit. Not that the very young pastor was blind to the social dimensions of the gospel he preached, but that he may have hesitated to proclaim those convictions in the context of worship. If so, North would have been true to his times. Washington Gladden was only fourteen years older and hardly beginning to fulfill a prophetic ministry; Walter Rauschenbusch had not reached his teens when North commenced his first pastorate. The Christian faith was still seen—and proclaimed—in almost totally individualistic terms, whatever wider responsibility might be implicit in it.

Yet, though he made no mention of a social or evangelistic mission for the church, North was not unmindful of it. "The Church must be 'in the world'—and the world shall hate it—but not overcome it," he warned (October 27, 1878). On the other hand, so frankly critical of the institutional church was the young Frank Mason North that his ecclesiastical superiors may well have regarded him as iconoclastic. On frequent occasions he wielded his rapier against his fellow clergymen. The following passage is but one example:

The man of God cultivates his eloquence and burnishes his shafts of wit and fills his sermon as full of fine points and lines as a steel engraving. He builds out of the richest materials—sciences for frame-

54

work—the arts for ornamentation—and clear diction and impressive manner for final touches. The effect is marked. It is a beautiful sermon. All are pleased—but no one is convinced—no one comforted—not one shamed—no one has been brought face to face with God—but the man is a fine orator (September 11, 1881).

His preference for old-fashioned Wesleyan simplicity shines through his distaste for all forms of aestheticism. For instance, "The Methodist Church has nearly lost one of its greatest opportunities by neglecting its birthright of earnest heartfelt song in the interests of sensual gratification by a mess of musical potage prepared by the hand of some supplanter" (September 11, 1881). With equal vigor he asserted, "I am, for one, convinced that in our own service the congregation has too little share" (September 9, 1888). The people should participate at least in responsive readings or a unison prayer of confession, he insisted.

At the same time, he was not disposed—in his early ministry, at least—to abandon any of the time-won or timeworn practices of the Methodist Episcopal Church. "The Sunday School is the greatest evangelizing agency the world has ever known," declared the son of *one* of the founders of Children's Day. "The Prayer meeting is the test of the church's health," he added. And the class meeting should be renewed and strengthened, even though four fifths of that particular congregation never attended, according to North (September 9, 1888). Even before he helped organize the Open and Institutional Church League, North deplored the practice of pew rents on Sundays and closed doors during the week. "Collectively the church makes the impression that it is a private concern," he complained (February 21, 1892). In one of his stewardship sermons (December 13, 1885), appealing for regular pledges instead of pew rents to support the church budget, he took as his text Paul's plea "that there be no gatherings when I come" (I Cor. 16:2). On another occasion he told the New Haven District Meeting that the "commercial theory of church support" made of the church a human institution, a corporation, a club, a benevolent society, a spiritual guild, or a clearing house. Not until he moved to the City Society, however, did he include among the essential tasks of the church

55

the creation of a social conscience. "Not long," he wrote in *The Christian City*, "can the church in the city avoid the responsibility of teaching social as well as individual ethics." [2]

"Even the sad mistakes of the church cannot destroy the influence of Jesus," North said in his first decade of preaching (April 11, 1881). But these probing criticisms of the institution by no means negate his profound commitment to the church as the Body of Christ, to the church as it should be and can be. In paying tribute to the stirring evangelism of Dwight L. Moody, William Taylor, James Thoburn, General William Booth, and Hudson Taylor, North particularly praised "the wisdom of Mr. Moody and the ablest of his compeers in refusing to cast discredit upon the church by ignoring it"—as so many evangelists did and do. Affirming his faith in the church as the "advancing host of redeemed souls," North added his own progressive hope and vision: "To overthrow the conventionalities of a church life—to instill a spirit of expectancy—to transform the conservative into the aggressive—this is not easy" (July 13, 1890).

If Frank Mason North appears, in such respects, extremely liberal and forward-looking for his day—and even for ours—he had also his human blindspots and prejudices. One of these lay in his attitude toward Roman Catholics on one hand and unorthodox sects on the other. Sometimes his attacks were couched in terms of passing comments or illustrations. Jesuitism, for example, "has spread a baneful influence wherever its silken covered iron hand has touched the centers of life and power" (February 8, 1874). In a sermon on adultery North denounced the "venal system of the Romish church" in which, through the confessional and penance, it "encouraged sin with one hand that it might be paid for forgiving it with the other" (May 20, 1876). Or again, preaching on "Christ the Only Saviour," he injected an attack on "the usurpation of Romanism wh. originates Divine decrees in the Papal palace and fulminates them from the papal chair, wh. presumes to forgive sin on the credit of saints wh. itself has made" (September 19, 1880).

On a few occasions the Methodist cleric devoted entire sermons

[2] September, 1900, p. 114.

to the threats of political Catholicism. When a Roman Catholic, W. K. Grace, had been nominated as mayor of New York, North felt it time for Protestant Christians to say: "Hitherto shalt thou come, but no further: and here shall thy proud waves be stayed" (Job 38:11). The issue is not, he insisted, one of politics or sectarian conflict or religious toleration; nor is it an imaginary danger or "bugaboo." A large share of New York patronage was already in Roman Catholic control, and the mayor's appointive power would include fourteen school commissioners, North pointed out—attaching to his sermon notes the newspaper clipping to verify his claims. Then, with extensive quotations from papal encyclicals, from the Second Plenary Council of American Bishops in Baltimore in 1866, and from other Roman Catholic documents, he declared that the threat to education had come from the hierarchy itself, that the confessional constituted a "denial of the right of private judgment," and that the Roman Catholic Church as a political institution was a "foe to liberty: intellectual, social, civil."

North was, on occasion, just as uncharitable toward other Christian sects which he regarded as morally or even doctrinally deviant. Chief of these *bêtes-noires* was the Church of Jesus Christ of the Latter-day Saints. Among three hopeful signs of progress cited in one sermon was the public demand to destroy Mormonism, "that organized iniquity" (July 2, 1882). Again he called it "organized disgrace . . . systematized immorality," one of the chief threats to freedom (May 30, 1886). Even in *The Christian City* he expressed the earnest conviction that polygamous Mormons should be excluded from Congress.[3] Another popular target was Christian Science, "a delusion in any of its many forms." Christian Science, North remarked sarcastically, would have dealt with Paul's "thorn in the flesh" by telling him to "think it out" (September 9, 1888). And in the issue of *The Christian City* cited above he referred to the "obnoxious doctrines . . . absurdity . . . insidious methods of interpretation" in Christian Science.[4] The following year, on the same subject, he commented that "the survival of humbugs has ever been one of the wonders

[3] March-April, 1899, p. 54.
[4] *Ibid.*, p. 78.

of history, and there is a strange vitality in religious error." [5]

These particular prejudices do not reflect a general attitude by any means. During the first year of his ministry he declared: "I have no controversy with sects. Let men believe as they will about non-essentials . . . so long as their chief effort is to bring the souls of men into personal union with Christ" (February 8, 1874). The difficulty lies, as always, in determining what constitute non-essentials. Thirty years before he joined with other Christian statesmen to inaugurate the Federal Council of the Churches of Christ, Frank Mason North voiced his own uncertainty about the meaning and goal of the ecumenical movement. Preaching on Philippians 1:27 ("With one mind striving together for the faith of the gospel"), he remarked: "We are very much urged to unity in these days—so much so that it has seemed almost as though a man had need to be ashamed at having convictions that placed him in one denomination rather than another. What is this unity?" (April 14, 1878). It is not, he insisted, intellectual belief ("The creeds of Christendom are compromises. . . . The heresy of opinion is less dangerous than the heresy of the heart."), not organization, not personal experience. It is One Spirit, the source of common inspiration, affection, work, and prayer.

Nevertheless, North somewhat tempered his hostilities as he came to associate more closely with representatives of other faiths and to realize that together they shared a common foe in secularism and sin. A few months before the founding of the Federal Council, he wrote that in dealing with Roman Catholicism one must "first acknowledge her as a true Church of Jesus Christ," not as mere superstition (which he himself had hardly been able to do thirty years earlier). Protestants should not, he suggested, attempt to proselyte Catholics ("an undertaking which halts both reason and faith") or to Gentilize Jews ("Gibraltar will fall first"), but to work with both groups in an irenic, not polemic, spirit.[6]

Even more than in sectarian prejudices, Frank Mason North proved himself a Victorian Christian in his moral standards. His basic guide was the Pauline text: "If meat make my brother

[5] *Ibid.*, February, 1900, p. 47.
[6] *Ibid.*, March, 1908.

to offend, I will eat no flesh while the world standeth, lest I make my brother to offend" (I Cor. 8:13). At least twice he used the illustration of a mountaineer leaping safely but thoughtlessly over a chasm, where others following him might plunge to destruction.

Clearly for this young preacher, as for Methodists traditionally, liquor is the greatest single evil—though it cannot be easily separated from its attendant sins. Admitting that abstinence is not based on any positive scriptural prohibition, North insisted that no man has the right to tempt others by indulgence, even in the "so-called moderate use of intoxicating liquor." In fact, "I believe today the responsibility of the drunkenness in our land lies upon men who never get drunk," he asserted, and "my belief is that every drop that goes into the system drives just that much true manhood out" (August 8, 1875). Drawing on the same statistics in 1876 and 1881, he charged that four fifths of the nation's paupers, four fifths of the crime, and one half of the idiots could be traced to liquor; that the $600,000,000 spent for alcohol would buy two and a half barrels of flour for every person in the country.

North's preaching included briefer, though equally vehement, condemnation of "the social evil." Justifying his boldness in mentioning such subjects as adultery and prostitution, he asserted: "There is a delicacy as harmful as is meretricious plainness" (May 20, 1876). On the one hand, he appealed—of course—for "humanity toward those who have lost their virtue"; on the other, he denounced especially the ownership of some brothels by nominal Christians and the dual standard of morality applied to men and women (June 27, 1880).

But Frank Mason North also included other "social pleasures and frivolity" among the "severest besetments of young Christians. . . . Ah! how many bright young souls have made shipwreck because of an evening's amusement!" (1878). Obviously, he conceded, "paste board with marks of different kinds on it is not sinful," but playing cards can lead to crime and debauchery (August 8, 1875). Since it is "useless to deny the utility and economy of Fashion," it would be "childish to condemn with one sweep," yet "the world knows no such tyranny as that of Fashion." Concern for hair or jewelry or costly array (even the anxiety of a Quaker lady over her cape and kerchief, North added whimsically) produces envy and extravagance (whereas renunciation of such vanity could turn the tide of the $7,000 debt on the church!) (May 16, 1880).

Dancing and the theater constitute still greater dangers for the Christian, the young preacher warned. "I speak advisedly and with absolute conviction" on dancing, he said, admitting that a quadrille is "very silly—but actually sinful in itself—No!" (August 8, 1875). Yet a few years later North fulminated against "real—flesh and blood—dancing of modern society" as one of the "unfruitful works of darkness" (Eph. 5:11). The round dance— "midnight gymnastics" he called it bitingly—is "essentially immoral" because of its appearance ("the modern school of immodesty"), its sensations, and its results (in dress, late hours, and extravagance). The square dance—"agility at the expense of intellect"—falls under condemnation because it leads inevitably to the round dance, from the home parlor to other places, from family and friends to unreliable strangers. A Christian who begins to dance, North cautioned, is like a man who, warned not to carry a lighted match into a powder magazine, discarded the match but carried in his lighted pipe, and "man and pipe and powder all went off together" (October 22, 1882).

Similarly, North confessed: "The benefits of the theatre have yet to be proved to me. Its attractions I can understand" (August 8, 1875). In a full evening sermon he insisted: "The general tendency of the theatre is evil. . . . Show me one period in any age in any land when the tendency of the theatre has been to elevate the moral life of men—and I will retreat from my position" (May 23, 1880). Condemning theatrical treatment of religion, the morals of most plays, the morality of the actors, North pointed out that most dramatists were not Christian (Moliére, Racine, Green, Congreve, Sheridan) and labeled "most of them men of blackest morals." Even Shakespeare, whom he greatly admired, North had to describe as "not immaculate," and he went on to add that Shakespeare's true greatness was as a philosopher of life rather than as a dramatist. Thus in the theater there can be only one answer to the rhetorical questions of Proverbs 6:27-28:

60

"Can a man take fire in his bosom, and his clothes not be burned? Can one go upon hot coals, and his feet not be burned?"

At one time North criticized even Sunday traffic, Sunday pleasure seeking, and Sunday newspapers (June 7, 1885). But unlike many moralists he did include in his list of ethical arenas the world of business. Christians must be involved in commerce, he said, and see in their vocations an opportunity for developing character. Most emphatically he denied the rationalization that it is impossible to be Christian in business, or that Christian ethics must be separated from business ethics. Admittedly the dangers of greed or neglecting other duties, of temptation to dishonesty and worldliness, are great, but "the *ultimate motive* of his industry must be the *glory of God* and the welfare of men" (June 20, 1880). It is noteworthy, however, that this sermon contains an application of the Golden Rule to honesty, but no reference to the exploitation of other men in industry.

Frank Mason North displayed strong—and unconventional—convictions in another area of preaching; namely, his treatment of political issues. Despite his insistence on the separation of church and state, he utilized the Sundays close to Thanksgiving and the Fourth of July for some very dogmatic political pronouncements. Theological justification for rabid patriotism is rare today, but North denounced as a prevalent error the idea that "the end of the Divine plan is the perfection of government . . . while men and their condition here and in the other world have little place—are errata in the problem." Instead he affirmed, quite naturally, his view that government is designed for man, for the development of the individual, that God rather than the people represent the source of power (November 26, 1874).

Furthermore, he rejected emphatically the "fallacy" of *vox populi, vox dei* (July 7, 1878); in fact he went much further to castigate popular democracy. On Thanksgiving Day, 1874, he affirmed: "In plain words universal suffrage wh. in the far future will be a glorious reality is in these days an ignominious failure. The world is not ready for it. Men are neither good enough nor wise enough to make it profitable." And on Thanksgiving Day, 1883, he deplored the "fallacious folly of universal suffrage" when one ninth of the population was illiterate. Majority rule is an

61

error, he asserted, when it allows only one sex to vote and denies the ballot to *men* of eighteen while granting it to *fools* of thirty (November 26, 1874). Intelligence and integrity ought to be factors in suffrage, he argued, though he offered no method by which these could be measured or enforced. He did stress the church's role, however, as a promoter of education, wisdom, and honesty.

Despite the corruption and ignorance so prevalent in government, North professed boundless faith in the divine destiny of the United States. "Our own loved land," he boasted, "seems to have been chosen as the stage for representing this method of government. I say *chosen*" through its natural resources, its isolation, its admirable European history, and its blending of Old World peoples in the best of *Aryan* (!) character (November 26, 1874, and November 29, 1883), "a character with grander possibilities of expansion and elevation than any the world has ever known" (July 2, 1876). "A mercantile facility, a love of liberty, and a true regard for true religion" are here combined with geography, culture, a common language, the practical arts, religious freedom, and the separation of church and state to produce a new chosen people.

On the other hand, North did not hesitate to confess from the pulpit his disappointments in the American scene. One of these was the gradual encroachment on religion in the public schools. "Secular education means irreligious education," he warned; "the one thing a child should know about is the one thing he must not be taught—on our theory of education" (Thanksgiving Day, November 29, 1883). Preaching on the text, "No man cared for my soul" (Ps. 142:4), he deplored the fact that—in the midst of government reform, social agitation, new emphasis on education— "the Bible must go out of our schools" (January 27, 1884). In a Memorial Day sermon on "Threats *of* Freedom" (italics added) North pointed to the tensions and conflicts between political liberty and restricted franchise, personal liberty and the liquor traffic, freedom of property and the popular despotism of both capital and labor, freedom of conscience and secular education. "Constitutional guarantees are insufficient to preserve the

62

balance between true liberty and false," he concluded (May 30, 1886).

One other theme of Frank Mason North's preaching must be illustrated here because of his later professional involvement; namely, his commitment to Christian missions. In fact, he claimed in one sermon that it was his custom to "turn at least once a year to scrutinize the terms of our Great Commission" (March 12, 1882).

Sometimes North's emphasis was on the factual situation around the world. On the basis of extensive reading he could point out the problems of caste in India; opium, state resistance, and "gross immorality" in China; a ban on foreigners in Japan; the climate, ignorance, and the "baneful influence of Mahometanism" in Africa; the "bitter opposition of the Catholic Church" in South America (March, 1879). He could introduce his listeners to the noble work of William Carey, Samuel Crowther, Robert Moffat, Melville Cox, James Thoburn, Allen Francis Gardiner; and he referred in 1882 to having recently "held by the hand Mr. H. M. Stanley," who had since departed for East Africa again via the Suez Canal.

Sometimes North's emphasis was on financial needs. He told his first parishioners that they were giving twenty-one cents per member per year for missions, when the New York Conference average was eighty-five cents—and he was therefore asking for twenty-five dollars that very day! His second congregation was contributing eighteen cents per member, while the Methodist Episcopal Church as a whole gave forty-six cents—and the Wesleyan Methodists in Great Britain gave two dollars a year. The average annual *increase* in wealth among professed Christians, he asserted in 1882, was seventy-one times greater than their missionary giving (March 12, 1882). The nation, he declaimed in 1889, was spending five million dollars for missions and a billion dollars for strong drink (March 17, 1889). For a Christian, he insisted, the tithe is an obligation and a privilege—but he raised no question as to the right of an individual to great affluence, or the ways in which philanthropists gained their wealth.

[The Christian] perceives that it is through consecrated money that the Gospel is to be brought to a dark world—that the self-denial required by a faithful discharge of his privileges in this matter is of the utmost importance to his own spiritual life—and that God in His word has therefore placed this matter of the use of His gifts to us in the very front rank of our obligations to Him (March 14, 1880).

But always, through Frank Mason North's preaching on missions, ran the challenging affirmation that "the evangelization of the world is not a matter of choice to the church. Christian missions are not a human device" (March 12, 1882). Or, as North put it one Christmas Sunday: "It is Divinely appointed that men should be the instruments in saving men. The duty of the church is your duty and mine. . . . It is not an obligation to the church to support our missions—it is a duty to God. Through us must His light shine" (December 20, 1874). Man is the instrument, "the sole medium by which the Gospel can come to the unsaved humanity" (March 12, 1882).

As North's theology of mission was broad enough to suggest "the Christian presence" in non-Christian cultures, so his concept of the church's task sounded remarkably like the "new approach" of eighty-five years later. On one hand, the transformations taking place on the world scene impose a new urgency on the church of Jesus Christ. "It has been reserved to our day to bring world and church into such relations of opportunity and power that the Commission of our Lord has its true significance," the young preacher declared. In contrast to early Protestant reformers, who sometimes argued that the missionary imperative belonged only to the first disciples, not to later generations, North commented simply: "Paul could not teach all nations—we can" (March 12, 1882). Citing the use of printing presses and modern medicine and agricultural tools, the revolutions in transportation and industry, the formation of some twenty-five women's boards of missions in England and America, the translation of the Bible into two hundred and fifty different languages and dialects, he recognized that "to those whose ideas of missionary work have not passed the day of—say 40 years ago—the present terms and methods must seem strange and significant" (March 12, 1882).

64

But repeatedly he returned to the theme of personal responsibility—above all, to the fulfillment of the church itself through missions. From Proverbs 11:24 he quoted: "There is that scattereth, and yet increaseth; and there is that withholdeth more than is meet, but it tendeth to poverty." Then, North asserted, with insight which attained widespread acceptance only in the mid-twentieth century: "The church is a Mission. . . . The work of the Gospel is one whether at our doors or at the Antipodes. . . . It is not more true that Missions need us than that we need Missions" (March 13, 1881). During his final pastorate Frank Mason North told his congregation in Middletown: "The call to tell the Glad Tidings is as surely a part of personal salvation as is the forgiveness of sins." The only question, he said, is where? (March 17, 1889). Three years later he was to be called to the greatest metropolitan mission in the church and two decades after that to the administration of a worldwide program.

O Morning Land of College Days

On vine-clad walls the sunlight falls,
And spreads right royally,
With cloth of gold a hillside old
For high-born company.
A vagrant breeze with minstrel heart
Awakes from silence long,
And strikes from June's sweet harp the chord
Of nature's wordless song.

Refrain

O morning land of college days,
O hill of golden light,
No other skies are soft as thine,
No other lands so bright.

From chapel tow'r the midnight hour
Has struck, and all is still,
Save where the song of merry throng
Breaks o'er the moonlit hill.
The silence rests on scholar's quests,
On lover's mem'ries deep;
Yields now the eager day to night
For thought and dreams and sleep.

Then, sing the praise of college days,
Let cheer on cheer ring free,
For springing life and eager strife,
And buoyant liberty.
This old hillside shall be our pride,
These paths of light we'll roam,
These friends shall be our friends for aye;
Cheer, cheer our college home!

Middletown, Connecticut
1891

4

"The Socialism of Christianity"

O Church of God! Awake! Awake!
The waking world is calling thee.
Lift up thine eyes! Hear thou once more
The challenge of humanity.

"More than any other person, he shaped the social policies of the Protestant churches of this country between 1892 and 1912." This tribute to Frank Mason North came at the memorial service (January 20, 1936) from his colleague of over forty years, Worth M. Tippy.[1] If there were rivals for this honor—and many of his associations will be indicated as the story moves along—such "competition" has been in the minds of friends or historians, not among the great souls who pioneered the social-gospel emphasis.

North's concern for applied Christianity and his interest in the socialist movement began early. In a letter to Tippy soon after her husband's death Mrs. North reported, "He was much amused lately to find among his college essays, written in 1872, a treatise on Socialism."[2] With all the fervor and all the turgid "over-writing" of youth, Frank Mason North pictured "the panorama of French history" as social revolution followed the political one:

The angry sky mutters sullenly. That speck no bigger than a man's hand, now fills the heavens, its "lurid lightnings" strike terror to many a breast, its thunders shake the world. The black cloud of

[1] *Frank Mason North* (Prepared and published by friends, 1936), p. 23.
[2] *Ibid.*, p. 19.

69

Socialism, which, for years has been absorbing the foul miasma from the sluggish, stagnating stream of social life, has burst in fury upon devoted France.

Citing Morelly's Code de la Nature as a forerunner of "this monstrous system," the college senior sketched the growing "despotism of capital" and counter-organization of labor. Among spokesmen for the new movement he listed "wonderful Proudhon—the apostle of anarchy—who thought by a single stroke of his pen to blot out every social principle which the finger of God has written in the great book of his law."

This was the tenor of most of the paper. Its language seemed to reflect the reactionary prejudices of a young capitalist. Its clichés were those of a typical ministerial student. Its description of socialism included all the stereotypes of that day— and this.

They asked for more than a proper adjustment of the relations of laborer and capitalist. They demanded the abolition of the right of inheritance, the leveling of all property, the total destruction of all personal and class distinctions, a community of goods, absolute equality, and entire uniformity. The individual must be lost in the state, there must be no reward of merit, no advantage from effort. All men, all things must be reduced to a common dead level. What must we think of the intellectual depravity of men who would deliberately destroy all the proper movements and adjustments of society by fastening upon it a system that ignores the teachings of both natural and revealed religion, destroys the family relation, suppresses genius, and dwarfs intellect; that changes patriotism to stupidity and gives no room for philanthropy; that, in a word, makes society a machine, man a cipher, God a bungler!

Finally, North examined the apparent failure of socialism: that it "thought to improve man's condition and commenced by subverting his nature; it meant to make *him* better and began by trying to destroy those divinely implanted elements which are the only true agents for reformation." He inquired what of the future, of the "tidal wave" among working people? He granted that the socialism of '48 "concealed a germ of truth which later years have developed into a power that threatens to revolutionize, not a single nation, but the world." Then he answered his question in a final sentence which puts a whole new perspective on the essay: "The destiny of the *Internationale* is to destroy the tyranny of capital, to break down the barriers of caste, to secure for *all* men equal social and political rights."

Two decades later a fully developed analysis of the subject indicates prolonged thought and reading in the field. At the request of Charles Parkhurst, editor of *Zion's Herald*, Frank Mason North produced a series of four articles, which were published weekly between January 14 and February 4, 1891, the first three on the paper's front page. Their four topics carry far more subtle significance than most such neat titles: "Socialism and the Christian Church," "The Christian Church and Socialism," "The Christianity of Socialism," and "The Socialism of Christianity." The balanced appraisal of both dangers and challenges, the openness to a changing world and the steadfastness of Christian faith, these are remarkable manifestations of a brilliant mind and a sensitive spirit. To make them fully contemporaneous one need only substitute for "socialism" the prevailing twentieth-century term "communism." But Frank Mason North (who referred occasionally to "communistic" ideas or programs) would recognize today that "communism" is a narrower word with far less affinity to the Christian gospel.

The theme of the *Zion's Herald* series appeared in an opening paragraph. A Mr. Ludlow, writing to the English "Christian Socialist," Frederick Maurice, from the Paris Revolution of 1848, reported that "Socialism was a real and very great power, . . . and that *it must be Christianized, or it would shake Christianity to its foundation!*" North went on to remind his readers that the church had often in the past encountered "forces which she herself should have marshaled and clothed in the uniform of the faith. For in Christianity are the creative ideas which must produce all the well-being of society, and it is a terrible indictment either of the church's perception or of her consecration when she becomes conscious of those ideas only through the teaching of 'them that are without'."

The first article then discusses five reasons why the church has

71

ignored or feared or shunned socialism. Primary among these is the "fundamental misconception" that the gospel is "a divine contrivance for redeeming men *from* this present world rather than *in* it," the half-truth "that Christ came . . . to rescue the individual, not to reform society; to extricate His *elect* from the meshes in which humanity had entangled itself, rather than to break the bonds and let the *world* go free." Specifically North cites the expectation of the early disciples for a speedy Second Coming, the alliance of the church with authority and wealth, the essential egoism of medieval piety, and the toleration of inequalities within a civilization called Christian. "Often," he noted, "the tendency of the church has been to substitute charity for justice, to ameliorate rather than to cure social ills; . . . the needs of the church have often excluded the needs of humanity."

A second factor in the conflict between Christianity and socialism lies in the fact that "for long centuries the church has been an endowed institution and a part of the established order." Because socialism proposes radical economic readjustments "which will affect all values," vested interests quite naturally resist such change. The writer quotes Karl Marx's devastating quip that "the English Established Church will more readily pardon an attack on thirty-eight of its thirty-nine articles, than one thirty-ninth of its income." As a third element in Christian opposition, North acknowledges that "Socialism in its measures and its men, if not always atheistic and anti-Christian, has rarely been other than un-Christian"; e.g., Rousseau, Voltaire, Fourier, Proudhon, Bakunin, John Stuart Mill. In the light of this avowed materialism, "it is less difficult to see why the church should have looked upon the whole socialistic propaganda as a menace to herself and her faith than why she has not herself averted the contest by the irresistible application of her own Gospel to social injustice."

Furthermore, it must be admitted that communistic experiments and other attempts at socialism under Christian auspices have often "excited contempt by their folly or their failure." "Finally, the church in America suspects Socialism because of her constitutional aversion to State interference with the private rights and the moral concerns of men." Indicting the type of

72

"sturdy and steady conservatism" which "depreciates the need of social reform," North sees capitalism and the church allied for self-preservation, demanding that the state protect their liberties but abstain from interfering with their functions.

The second article in the series begins by deploring the widening gulf between the sacred and the secular, with art and science and the political and social orders relegated to the latter category. Praising the reforms of Wilberforce, Howard, and Shaftesbury, North asserts: "It was a *Christian* conviction which commanded the liberation of the slave, the relief of the prisoner, and justice to the poor." He then proceeds to emphasize three truths which "seers if not the whole church" understand: (a) "*every* phase of human life is a concern of the church;" (b) "this well-being is not a demand upon individuals alone, but upon the church as the formal expression and instrument of the Spirit of Christ;" (c) "the problems are not those of Christian *charity* chiefly, but those of human justice." These are profound insights for a pastor writing in 1890, insights which have yet to be attained by many people in our churches today.

Frank Mason North rejected the charge that benevolence is a handicap to reform, but he stressed that it can no longer be accepted as the last resort of the poor or the chief virtue of the fortunate. Thanks to men such as Frederick Maurice, who proclaimed man's essential sonship and brotherhood as the "primary condition of humanity," North said, there is at last a "reversal of tendency to ignore the second great commandment." Among leaders who were stimulating the Christian enterprise to cope with social ills, he named Elisha Mulford, an Episcopalian; T. T. Munger, at United Church, New Haven; Washington Gladden; Lyman Abbott; and Phillips Brooks.

"The church is turning its face toward the industrial problems," declared the man who eighteen years later would see his report on "The Church and Modern Industry" become "The Social Creed of the Churches." North spoke also of the Social Democrats in Germany, the Christian Social Union in Britain, the eagerly awaited papal encyclical on social questions (*Rerum Novarum,* May 15, 1891). He referred to the amount of "time devoted in recent session of the Evangelical Alliance to social questions," to

"Count Tolstoi's startling application of the literal gospel to modern life," and to the discussion of *Progress and Poverty* by Henry George (who had run for mayor of New York in 1886). In these he saw evidence of "a new political economy" in which "the conception of man as an inexorably selfish machine gives place to that of man as a living soul." "Its advocates, even when they deny Christ, urge the Christian's ethics under the name of 'altruism,' " North claimed, "and many of its foremost teachers are treating social questions from the Gospel point of view."

What, now, of our own Methodist Church? It inherited from its founder a mission to the poor and the oppressed. Methodism was a social as well as a spiritual reformation. That quaint document we call the General Rules is packed with the seed principles of a new social order. . . .

If any organized body in the world today is prepared by its genius, experience and contacts to study social and industrial problems and apply the Gospel to their solution, it would seem to be the Methodist Episcopal Church. . . .

[Yet] its colleges present few advantages for adequate study of the science of society. As far as can be learned, not one of its theological schools, where are trained the men whose very first hand-to-hand encounter with the world of their work will be with other men who hunger and toil and curse a social order which often denies them manhood's first right, gives any specific attention to the living problems of sociology. . . . Methodism awaits thought-leadership in these themes. . . .

On the contrary, Methodism tolerates and approves a system of church management which practically excludes the poor, deepens the lines drawn by the caste-spirit of the world, withholds the millions which would unlock the secret of dealing with the "downtown" populations, and looks with suspicion upon men who assert that the "kingdom" for which Christ taught us to pray will certainly not "come" until we help Him answer the other prayer which to millions of our fellow-men seems so necessary and so vain, "Give us this day our daily bread." . . . In a word, Methodism has long been conscious of its mission to regenerate souls. Let it now realize, also, that God calls it to regenerate society.

74

Here is the concern about ecclesiastical policies which was soon to help organize the Open and Institutional Church League. Here is an awareness of "down-town" populations and their challenge to the church that begins to "catch fire" only now, after seventy-five years. Here is a recognition that the gospel of Jesus Christ has social as well as individual implications. Here is the vision which was to lead Frank Mason North back to the city the following year.

To write on "The Christianity of Socialism" took as much courage in 1891 as it does today to speak of any positive relationship between Christianity and communism, of mutual challenge instead of black-and-white contrast. Suggesting that the watchwords of socialism and the gospel are the same—equality, liberty, fraternity—North in his third article made the bold assertion: "And thus amid all the absurdities, the omissions and the positive menaces of much that is called Socialism, one cannot look upon it long and earnestly without discerning in it genuine marks of its kinship with the Christianity of Christ." Aware that critics would ignore his clear recognition—and rejection—of fallacies and dangers, he nevertheless focused attention on the positive affirmations of Christianity and socialism.

In terms of community North admitted, "the ideal of the former [Christianity] is certainly immeasurably superior, yet neither has with complete success worked its principle into actual life." Even today no one can claim that the church has sufficiently realized the brotherhood of man. While Christians often fail to act as good Samaritans, North pointed out, Socialists often scorn to acknowledge God as the source of humanitarian concerns. But the law of mutual help by which they operate is "a fundamental principle in the whole structure of the Christian life."

Specifically, this third article dealt with three "socialistic" policies: substitution of industrial cooperation for competition, arbitration to suppress and supplant war, and a more equitable relation between "weal and wealth." It cited concrete examples of families earning five dollars per week, of laborers working fourteen hours a day at seven cents an hour, of products which sold for seven shillings (nearly a dollar) but netted the actual maker three cents. Intrinsic evils such as these, North implied, are at last being seen as injustices, not as the faults of their victims. And they are leading to demands for fundamental changes in the social and economic system: profit-sharing, cooperative stores, "communistic" societies. "Is, then, this whole mighty movement anti-Christian?" he asked; "Is it even un-Christian? Is it not in essential harmony with the teachings of Christ?"

In the realm of international peace North saw another common goal shared by socialism and Christianity. True, he admitted, some forms of socialism "know no compromise save the torch and the bomb," but "the best, the coolest, the dominant thought" seeks arbitration among governments and peoples.

In the third area of kinship North described the Bible as "in part a treatise upon the uses and misuses of wealth. Its descriptions of the power, the peril, and the effect of money-loving and money-getting are irresistibly accurate." He went on to argue that the Bible stands squarely against monopoly (those who join house to house and field to field, Isa. 5:8), and concluded: "On every problem of political economy—the ownership of land, the question of interest, the rights of labor, the treatment of poverty, the principles of taxation, the danger of capital—the Bible has its utterance." Such an interpretation runs counter to many today who spurn biblical ethics on the ground that explicit guidelines are nonexistent or irrelevant.

In summary, North pointed up the inherent contrasts between socialism and Christianity and arrived nevertheless at a provocative conclusion:

The ends for which Socialism are striving are essentially those which are central in the "promise and potency" of the Gospel. The contention is not that all Socialism is Christian. There is a Socialism that is as subversive of the Sermon on the Mount as it is of the Decalogue. Nor do we find wisdom, justice and mercy in all the diversified schemes by which theoretical and practical reformers seek social perfection. And even should true Socialism attain its highest ideal, it would not be Christianity—since the one deals with the humanity of one world, the other with the humanity of two. Yet, none the less, within its limitations Socialism is not the foe, but the brother, of Christianity.

The final article in this prophetic series bore the startling title, "The Socialism of Christianity." It asked bluntly: "If the contention be admitted that touching this present world the essential aims of Socialism and Christianity are identical, what are the practical methods by which the church can assume and retain its true place as the leader in social reform?" Any such methods must rest on the conviction that personal regeneration and social transformation go hand in hand. They must recognize what has heretofore been often overlooked; namely, the "tremendous influence of environment on character."

Ideas must harden into facts. Principles must put on form. Liberty creates institutions. Justice becomes courts of law. Charity is organized into hospitals, and the Gospel must govern life. It is not true that we are to be content with the fact that the ideals of a perfect society are in the Gospel. . . . Only, then, when the church acts from the conviction that Christianity relates itself to the life both of the individual and of the community, can its true mission be accomplished. It must cure its fevered patient and at the same time drain the marsh where lurk the germs of the disease.

Such a philosophy of mission was half a century ahead of its time. It has not yet achieved universal comprehension or commitment. Frank Mason North not only felt its imperative, but focused its endeavor. First, he declared, there must be a more urgent application of Christ's teaching to personal, domestic, commercial, political, and social affairs. Deploring "the fiction of a dual conscience, of which one part acts in the business world and the other in ordinary life," he called for an end to extravagance, to the tyranny of power, to the slavery of domestic workers, to unjust wages, etc. "This, then, first, is the church bound to do," he asserted, "to apply its own ethics to life." Instead of inviting—and inciting—drastic measures by divorcing business from Christian principles, North appealed: "Let Christians live Christianity; let the second great commandment have the right of way, and Socialism will find its occupation in part gone; for its problems will be nearing solution."

As a second concrete step, the church itself must practice the same Christian ideals which it demands of individual members.

77

North condemned monopoly of the Lord's house by class privilege, support of wealth and capital in ecclesiastical polity and policy. Specifically, "the pew system [i.e., support of churches through rental of seats] is wrong in principle and terribly pernicious in its results." There is no shrewder device, he continued, for creating a false opinion of Christianity and excluding the masses from Christian fellowship. "The Gospel stands for brotherhood, simplicity, humility, helpfulness, self-sacrifice. The church belies it when it encourages caste, extravagance, pride, exclusiveness, selfishness."

Thirdly, the church must be directly concerned with the betterment of social conditions.

Do we mean by entering politics? No, assuredly. By secularizing the church? Never. But we do mean that the whole force of Christian thought and action should be turned upon the world's wrongs and miseries; that it is the church's duty to make social ethics a prime study in our colleges and seminaries; to treat sympathetically all honest effort for reform; to agitate against the overcrowding of the poor, the false methods of business, the public crime of monopoly, the injustice of the competitive system, the cruelty of child labor; to plead for the community control of what concerns the community as such, for the reorganization of labor on some co-operative basis, for the radical change of our treatment of criminals, for the reduction of the hardships of toil, for the abolition of pauperism, and the prohibition of the liquor crime.

Such eloquent elucidating of the social gospel—or even of "Christian socialism," if you will—had not been voiced before. It would be sixteen years before Walter Rauschenbusch published *Christianity and the Social Crisis,* although he began his first draft of that masterpiece very soon after North's series appeared in *Zion's Herald.* Frank Mason North, just turned forty, was at mid-life but hardly at mid-career. Although he had served pastorates in the "inner city," one might have expected his first "blueprint" to appear *after* he had worked awhile in the City Society. Or his treatment of socialism might well have remained a theoretical and historical analysis from the campus of Wesleyan University. Instead he moved forcefully from the scholarly references of the opening articles to the fervent exhortations of the finale. This, too, was typical of Frank Mason North.

There will be disagreement as to methods, and perhaps specific contentions; but the church—in its pulpit, through its press, in its legislative discussions, and in its guidance of the thought and action of the individuals who compose it—must accept the challenge thrown down to it by the spirit of this age and become the antagonist of all evils, the protector of all the unfortunate, and the avenger of all the wronged.

The pride that despises labor must go. The selfishness which seeks men simply to use them must die. The customs which put the silken glove upon the iron grasp of human greed must be abolished. The laws which ennoble riches and degrade manhood are to be abrogated. The wealth which belongs to all should be held for all, and the rights which belong to each should be withheld from none. The rivalry which begets hate and issues in death must be supplanted. The hand which shackles souls before they see the light must be cut off. The avarice which buys up virtue for gold and makes merchandise of vice must be foiled. Entailed poverty and enforced starvation must be prevented by the community which now barely relieves them. For each soul there must be a living chance in this world and a reasonable opportunity to secure in the world to come "life everlasting."

All this Christ came to accomplish; most of this Socialism is seeking to do. Upon the church the age lays a two-fold demand—that it *prove the truth of its faith,* and *apply its morals to life.* Many are busy about the former; the latter is the responsibility of the whole church.

Any attempt to evaluate North's thoughts on Christianity and socialism, as a foundation for the social gospel he preached and practiced so effectively for another forty years, must begin with this *Zion's Herald* series, but it cannot stop there. The significance of these articles lies primarily in their timing: in North's own career *before* he left Middletown, Connecticut; in the development of Christian social thought;[3] in the rapid industrialization and urbanization of American society.

Frank Mason North was never one to leave his convictions to mere words, however eloquent. Perhaps at his initiative, perhaps

[3] Cf. Charles Howard Hopkins, *The Rise of the Social Gospel in American Protestantism, 1865-1915* (New Haven: Yale University Press, 1940).

on the inspiration of his recent writing, a resolution was introduced by North and two of his colleagues at the New York East Annual Conference in April, 1891, to this effect:

Believing that the general unrest prevailing among the laboring classes of our time and the urgency voted by public opinion to social questions justly claims the prayerful and studious investigation of all Christian men, and of the public teachers of religion especially, we move the appointment of a committee of five—to report at the next session of the Conference—to consider the relation of the Church to the various phases of what is called Socialism.[4]

Such a committee on the Relation of the Church to Socialism (later renamed the Church and Social Problems) was appointed forthwith. Reminiscing clearly sixty-seven years later, Bishop Herbert Welch called it "a strong committee" made up of "prominent members" of the Conference:[5] F. M. North, chairman; John Rhey Thompson; Joseph Pullman; Bradford P. Raymond, president of Wesleyan University, 1899-1908; William North Rice, long-time professor of geology at Wesleyan.

The report of the committee was submitted to the next session of the New York East Annual Conference, on April 4, 1892. Frank Mason North composed approximately half of the statement alone and shared in all but seventy-one lines of it. Quoting Professor Richard T. Ely of Johns Hopkins University, author of *Social Aspects of Christianity* (1889), to the effect that "extreme individualism is immoral," the report presented a revolutionary explanation of social ills:

Although many are poor because of indolence, intemperance, or incompetency, it is also true that multitudes are poor because the economic system itself has not brought to them a fair share of the products of their own labor. The conviction is certainly growing that many of the evils of society may be cured, or at least greatly mitigated, by such modifications of the existing social system as shall secure to the industrious and temperate better conditions of life, better homes, more comforts, and larger opportunities for intellectual and moral

[4] *Journal,* New York East Annual Conference, 1891, pp. 24 and 28.
[5] Personal interview, New York, January 21, 1958.

improvement. Many of the utterances of the socialists themselves . . . contain much which we as Christians can heartily indorse (North and Rice).

Then followed a review of distinctive Methodist qualifications for social leadership, some of it taken verbatim from the *Zion's Herald* series. John Wesley was, the report asserted, "both in theory and practice, one of the few great humanitarians." The resolution to be submitted to General Conference appealed for "fearless discussion" of four main points.

First, "the rights and correlative duties of property ownership." "While maintaining firmly the sacredness of individual rights of property and resisting any communistic scheme of general confiscation," Rice had written, "we believe that the prodigious inequality in the distribution of the blessings of life is a frightful evil." North himself added:

This is not the plea of the reckless leveler. It is not even asserted that the aggregation of wealth is in itself an unmitigated evil. Yet . . . monopoly in land, in the natural resources of the earth, in the necessary instruments of production, must be strenuously resisted. Corporations should be placed under the most observant control of government. Taxation should be distributed so as to fall more heavily upon the rich . . . and there should be a graduated tax on large inheritances.

Second, "in spite of the selfish instinct and the tyrannical spirit which are often prominent in the combinations of labor as well as in those of capital," the church should "greet cordially the many principles of the labor organizations which are in harmony with the teachings of the Gospel": on one hand "the right of workmen to combine for mutual well being," on the other "the need . . . for strict governmental regulation of employment of children and of women . . . and employment in unwholesome and dangerous occupations" (North and Raymond). "The influence of poverty upon character," said North in this report, "is as important as that of character upon poverty. It is the Church's duty not merely to give the dole of charity and to teach contentment, but to agitate for social justice, and demand for the very humblest the right to a fair chance."

81

Third, "we approve of the principle of profit-sharing and co-operation in all practicable forms." Furthermore, "the principle of arbitration ought to be encouraged as a means of settling many difficulties between capital and labor." Such precepts are taken for granted today; they were not even widely familiar in 1892.

Fourth, the church herself must expel the caste spirit and all elements which emphasize social distinctions. "It is wrong to tempt the poor to envy or the rich to pride. We believe the pew system is a barrier between the masses and the churches, and urge its condemnation as contrary both to good policy and the true spirit of the Gospel." "The Church should never forget that her chief mission is spiritual," the chairman wrote, "but the exigencies of society demand that our churches shall also be centers of social, educational, and philanthropic influences, and shall concern themselves with human welfare in this world as well as in that which is to come."

The report was enthusiastically adopted by the New York East Annual Conference and sent as a memorial to the General Conference of 1892, which took no action. Four years later the New York East Annual Conference renewed its resolution. As Herbert Welch, this time a member of the committee, recalls the process, he had become—in association with various industrialists—"rather more conservative than some of my brethren" (notably William North Rice). Because he wished neither to cause division on the Conference floor by bringing in a minority report nor to sign the original version of the report, Welch offered to resign from the committee. Apparently North's tact and moderation prevailed, and the more extreme statement was modified so that Welch could conscientiously sign it. "North was recognized as the leader," Welch insisted, "though *not* the most radical." [6]

The distinction between charity and justice constitutes the practical key to the social-gospel protest against previous—and present-day—pietism. In this vein, North wrote for the *Zion's Herald* in 1893: "The problem of poverty lies very close to the problem of sin. Sin is a primary cause of poverty, poverty a

[6] *Ibid.*

82

constant occasion for sin." [7] Fourteen months after his series on Christianity and socialism was published, North became corresponding secretary of the New York City Church Extension and Missionary Society. In his inaugural address on April 21, 1892, he returned to this theme, using some of the identical sentences he had published in *Zion's Herald:*

Somebody has said that the distinction between the Socialist and the Christian is this: "One seeks to improve character by better conditions; the other, conditions by better character." So there are many who think the Church is going beyond its commission when it is other than directly evangelistic. Its business is to rescue men and get them safe to the shore. It has nothing to do with teaching them how to sail or swim or pour oil upon a troubled sea. On the other hand are many who have no hope for human character except in the change of the besotting, carnalizing conditions in which human life is so often lived. Now both views are right and neither is complete. The middle ground is the only true one. The evangelist and the humanitarian must come together. It is perfectly absurd to think of saving the world simply by preaching and revival meetings. The Gospel must be put into institutions and become an organized and visible force. So it is equally absurd to think men are redeemed when they are fed and clothed, get work, and become educated. All this without the transformation of character is utterly void. . . .

Let us admit that the work assigned us is not merely rescue work. It is not ours alone to show men a path through the desert, but as well to plant the seed which will some day make the desert blossom as the rose. The battle will not be won by guerilla tactics, but a plan of campaign with careful note of the key positions, with massing of troops, and well timed attack, and ample care of the commissariat, must be adopted and worked.

During the next twenty years Frank Mason North was caught up in the administrative details of his vast metropolitan parish. His frequent speeches, his continuous stream of articles, constantly confronted the church with its social responsibility. But he retained his theological perspective and his ethical stability precisely because he had long since hammered out the implications

[7] "City Missions and Poverty," p. 33.

of the gospel for human life. He was ready, willing, and able to add his support to the Methodist Federation for Social Service in 1907, to the Federal Council of Churches in 1908, because he had already composed his own social creed in the quiet of a small New England town. No wonder Worth Tippy was able to say, in that farewell service of memory: "Dr. North definitely fused social and spiritual passion. He had technical knowledge of the field in which he worked. He had balance and courage, and he never swerved from his loyalty to Christ. He kept the faith to the end." [8]

[8] *Frank Mason North,* p. 24.

A Prayer for the Multitudes

Where cross the crowded ways of life,
  Where sound the cries of race and clan,
Above the noise of selfish strife,
  We hear Thy voice, O Son of Man!

In haunts of wretchedness and need,
  On shadowed thresholds dark with fears,
From paths where hide the lures of greed,
  We catch the vision of Thy tears.

From tender childhood's helplessness,
  From woman's grief, man's burdened toil,
From famished souls, from sorrow's stress,
  Thy heart has never known recoil.

The cup of water given for Thee
  Still holds the freshness of Thy grace;
Yet long these multitudes to see
  The sweet compassion of Thy face.

O Master, from the mountain side
  Make haste to heal these hearts of pain;
Among these restless throngs abide,
  O tread the city's streets again;

Till sons of men shall learn Thy love,
  And follow where Thy feet have trod;
Till glorious from Thy heaven above,
  Shall come the City of our God.

New York
1903

5

"The Christian City"

O Master, from the mountain side
Make haste to heal these hearts of pain;
Among these restless throngs abide,
O tread the city's streets again.

Frank Mason North knew what it meant to leave the mountainside and tread the city streets again. He had been supremely happy in the college pastorate at Middletown, Connecticut—happy with his ministry in the quiet, rustic community, happy with his new family. But he had grown up among the urban cries of race and clan, and his heart—like that of his Master—had never known recoil. Charles Randolph North, his elder brother, had served for less than a year as corresponding secretary of the New York City Church Extension and Missionary Society when he was killed in a railway accident on Long Island in 1889. Three years later Frank Mason North was elected to the same post.

"Men speak as though Methodism were a balky horse, which will travel well enough on all other roads but refuses to go when he strikes the pavements of the metropolis," North wrote soon after his return to New York.[1] He was not the only Methodist statesman concerned with this growing problem, but he saw clearly that it represented a *new* problem, requiring new insights and new techniques, for gigantic cities are a modern phenomenon, and an evangelistic "flying column is no longer adequate. The Christian Church must become an army of occupation."

[1] "New York Letter by Knickerbocker," *Central Christian Advocate*, November 15, 1893, p. 9.

One of North's major responsibilities in the City Society—and one of his principal channels of influence—was the editorship of *The Christian City*. Soon after taking office he discarded the title of the insignificant "house organ," *Aggressive Methodism,* and with occasional lapses *The Christian City* appeared monthly until North's resignation in 1912, when it became a bi-monthly until 1918.[2] In the first issue after reorganization the editor expounded his philosophy as follows:

Our aim in this new departure is to concentrate, as far as our influence extends, the thought of the church upon the fundamental principles of the gospel as applied to the conditions of the social order of our own times, especially as it exists in the cities, and, among the cities, in New York in particular. We believe that the coming of the Kingdom depends not alone upon God's purpose but upon man's apprehension of that purpose. The church must not only work—but work to a pattern.[3]

This theological perspective dominated the publication throughout, but the magazine proved also to be a fascinating window on metropolitan life and times. Advertisements ranged from Constantine's Pine Tar Soap and Stodder Punctureless (bicycle) Tires to Bishop McCabe's testimonial that " 'I never allow myself to be without Dr. Janes' Headache Powders.' (They relieve instantly. No evil effect.) " *Youth's Companion* announced among coming attractions for 1897-98: "The Life of a Senator" by Henry Cabot Lodge, "Training the Voice" by Lillian Nordica, plus stories or articles by Rudyard Kipling, Stephen Crane, Hamlin Garland, the Honorable Theodore Roosevelt, Edward Everett Hale, and Lt. R. E. Peary. The Vir Publishing Company of Philadelphia introduced a "Self and Sex Series" by Sylvanus Stall, D.D., and Mrs. Mary Wood-Allen, M.D., designed to promote purity and truth by explaining "What a Young Boy (or Girl) (or Husband) (or Wife) (or Man of 45) (or Man of 65) Ought to Know": "These books will create an Antiseptic Atmosphere in which Evil Thoughts cannot live." By 1906 subscriptions

[2] Cf. *The Christian City* (revived and revised), March, 1965, p. 1.

[3] January, 1897, p. 50.

to *The Christian City* were being offered in a quadruple bargain along with *The Review of Reviews, Cosmopolitan,* and *Woman's Home Companion* (all for $3 instead of the regular $6 for the other three alone) !

Bits of "urbania" sprinkled through the magazine contributed intentionally or otherwise, to the vividness of New York's challenge to the churches. Readers were told that on Tenth and Eleventh Avenues (in 1898) there was one bathtub for 440.3 families. Word that one cent more for knee pants would *double* the starvation wages of 2,300 workers on strike was contrasted with a Christian Science meeting at which the leader arose after a hymn and prayer to suggest: "Friends, let us surround with beautiful thoughts those living in the slums below Fourteenth Street." [4] In 1904 the editor speculated about the probable effects of the new subway which could transport passengers from 125th Street to Brooklyn Bridge in twenty to twenty-five minutes. It was noted that New York contained as many Italians as Venice, and that one in every four Manhattan residents was a Jew. An editorial on "Public Baths and Public Comfort" discussed a municipal report from the Mayor's Committee—and nothing has been done on this problem after sixty years!

A sensitive Christian sees the city in still more graphic terms:

He finds the men to whom he is sent debauched by drink which is given them under the authority of law. He discovers that family life is destroyed, its sanctities gone, its control overthrown by the impossibility of home, impossible under what is known as the sacred rights of property. He looks into the eyes of men and women gaunt with hunger and clothed with rags, cursed by the poverty of vice, some of them,—but more, ground into the dust by the inequities of industrial injustice and the cruel pride of social caste. About him swarm myriads of children doomed to warped lives and vicious surroundings from their birth; children with no home when night comes; the alleys and thoroughfares their playgrounds by day; the oaths and vulgarity of reckless sin the most familiar sound in their ears; children whose souls are saturated with evil before ever they know that sin is sin, or that God is God. He marks crowding the streets aliens whose very

---

[4] *The Christian City,* August, 1897, p. 219.

89

first knowledge of the freedom of our land is in the licensing and protection of vice, and who enter the national domain by way of the purlieus of crime. He feels quickly that the great masses here are swayed by passion, ignorance, prejudice—that they love not God and hate the church—and in the main believe profoundly that no man cares for their life.[5]

This, then, was the mission field for the New York City Church Extension and Missionary Society, the new parish which North had come to serve. "The Society is Methodism at work," he remarked in his fifth annual report. Organized in 1866 as the New York City Sunday School and Missionary Society, it changed its name five years later. Under this agency the Methodist Episcopal Church in the metropolitan area carried on a multi-phased program: ministry to immigrants (most notably the Church of All Nations), rescue missions in the Bowery, settlement houses, institutional churches, a total of more than thirty centers. In his inaugural address, delivered on April 21, 1892, North declared:

The Church has never met greater problems than those which confront her on Manhattan Island. The kingdom of Christ must be established in the great social, commercial, industrial and intellectual centers and dominate their life, or be relegated to the rank of a fourth rate power among the forces which control human destiny.

This was more than a sociological observation; it was a fundamental theological affirmation. Although North seldom if ever talked about "building the Kingdom of God"—that phrase so objectionable to later critics of the social gospel—he made abundantly clear his faith that man is in partnership with God, an essential instrument in fulfilling his Will.

If we imagine that God can finish his work on this earth without either saving or destroying this great and wicked city, we are not arguing according to the analogy of history. We are equally astray if we suppose that he exempts our own Church from the high privilege of

[5] F. M. North, "The Gospel for the City; Larger Ideals As Well As New Methods," address to the National City Evangelization Union, November 17, 1892.

doing his will and work *here*. Whether he will destroy or save depends quite definitely upon what we do; and what we do depends upon our conception of his plan, our conviction of our own duty, and our consecration to his service.

This human responsibility within God's purpose North saw reflected and verified in changing secular concepts as well. He was always quick to recognize and emphasize movements outside the church which seemed to reinforce the second Great Commandment. One of these was a new understanding of human rights. "It is now denied in very reputable quarters," he asserted in this same inaugural address, "that a man has a right to all he can get; that society is a scramble and a survival of the strongest and the best fit; that laws should be made for the strong rather than the weak." A second firm conviction involved social and preventive reforms as distinct from individual, curative philanthropy. "The whole social movement with all its vagaries," he said, "has a central thought which would do no discredit to the Gospel itself . . . not temporary relief, nor incidental benefit, but well-being and character and changed conditions in this world, the redemption not only of souls, but of life."

Over and over the secretary of the City Society returned to his central theme of God's presence in the midst of all human life. "There are people," he bemoaned in 1892—and would still find today—"who do not perceive that God is at work in the secular world as truly as he is in the religious." Frank Mason North never doubted this divine activity. Nor did he ever slacken in his own activity in response to God's concern. The New York City Society covered a gigantic enterprise, a polyglot family in which (as North himself put it) "the Swedish, German, Italian, Chinese, Russian, Hebrew, Polish and *Jargon* were represented."

In addition to editing *The Christian City,* Frank Mason North served as metropolitan commentator for a number of church publications. Here he amused himself (but probably fooled few readers) with a variety of *noms de plume.* As Calamus Currens he contributed "Gothamite Notes" for the *North-West Christian Advocate.* As Curren T. Calamo he wrote intermittently a "New York Letter" for the *Central Christian Advocate.* In one of these he poked sly humor at an earlier—and later—pseudonym: "Knickerbocker . . . seems for some months to have laid aside his pen. Has he wearied of life in the great city? Perhaps he is writing a book or building a church, or possibly . . . for a time has fled the country." None of these suggestions accurately portrayed the manifold concerns of the city secretary at this particular period. In fact, in the same issue of his "New York Letter," he condemned St. Paul's Methodist Church for tying up $300,000 in capital in the midst of a depression in order to build "a stately church . . . far out of the center of need and away from the rushing currents of the city's life."

"Knickerbocker" North knew his New York. In a two-part "Story of New York Methodism" [6] he sketched the needs of the city—and the handicaps of the Methodist Church in meeting those needs. Within a radius of thirty miles from Grand Central Station, he pointed out, the population (four fifths of it foreign-born or children of foreign-born residents) had increased 134% (to four million!) in thirty years, whereas Methodist growth had been only 120%. But on the East Side, where total population swelled by 30%, Methodist Church membership had gone down by 60%, and below 14th Street, in an area of 20% growth, Methodist membership dropped 40%. Here were unmistakable signs, even before the turn of the century, of Anglo-Saxon middle-class Protestantism losing its hold on the "inner city."

North recognized some of the reasons, too, and did not hesitate to point them out. Although "doing good" had been a requisite among the early Methodist rules of John Wesley, organized agencies for philanthropic service had not been developed, and North offered several explanations. One was the limited economic status of the people called Methodists. They had been late in arriving and were poor in resources, at least as compared with some other wealthy, highly endowed denominations. The largest single gift for the first Methodist Church in New York had been thirty pounds. Even the great philanthropists of the latter nineteenth century had "first-generation fortunes"—though New York

---

[6] *Christian Advocate*, November 7-14, 1895.

Methodists averaged $23 per member in annual church gifts, three times the denominational average for the country.

A second factor North cited was fear of "humanitarianism," lest it might be interpreted as a doctrine of salvation by works. "It is time the spectre of humanitarianism was chased from the field of our endeavor," he declared in 1892. "Methodists have been frightened by it long enough. . . . The world's great humanitarian was Jesus Christ. Who would know much of God must do much for men. . . . The truth is that the place of highest service belongs to that Church which cares most for *human welfare.*"

Closely related to this was the emphasis in Methodist theology on free grace and on the world to come, an emphasis which tended to exclude or minimize social responsibility. But Frank Mason North, his own work undergirded by a circle of wealthy and benevolent friends, looked into the future and wrote: "Who can doubt that when the twentieth century is half gone the historian of Methodism—then, please God, a united Methodism—will need not a page or two, but a volume, fitly to set forth the greatness of the philanthropies of Methodism?" [7]

North also found weaknesses in the structure and polity of the Methodist Episcopal Church. On one occasion he discussed briefly a proposal that an Order of Deacons should consist not of a second level of clergy, but of a fellowship of lay ministration.[8] A more serious threat to effective evangelism, in his view, was the insistence on Methodism's annual appointment system, even for special ministries. North commented sharply on the General Conference action of 1900:

The one year plan of appointment—with no limit to the number of successive reappointments—will receive its severest tests in the large cities, the very field where its benefits were expected to be most evident. It will be found that long-term opportunity requires long-term capacity. It may take a score of years to provide the latter in sufficient fulness to meet the former.[9]

[7] *The Christian City,* July, 1899, p. 118.
[8] *Ibid.,* December, 1901.
[9] *Ibid.,* January, 1901, p. 49.

But he concluded the same article with a vigorous reaffirmation of the Christian imperative: "For her [the Church] to assert moral convictions, in the market-place, in the forum, in legislative halls, and to create in men's minds a hunger for righteousness and a shame for sin, is not intermeddling with what does not concern her. It does concern her—for it concerns the Kingdom of God." [10]

If the Methodist itinerancy failed to build strong, permanent church institutions, this was especially so when Methodist work in the metropolitan area (presumably because of linguistic and ethnic segregation) was divided under six bishops and five presiding elders (district superintendents), and in the preceding decade fourteen bishops had presided over the two New York annual conferences. Still worse, only one of the six bishops and one presiding elder actually lived within the city; or (to take a single example) the East German Conference of the Methodist Church had a denominational center with thirteen people in the office staff, only three of whom lived in New York. Ecclesiastical absenteeism!

No wonder the secretary of the City Society was eager to find—and to glorify!—the "city missionary" as a man with a *mission to the city,* like Jonah of old, not a creation of episcopal assignment. His is "a work overwhelmingly important and specialized as definitely as is that of missions to the heathen in foreign lands." [11] It may take many forms and use many facilities—schools and churches, settlements and rescue missions, deaconesses and social workers. "This man with a mission to the cities must be evangelical in faith and evangelical in method," North continued; "he will be a gospel-man in what he believes and in what he does."

This does not sound like the later stereotype of the social gospel. Rather it was—and is—an attempt to awaken the church of Jesus Christ to her essential mission. "The application of the gospel to the cities is a process which has been very vaguely understood by the Church of the past and is only divinely [sic!—"dimly" as North corrected the text in the margin of his clipping!]

[10] *Ibid.,* p. 50.
[11] *Central Christian Advocate,* January 4, 1893, p. 3.

94

comprehended by that of the present." Salvation of souls, he asserted, has social, educational, and economic meanings, too.

The man with a mission to the cities must have knowledge as well as zeal, breadth as well as intensity . . . must be awake to the progress of social and economic ideas. . . . He needs to see humanity in the mass as well as the individual in the masses. . . . He stands in some dark, fetid court surrounded by the barracks, owned by, no one knows whom, but reeking with the filth and immorality of human degradation and he is bound to scrutinize that precious idol of the economist—the right of private property. He kneels at the bedside of the dying child, who lies scorching with scarlet fever or choking with diphtheria, and with his very prayer mingles indignant protest against the neglect of sanitary science by landlord and municipality. He traces everywhere the relation of the corner liquor saloon, protected by law, to the vice of brothel and the squalor of homes and better than senators understands the basis upon which the law should settle forever the status of this licensed crime. . . . He deals with working men. He is familiar with the red flag. . . . It is through his heart, warm with the divine love, and his mind, intelligent with the wisdom which is from above, that the world must gain the knowledge requisite for the solution of the mighty problems which confront its progress.

In official tribute on Janurary 10, 1936,[12] the Board of Managers of the New York City Society summarized North's own contributions under four main headings. The first was his *evangelistic concern.* Immediately after assuming office North laid plans for a Metropolitan Evangelistic Campaign conducted by Charles H. Yatman for six months in Union Square Theater. According to contemporary reports, "1,000 souls were led to Christ." But this was no momentary interest for Frank Mason North. The annual reports of the City Society usually listed "the number of souls who had come to the altars of the churches owned and operated by this Society": 17,000 in the first thirty years, another 1,000 in 1896-97. North rejoiced that these active welfare institutions and recreational centers were also holding two hundred

[12] *Frank Mason North,* pp. 54-58.

services each week and claimed a total membership of 3,500 in the churches, 6,000 in the Sunday schools.

The second distinctive contribution cited by Frederick B. Newell, then secretary of the City Society and later bishop of the New York Area, was the policy of *local ownership*. Whenever a congregation showed itself stable and ready to undertake self-support, the City Society would transfer the property title to the church with only an ecclesiastical mortgage; i.e., without indebtedness or interest *unless* the property ceased to be used for church functions, in which case a regular mortgage came into effect. In 1895-96 the congregation of St. Mark's moved to West 53rd Street and received full title, free of debt except for the ecclesiastical mortgage. By the time of North's death it had become one of the great centers of Methodism, with a membership of over two thousand, and (in Newell's words) "unquestionably this [policy of independence] had much to do with the rise of this great Negro church to its present position of distinction." During North's administration nine other churches received title to their property from the Society.

In the New York City Society office hangs a painting of Frank Mason North. Wearing a Prince Albert coat (which at least two informants recall as his invariable garb at this period), with a gold chain strung across his vest, he holds in his hand a document bearing the one legible word: "Agreement." On inquiry, Leland Cary, a later successor as secretary, surmised that the paper was probably an ecclesiastical mortgage, a hallmark of North's enlightened policy. No wonder Newell suggested, in his final tribute, that "we pause to admire the wisdom of his strategy."

Third, among the highlights of North's administration, was a word—and an attitude—conspicuous in his reports: Forward! Time and time again, his accounts of particular churches or programs included the assurance: "During the past year this church has moved forward into new ground." Out of the initial Yatman evangelistic crusade came the Forward Movement of 1897-1900, which brought S. Parkes Cadman from London for revival services. Five hundred to 3,000 people crowded into the Academy of Music for three Sunday services. Evening preaching and noonday prayer meetings were held daily. Over 2,000 inquirers responded, and 350 new members joined local congregations.

In addition to its evangelistic aims, however, the Forward Movement had financial and organizational dimensions. Designed to supplement and extend the work of the City Society, it provided aid for a number of churches outside the established structure, as urban evangelization moved forward into the twentieth century. This accent on advance was more than a slogan or activity for Frank Mason North; it characterized his vision and his faith. In observing the centennial of Yale Divinity School in 1922 he said simply: "We commemorate but we march."

As a fourth contribution, Newell declared, Frank Mason North was "essentially a builder" During two decades in office he supervised the building or land purchase for eleven congregations. One of these was Jefferson Park Church for the Italian community on East 114th Street near First Avenue. This $110,000 building, dedicated in 1907, included the usual sanctuary and Sunday school facilities, plus a roof garden, gymnasium and baths and locker rooms, a music room, a parlor for weddings and funerals, a center for settlement workers. "To understand the far-reaching influence of this man's ministry," said Newell at the Society's memorial service, "we should remember the thousands and thousands of men, women, and children who have gone in and out of the portals of Jefferson Park Church for Italians built in the heart of Little Italy."

One could say the same for other groups. Japanese work was initiated in Brooklyn and Manhattan in 1901-2; the following year work among Chinese, started previously, moved to Mott Street and eventually became a department of the Church of All Nations. The story is still told of a Negro pastor, Frederick A. Cullen, who was growing discouraged over the problems of his struggling little Salem Church. When he had a vision to "Go North!" he responded by going south on Manhattan to appeal for aid from Frank Mason North. With the support of the Society Salem Church flourished and grew to a membership of 4,000, ultimately taking over the West Harlem building of Calvary Church, which North himself had built in his last New

York pastorate (1884-87). Of this particular achievement, Bishop Newell recollects:

In those rare and beautiful moments, when Dr. North soliloquized from time to time with the Secretary of this Society, there used to come into his face a remarkable light as he told of his great joy that members of the Negro race had been aided by his activity, both in building that church and in serving this Society.[13]

Obviously North would not have been continued for so many years as chairman of his Conference Endowment Fund Commission and of at least three boards of trustees if he had not displayed unusual skill at finance. Yet, by the cruel irony of history, both the City Society and, later, the Board of Foreign Missions faced critical debts which were not covered until many years afterward. Frederick B. Newell, the man who bore major responsibility for paying off the City Society mortgages up to 1950, offers this generous and convincing explanation:

The world of his day had a custom of placing mortgages on property with the expectation of allowing the mortgage to continue without amortization for long periods of time. Dr. North could not have been expected to forsee how dangerous a policy this was. In fact the savings banks themselves didn't see the weakness of this policy until the great depression of 1929 brought them to their senses. Dr. North was a man of his time and the debt he left was part and parcel of the financial custom of the day.[14]

Others have mentioned as a further factor in this picture the death of several philanthropists who had supported the City Society program in earlier days. One conspicuous feature of North's career was the wide variety of friends whom he influenced profoundly. Recurring references indicate that he held prayer services in the home of John B. Cornell, that he often took John S. Huyler to kneel among the "Bowery bums" at Wesley (later Hadley) Rescue Hall, that at least two friends (possibly Huyler and Samuel W. Bowne) contributed $25,000 each to the

[13] *Ibid.*, p. 54.
[14] Letter to the author, July 8, 1965.

Twentieth Century Thank Offering Movement in 1900. His friendships, his boundless interest in people, were never limited to rich and influential men. But the work of the New York City Church Extension and Missionary Society rested largely on the fact that North charmed and challenged financial leaders of his day into generous support of ministries among the alien, the downtrodden, and the lost. When these men gradually left the scene or lost their fortunes, an entirely new pattern of support had to be developed amid changing social and economic conditions.

With the wisdom of hindsight, other critics have found fault with North's judgment in meeting the twentieth-century shifts of urban population. "There were and are those," writes a later colleague from Centenary days, "who have said that Dr. North's job was that of presiding over the closing of many Methodist churches in Manhattan, and the consolidation of churches." [15] But opinion is divided as to whether, in so doing, he showed financial and political genius, or whether some strategy could have been found to preserve some of these "old structures . . . from becoming warehouses" and thus have them available for today's renewed emphasis on inner-city parishes.

In Christian concern a few Methodist laymen and ministers met in 1891 to discuss city evangelization. North was probably not among them, since he had not yet been elected to the New York City Society, and it is therefore doubtful if he participated in the initial organization of the National City Evangelization Union later that same year. But from the assumption of his responsibilities in Manhattan in 1892, North became the undisputed leader of the new federation. When, in 1897, it was proposed that the Union should employ Frank Mason North as its full-time executive, he replied simply: "It is a tremendous duty to help save the metropolis of this great nation. That sense of responsibility keeps me where I am." But the following year he accepted the office of corresponding secretary and retained it until 1912, when the Union turned its work over to the Board of Home Missions and Church Extension of the Methodist Episcopal Church.

[15] W. W. Reid, letter to the author, June 12, 1965.

To the first formal session, November 17, 1892, North repeated many sentences *verbatim* from his articles in *Zion's Herald:*

It is not difficult to assume that the man who ventures to discuss *ideals* has nothing *practical* to propose. Our own age is so keenly devoted to actual performance that the theorist seems a visionary. . . . Methodism started with a great ideal—"to spread Scriptural holiness throughout the land." There is no larger ideal. Its realization may require the increase of the number of churches, and it may not. Holiness is sometimes more directly attained by excision than by accession. It may or may not include the expansion of the denomination in lines of wealth and education. It certainly does mean bringing, by some way, the Gospel of Christ where men individually may understand it and accept Him, but vastly more, it includes the sanctification of law, the establishing of divine justice in human affairs, the control of industry and thought and life in the interests of that kingdom of Redeemed Humanity in which the Eternal Son of God has with His own precious life bought the right to dwell forever. "Scriptural holiness" . . . deals not alone with man, but with humanity.

North then went on to inquire whether, in unprecedented conditions, the Methodist is to be "in the technical and somewhat threadbare phrase, 'a soul-saver'?"—whether he is to "rejoice in the growing light of the suburbs while the shadows deepen and lengthen upon the heart of the city?"

In language prophetic of a later emphasis on "the Christian presence" North declared: "Methodism must reach both ways; she must touch God on one hand and on the other the people. Nay, the figure is false. God is with the people, and Methodism can find each only by seeking the other." Despite "didactic theology in its pulpits" and "commercialism in its pews," he said, the church must be "always and everywhere *evangelistic.*"

But what is evangelism? Is it not the contact of saved souls with the unsaved? . . . The Church of *Christ*—of Christ who went about *doing good*—must walk about the streets, and go down upon the East side, and enter into poverty's home, and chat with the workingman over his hardships, or enter into his aspirations for a better job; it must help the bright boy to an education and the bad boy to escape from his surroundings; it must, by a membership vital with the di-

100

vine life, establish relations of sympathy and helpfulness, in *all possible ways,* with the individuals in the dense mass of humanity which, like an impenetrable wall, confronts it. . . . It must wipe out the fine distinction between *iniquity* and in-*equity.*

Continuing this theme a few months later, North wrote: "To that Church which solves the difficult problem of harmonizing the most intense and spiritual evangelism with the broadest humanitarianism the future belongs." "No organization or order of men on the face of the earth must be permitted to usurp the place of the Church of Christ as the champion of human rights." [16]

But while he recognized the need for clothing, for nickel meals, for other relief measures in the midst of a deepening depression and critical unemployment, Frank Mason North believed profoundly that such charity was not enough:

This treatment of symptoms will not deceive the thoughtful among the distressed classes, and many a wage earner will be asking with increased earnestness that something be done not to relieve the pain, but to cure the disease. . . . Why in New York one man can put $2,000,000 into one house for one family on Fifth Avenue, and within a short walk can be found crowded into an equal space a hundred families.[17]

With his awareness that the structure of society itself was out of joint North coupled an equally sincere conviction that the gospel of Jesus Christ does hold an answer—*the* answer—and that the servant of Jesus Christ must be the agent. To the "deepening convictions of men everywhere that some reconstruction of the social order is at hand," the City Secretary added: "Verily, changes must come, so fundamental and wide-reaching that there will be in the social world a new heaven and a new earth."

The possibilities of the applied Gospel in curing social inequities seem to him [the city missionary] less distant and the socialism of Christ more reasonable than to many who are following the Master and studying his teachings where the crowds cannot jostle thought or

---

[16] "City Missions and Social Problems," *Methodist Review,* March-April, 1893, pp. 238, 237.

[17] "Letter from New York by Knickerbocker," *Central Christian Advocate,* December 27, 1893.

disturb complacence. . . . In this process of social transformation, no man can better serve God and humanity than he who stands as the apostle of Jesus amid the surging crowds of our great cities.[18]

In pleading for effective evangelization, Frank Mason North took pains to clarify his terms. The word *"evangelical,"* he declared, deals with "theological theories, with orthodoxy rather than action." *"Evangelism"* he defined as "action rather than mere doctrine, but it is action limited to certain forms of religious appeal and concrete methods of service. The revival idea underlies the word." The third term, *"evangelization,"* he explained, includes both the others but is much broader in significance, as John R. Mott pledged the Student Volunteer Movement to "the evangelization of the world in this generation." "Evangelization means truth and honesty and justice," North insisted.[19] The church may need to show the way, to be a good Samaritan when the government is at fault, when justice is defective, when the public does not care.

But this should never imply a rejection of public services. The community must protect human rights and promote social betterment, even at the risk of government paternalism, the speaker affirmed. Sanitation, vice, the penal system, housing, labor violence, all are public issues which demand social solutions. Conversely, acceptance of government responsibility can never eliminate the role of the church. "Humanity extends beyond system; love makes its own channels," North said. "Ministration is as true a function of the Church as teaching or worship."

In order to meet this new challenge of the city, the secretary warned, evangelization will destroy more than sin. It will, firstly, shatter old molds of language—and he suggested, with typical quiet humor, that theological seminaries need a "Chair of Common Speech." Secondly, "property, it is likely, must be transformed." Some churches, he proposed, should be investing in lives instead of corner lots and ornate architecture. Thirdly, ecclesiastical "modes of administration" may need to be changed,

[18] "City Missions and Social Problems," pp. 237-38.
[19] "City Evangelization: Its Meaning, Its Method, Its Motive," at the International Convention of Y.M.C.A.'s in Theological Institutions of the United States and Canada, Rochester, N. Y., November, 1903.

as effective ministries take on multiple staffs with diverse training and functions. Finally, evangelization will demand a vastly increased "consecration of money and men—the best men, working in heavily endowed institutions of service."

In the famous Hall of Philosophy at Chautauqua, New York, then (1909) at the height of its popularity, Frank Mason North deplored the failures of education:

Out of the public schools we have, in hundreds of cities, thrown the Bible. Into our Sunday schools come a minority of the city's children for an hour one day in seven. Tens of thousands, yes, hundreds of thousands, of the boys and girls of our cities are growing up into citizenship and home-making, with no spiritual sanction for conduct, no conception of God, no knowledge of the Bible, no reverence for essential truths, and with an atrophied moral sense. Until education as a system of instruction and discipline can find a way, either through religious institutions or by direct methods, to put into the child heart and mind of our cities the primary facts and principles of religion, education as a phase of civilization is an abject failure.[20]

But North was the last person to leave the blame and the responsibility on the schools—or any other secular institution. He was speaking to Christians—for Christ:

This institution, the church, will default and miserably fail if, a conqueror everywhere else, it goes down to defeat in the cities of the world. . . . A scheme of campaign which plans to ravage remote fields or to capture defenseless towns and leaves untouched the heart of empire may give men exercise at arms and increase their tactical skill, but brings neither the full glory nor the final conquest. The nation may strengthen its commerce, perfect its policies, build large and strong ships, discipline its armies. Its destiny—who can not see it?—will still be wrapped up in the thronging life of the cities. The church may build its schools, lift towers symmetrical and strong, endow its vast charities and organize ministry in a system, and harden truth into symbol and creed—and still it will be true that the crowd, the seething, restless crowd of the cities determine the future.

[20] Cf. "The City and the Kingdom" in *Social Ministry*, Harry F. Ward, ed. (New York: Eaton & Mains, 1910), pp. 310-11.

One of the most crucial social issues in urban areas at the turn of the century—as today—was race relations. One might expect to find this comment in any contemporary discussion of New York's problems:

How closely you have studied our race troubles here, I do not know. The conflict between hoodlum toughs and vicious Negroes is simply inevitable at the points of contact in the sections where both thrive. Social and municipal conditions must be transformed before this danger is past.

Yet the report comes from North's column, "Metropolitan Matters" (under another *nom de plume,* Grapho) in the *Western Christian Advocate* for September 26, 1900. In talking "the other day" with Booker T. Washington, whom he greatly admired, North agreed that "industrially, the Negro has far less opportunity here than in the Southern States. Excluded from the trades, shut up to the occupations of service, the tendency toward deterioration, toward loss of self-respect, toward idleness and vice becomes strong indeed." Believing that the increasing migration northward was "perilous to virtue and integrity," he urged Washington to emphasize "here as in the Southern States the gospel of industrial education and opportunity for the Negro."

Evidently the atmosphere was strikingly parallel to that of New York in 1964, when the killing of a Negro boy stirred up a demonstration of protest in Harlem and beyond. North referred to an attack "by both mob and police upon innocent and absolutely unoffending Negroes" and then launched into a denunciation of shame to the police and to "Tammany which controls them, and to the citizenship which tolerates the Tammany tyranny. The most painful element in the miserable business," he added with typical candor and sensitivity, "is the apathy of the citizens and the indifference of the Church." But in such a situation Frank Mason North seldom rested his case with words. In consultation with Dr. W. H. Brooks, pastor of St. Mark's Methodist Episcopal Church, and aided by the legal advice of one of his many lawyer friends, Frank Moss, he sought (in vain?) "to secure redress in the punishment of the guilty police officers."

104

"New York is potentially in chains," North commented on the stranglehold of a corrupt Tammany. Even more practically, according to Walter Muelder, dean of the School of Theology at Boston University, "North's was one of the few voices who heralded the founding of the N.A.A.C.P." [21]

The secretary of the New York City Church Extension and Missionary Society was obsessed and sometimes oppressed by the weight of this polyglot, multiracial population and its need for superhuman patience and wisdom. Almost wistfully he remarked in Nashville, Tennessee, in 1903, after citing the 600,000 Jews and burgeoning Italian community of New York: "It is refreshing to see here in the South that you are dealing with a native-born population sixty per cent of which is white." But he knew full well—and never failed to add—that "the gospel is a message to every man on the face of the earth . . . every one of whom has a soul," be he Negro or white, immigrant or native-born.

Again in *The Christian City* North declared: "If, as some believe and assert, this race problem is to be solved first in the North, that solution will be settled aright only by the moral and religious forces which center in the evangel of Jesus Christ." [22] He did not mean merely pious and pietistic revivalism, which characterized the period of James Baldwin's youth, for example. "When the boys and girls come to the city," North explained, "they must find, if they are to be held, centers of life that are something more than Salvation Army barracks or the mourner's bench."

Frank Mason North also recognized the broader implications of the racial crisis. In keeping with his times, he accepted cultural and ethnic differences as inescapably real, but he was confident that good sense, human reason, and simple justice, as well as Christian brotherhood, could overcome them. In a symposium edited by Harry Ward he affirmed this faith in words that have a contemporary ring:

The amazing progress of forty years must not betray us into a denial

[21] *Methodism and Society in the Twentieth Century* (Nashville: Abingdon Press, 1961), p. 60.
[22] November, 1904.

of present facts. . . . The negro will not be a successful factor in our modern civilization unless he can survive the test of the city. On the streets of our cities, not upon the plantations of the Southland, will he find his birthright. Unless a character be developed which shall emerge from the complex conditions of our civic life unsullied, the citizenship of the future is not his. . . .

But to the test of the complex life of these vast American communities these [Anglo-Saxon?] traits come now to association with the characteristics of other races. The majorities in these cities are no longer American or English born. Here peoples separated by ages and by hemispheres are discovering one another and sharing a common life. No strengthening of the bars on the gates of Ellis Island will keep America forever Anglo-Saxon. Indeed, are not other peoples also to go forward into the Kingdom? Are not human rather than racial traits, after all, the elemental powers of the new character? Through the cities the people must together go and find one another and their destiny as they aspire and struggle and win. In the American city will be worked out that problem which belongs to the beginning of the better time, the oneness of the race.[23]

As this indicates, North quite understandably saw the racial challenge to the church at least as sharply in the lives of immigrants from abroad as among Negro migrants from the South. He was an ardent advocate not of America for Americans but of "America for the whole world." Over and over he appealed to his constituency to intensify the organized program for evangelizing all of these groups. If there is too close a link between Americanization and christianization—not to mention "Methodization" (note the capitalizations in the paragraph below), at least these appear to be in series rather than in apposition. And if critics of the social gospel choose to pounce upon the phrase, "to establish the kingdom of God," it should be pointed out that these are "vital forces," a sort of historical determinism, which may imply divine and/or human participation.

The purpose to Americanize, to christianize and so far as may be to Methodize the foreigners who crowd certain quarters of our large cities, has won the approval of the church at large and of its repre-

[23] "The City and the Kingdom," pp. 311-14.

sentative societies. . . . If it is important to send across seas our bishops to promote and superintend our mission to the far lands, it is imperative that the immense mission fields created on this continent by the progress of civilization should be the heart burden of some who lead in our denomination . . . a policy which ought to conserve and direct those vital forces which are eagerly moving forward to establish the kingdom of God in the cities of our land.[24]

Still another social problem corrupting "the Christian city" was the liquor traffic. As early as 1897 North wrote an editorial urging his readers against buying any goods from stores which sold liquor.[25] Two years later he expressed concern about the sale of beer on warships and at army canteens, citing the secretary of the navy and four generals as favoring a ban on such sales.[26] That same season an editorial proposed that a "popular non-alcoholic drink" (the forerunner of "soft drinks" today; note the designation of "pop"!) be provided for workingmen as an alternative to iced beer or warm Croton water.[27]

In many respects the arguments for and against the opening of saloons on Sunday paralleled arguments for and against prohibition two decades later. North considered alcoholic beverages a serious threat to the moral, social, and financial welfare of the laboring class. Contentions that the Sunday closing of saloons were not being enforced or, conversely, would not effectively prevent Sunday drunkenness appeared to him highly spurious. An exception for Sabbath trade in alcohol he labeled "class legislation" for the benefit of liquor dealers.[28] At the same time, North was realistic enough to recognize the necessity for moral controls in this area. "This is not to say," he wrote in 1903, "that the problem of drink and drinking customs can be solved by an ethical formula or some lofty mandate of authority." [29]

One further area of social challenge constantly interacted with race and immigration, slums and alcohol: the problem of or-

[24] *The Christian City*, April, 1900, p. 79.
[25] *Ibid.*, July, 1897.
[26] *Ibid.*, March-April, 1899.
[27] *Ibid.*, June, 1899.
[28] *Ibid.*, March, 1909.
[29] *Ibid.*, February, 1903.

ganized labor. It is indicative of the times in which North lived that "The Social Creed of the Churches" should have been presented in the form of a report on "The Church and Modern Industry." So significant a milestone in American religious life deserves a chapter to itself (see chapter 7). The avowed concern of Frank Mason North reached far back to his interest in Christian socialism, the resolutions he introduced as early as 1892 at the New York East Annual Conference, and the declarations of ecumenical groups at work in the cities.

Yet North was never radical in his commitments. His loyalties were always directed to Jesus Christ, his Lord, rather than to human agencies or organizations as ultimate. He did not believe that institutions *necessarily* served the physical or spiritual welfare of the individual. This caution in endorsing specific causes or structures he affirmed at the eleventh convention of the National City Evangelization Union:

There is a difference between our standing by the labor unions— the conventions of men who are appointed and bonded together to secure their rights—and our sympathy with the conditions of the workingmen. And if we test the Church on the one basis, without remembering to test it on the other, we are making a grave error. . . . I find that workingmen are unwilling to believe in the sympathy of the Church because we do not always stand for the special contentions of their labor unions. I have no opposition to the union of labor except when its position is wrong and un- righteous. But to test the fact of the Church's sympathy with the needs of the labor by the Church's formal relation to the labor unions is a narrow application of a very important principle.[30]

Yet all that has been said so far, all that is expressed in the now-famous Social Creed, denies the assumption of a narrow, pietistic individualism. Long before he heard of Reinhold Niebuhr, Frank Mason North sensed—even more than he for- mulated theologically—the fact that all finite structures are open to corruption and abuse. His was neither a superficial optimism nor a naïve trust in human systems.

This did *not* mean, ever, a rejection of the social dimension,

[30] *Ibid.*, December, 1901.

the social demand, of the Christian gospel. His personal creed was seldom put more positively and succinctly than in "A Statement to the Church" contained in an editorial on the brand new Methodist Federation for Social Service: "Industrial peace, social justice, commercial morality, political integrity, open opportunity to decent and happy conditions of life and of labor for every man, do not yet prevail. Until this comes to pass, the Kingdom of God, which is righteousness and peace and joy, cannot be supposed to have fully come." [31] Precisely because he believed in the transcendent, eternal kingdom of God, Frank Mason North devoted his life to proclaiming the material *and* spiritual conditions essential for the Christian city. During twenty years of his career, while Walter Rauschenbusch wrote and taught the social gospel and Washington Gladden preached it, North *was* the city missionary at work.

[31] *Ibid.*, March, 1908.

The Students' Hymn

The world's astir! The clouds of storm
Have melted into light,
Whose streams aglow from fountains warm
Have driven back the night.
Now brightens dawn toward golden day;
The earth is full of song;
Far stretch the shining paths away;
Spring forward! Hearts, be strong!

Where lies our path? We seek to know,
To measure life, to find
The hidden springs of truth whence flow
The joys of heart and mind.
We dream of days beyond these walls,
The lure of gold we feel;
Life beckons us and learning calls,
Loud sounds the world's appeal.

But Thou, O Christ, art master here;
Redeemed by Thee we stand;
We challenge life without a fear;
We wait for Thy command.
For Thy command is victory,
And glory crowns the task;
We follow Thee, and only Thee,
Thy will alone we ask.

Give us the wisdom from above;
We pledge our loyalty.
Change flash of hope to flame of love
And doubt to certainty.
In Thy great will, O Master Mind,
In Thee, O Master Heart,
Our guerdon and our guide we find,
Our Lord, our King, Thou art.

1917

6

Forerunners of Federation

Here stand we at the century's crest;
Shine Thou upon us, Lord of light;
Out from the ways that Thou hast blest
New paths are broadening to our sight.

"However late 'Federation' has been drafted into Christian service, there can be little doubt that in the Church of Christ it will find a broader and richer field than it ever has gained among the states and nations of the world." [1] In an address before the Federation of Churches and Christian Workers at Philadelphia (February 5, 1901) Frank Mason North reaffirmed a conviction which he had voiced through many channels for more than a decade. Citing the values of "unity in variety" for religion and art, without surrender or concession, he stressed that such ecclesiastical federation would have no authority beyond the One Lord.[2] Two years earlier he had declared in an editorial: "Whatever may be the power of the competitive system in the social and economic world, it is a curse in the church." [3]

North was a loyal and occasionally defensive Methodist, as other citations in this study show. But he was one of the first to plead that his denomination should enter into full and active cooperation wherever the church of Christ could speak or serve

---

[1] "Federation in City Evangelization," *The Christian City*, March, 1901; Christian City Leaflet, No. 5.

[2] Cf. almost identical language in his speech to the Inter-Church Conference on Federation in 1905 in Elias B. Sanford, ed., *Church Federation* (New York: Fleming H. Revell Company, 1906), pp. 501-9.

[3] *The Christian City*, November, 1899.

unitedly. In the same issue of *The Christian City* where he deplored competition as "a curse in the church" he remarked in the column "Side Lights" that there was need to "bring to book" those who use Methodist platforms "to bring railing accusations against their brethren."

Men who see God's light through a slit in the shutter which by their own hands they keep tightly closed, are hardly competent to characterize the vision of other men who look out through a window flung wide open. That there exist among us these "other men" is a blessing for which Methodism should be not only secretly but publicly grateful.[4]

Even before he left his pastorate in Middletown to return to the metropolis, Frank Mason North sought to organize and to implement his social concern. Significantly, in the light of the quoted exhortation to his Methodist brethren, he consulted colleagues in other denominations. Although North's original letter is missing, Charles A. Dickinson, pastor of Berkley Congregational Temple, Boston, replied in this vein (on November 18, 1891):

Concerning the matter of concerted study on the social aspects of Christianity, I should be very glad to do what I could to forward such an enterprise. . . . There are men all over the country who are deeply interested in this subject, and who would be very glad I presume to form some kind of a league through which our views might be more clearly defined, and more effectively presented to the public. What is your thought about it? What would you suggest in the way of special organization?[5]

On December 28, 1891, he wrote again, as follows: "In regard to books, I will say that Barrett's 'Practical Socialism', Loomis' 'Modern Cities', Rev. L. A. Banks' 'White Slaves', Jacob Riis' 'How the other half Lives', and Booth's 'In darkest England', are valuable helps in this line you suggest."[6] Dickinson then added:

---

[4] *Ibid.*, p. 100.

[5] Letter to F. M. North ("Social Service" files, Federal Council archives).

[6] The last two, by Riis and Booth, had been cited almost a year before in North's series for *Zion's Herald* (cf. chapter 4).

I feel with you that now is the great opportunity for the church to strike a telling blow in the interests of the common people, and I wish that something might be done to organize the sporadic aggressive movements which are springing up all over the country into a league or association of some kind.

Two years later, on March 6, 1894, North joined with Dickinson and with Charles L. Thompson, pastor of Madison Avenue Presbyterian Church, New York, to call a meeting on Christian Federation. "The time appears ripe," the invitation said, "for an organized advance along the lines of practical church work. . . . What we need now is co-operation and aggressive action on the part of these churches." [7] Three weeks later about fifty church leaders gathered at the Madison Avenue Church from all the states between Boston and Philadelphia. North was chosen temporary secretary and treasurer. Among other participants were Josiah Strong, later chairman of the Commission on the Church and Social Service in the Federal Council of Churches; Leighton Williams for the Baptists; Washington Gladden and Elias B. Sanford, Congregationalists; John P. Peters, Episcopalian; Sylvanus Stall, Lutheran (see p. 88) ; John B. Devins, in charge of mission work on New York's East Side; and Gaylord S. White. These men "hoped to bring about social salvation by means of an aggressive evangelistic, educational, and 'institutional' program." [8]

To this end they organized, at a second meeting that fall in Boston, the Open and Institutional Church League, with Charles Dickinson as president. The word "open" was chosen to condemn the widespread practice of charging pew rent and thus maintaining the class character of American churches. The Rev. William S. Rainsford had begun to abolish pew rents in St. George's (Episcopal) Church, New York, in 1882, while stressing continuous weekday use of the church plant and a program designed for the needs of the neighborhood. At the initial meeting in March, 1894, Frank Mason North had spoken of Calvary Methodist Episcopal Church (and all but one or two of those under the New York City Church Extension and Missionary

[7] *The Open and Institutional Church League* (Boston: Everett Press, 1894) .
[8] Hopkins, *The Rise of the Social Gospel*, p. 154.

115

Society) as now providing "free sittings." In order to replace the lost revenue Calvary had collected over $18,000 *per annum* in voluntary offerings, apparently a novel idea in those days, and had managed to avoid any "deficiency collection." Others were experimenting with "offertory calendars" to stimulate regular giving, and many reported gains in attendance (and in collections?) from having free pews.

Josiah Strong had referred to *institutional* as "a word we all dislike but all have to use." [9] In a speech before the Itinerants' Club in Buffalo (May 4, 1894) North defined the purpose of the new movement in these terms from the proposed platform: "The open and institutional church aims to save all men and all of the man by all means, abolishing as far as possible the distinction between the religious and the secular and sanctifying all days and all means to the great end of saving the world for Christ." [10] Agreeing with Strong that "the institutional church" was an unsatisfactory designation, he explained that its advocates were concerned with spirit and principle rather than methods and organization.

We are beginning to interest ourselves in men because they are men, the children of the Almighty Father, not because they wish to be converted or wish not to be converted, not because they are in the church nor because they are outside the church. . . . Should it be alleged that what Christ would have the church be in the world is impossible under "our economy" [polity], the answer is at hand. The economy is not of Divine right, the world can do without it; system, method, economy, are of value only so far as they enable men to express Christ's will. . . . Let the economy fit the purpose of God. . . . Be not conformed . . . be ye transformed.[11]

At the second convention of the Open and Institutional Church League (November 5, 1895) Charles Thompson, later to serve as secretary of the Presbyterian Board of Home Missions, a founder and president of the Home Missions Council, was elected

[9] Elias B. Sanford, *Origin and History of the Federal Council of the Churches of Christ in America* (Hartford: S. S. Scranton Company, 1916), p. 39n.
[10] "The Institutional Church," *The Christian City*, March, 1908.
[11] *Ibid.*, pp. 118-19.

116

president, with Elias Sanford as corresponding secretary. Sanford himself says of these ministers and laymen: "The men who founded the 'League' were practical idealists." [12] He also reports that the League was given office space in the New York City Society, closer to "secretarial headquarters" of the various denominations; "through the kindness of Dr. North my desk soon found a convenient nook in the room that opened into his office." [13]

The platform of the Open and Institutional Church League read in part:

Inasmuch as the Christ came not to be ministered unto, but to minister, the open or institutional church, filled and moved by his spirit of ministering love, seeks to become the centre and source of all benevolent and philanthropic effort, and to take the leading part in every movement which has for its end the alleviation of human suffering, the elevation of man, and the betterment of the world. . . .

It stands for open church doors every day and all the day, free seats, a plurality [multiplicity] of Christian workers, the personal activity of all church members, a ministry to all the community through educational, reformatory, and philanthropic channels, to the end that men may be won to Christ and his service, that the Church may be brought back to the simplicity and comprehensiveness of its primitive life, until it can be said of every community, "The kingdom of heaven is within you," and "Christ is all and in all." [14]

In an address on "The Twentieth Century Pastor" in 1897 North commended the practical projects which arose from the League's concern: nurseries, gymnasiums and swimming pools, sewing and industrial classes, language practice for immigrants, clubs, and lectures. He praised Episcopalian vestries for buying family pews from descendents in order to make them available to the public, and Trinity Parish in particular for devoting $38,000 of its $48,000 budget for the needy, for schools, and other community services. "Here the life of the church has not centered itself upon creeds and symbols," North noted in *The Christian*

[12] Sanford, *Origin and History of the Federal Council*, p. 39.
[13] *Ibid.*, p. 52.
[14] *The Open and Institutional Church League*, p. 14. Cf. Sanford, *Origin and History of the Federal Council*, pp. 397-98.

City, "but has expanded toward the world in obedience to the inevitable demand of the law of ministration." [15]

After slightly over a decade the specific principles of open pews and institutional service had been accepted, at least in theory in urban areas, and other agencies had assumed responsibility for such activities. Toward ecumenicity, says C. S. Macfarland, second general secretary of the Federal Council of Churches, the League "marked a step in advance in that it brought churches as such together rather than simply uniting individual Christians as the previous movements had done." Not only did it lay foundations for successive federations, but in drawing ecclesiastical statesmen into personal fellowship, it provided "a brief but significant stage in the movement for unity." [16]

Almost simultaneously other Christian federations were being formed, often involving the same personnel. John B. Devins organized a Federation of East Side Workers about 1894, but it was soon to merge into a larger body. When the Union Seminary Alumni Club gathered for its monthly meeting on March 18, 1895, its members heard a shocking paper by J. Winthrop Hegeman, rector of Christ Protestant Episcopal Church in Riverdale, New York. Dealing with racial, social, and religious conditions in the slums, it was entitled "What Are the Churches Going to Do About It?" On May 13 and again on October 21 a small group met to try to answer that challenge, men such as Josiah Strong and Henry A. Stimson, pastor of Manhattan Congregational Church. There were no Methodists present at the formal organization of the Federation of Churches and Christian Workers in New York City, but a commentator noted: "Among those who at once appreciated the Federation's purpose and possibilities were two men whose daily work dealt with the problem of the city as a whole, the late Robert R. McBurney, Secretary of the Y.M.C.A., and the Rev. Dr. Frank Mason North, Corresponding Secretary of the Methodist Episcopal Church Extension and Missionary Society." [17]

[15] January, 1897, p. 4.
[16] *Christian Unity in the Making* (New York: Federal Council of the Churches of Christ in America, 1948), p. 24.
[17] *Federation,* November, 1905.

North addressed the first public meeting of the Federation on December 2, 1895, was elected chairman of the Executive Committee the next year, and served on the Board of Directors through its first decade. The organization was composed initially of ten religious communions and thirteen Christian agencies (such as the Children's Aid Society and the Y.M.C.A.), with a formula for representation which foreshadowed the Federal Council of Churches: one clergyman and one layman from each participating group, two more if over fifty local churches were included in the constituency.

The Federation took as its first task an investigation of conditions in one of the most populous districts of the city, lying roughly between the Hudson River and Eighth Avenue, from 43rd to 53rd Street. Surveys were made of home conditions (the area included the second and third most densely inhabited blocks on the island); church affiliation (53.9% church members, but over 67% of them Roman Catholic, 7% Episcopalian, 6.5% Lutheran, 3.1% Methodist); ethnic background (27 nationalities, only one third of the population having American-born mothers); occupations (only 31% wage earners, 19% working on Sundays); education (69% of the children in school); saloons, "parks (or absence of them)," sanitary conditions, etc. But the "aim of the Federation [is not] analytical alone; it is also constructive," and the writer (probably North himself) added that this was "not a new charitable organization," but rather was designed to report to its constituent denominations and other charitable agencies and then to help coordinate plans for relief.[18]

However meager concrete accomplishments may have been, there developed widespread agreement that this cooperative pattern represented the wave of the future. Almost always this conviction found expression in practical rather than theological terms. In June, 1899, the editor of *The Christian City* wrote: "The suggestion that the time is at hand for the formation of a National Federation has received favorable consideration . . . a remarkable unanimity of conviction and desire for the initiation of some plan by which federative cooperation may be secured as a

---

[18] *Christian Advocate*, October 15, 1896.

fundamental principle in the church work of the future." [19] Out of such prodding came preliminary conferences in December, 1899, and February, 1900, sponsored jointly by the Open and Institutional Church League and the Federation of Churches and Christian Workers in New York. Said the invitation to the meeting in 1900:

It has thus, and could have at first, no official relation with any denominational body. But it is desired that it may be the forerunner of an official Federation of Churches to which it shall give place. . . . May we not also look forward to a National Federation of all our Protestant Christian denominations, through their official Heads [sic], which shall utter their declaration of Christian unity, and accomplish in good part the fulfillment of the prayer of our Lord that "they all may be one, that the world may know that thou hast sent me"? Too long have our churches been working along independent lines, and their divisions have too long given point to the gibes of the enemy. It is to bring these churches together, in testimony and in service, that these local and this National Federation of Churches and Christian Workers have been organized. They appeal to the sensitive and earnest Christian conscience of those who are drawn together because first drawn to Christ.[20]

Knowledge of these developments, North commented in an editorial, "will be a help to all Christian workers who, reading with sufficient clearness the signs of the times, know that some forms of federative action are inevitable." [21]

These meetings led in turn to the official establishment at Philadelphia, in 1901, of a National Federation of Churches and Christian Workers—

to secure cooperation among churches and Christian workers throughout the United States for the more effective promotion of the interests of the kingdom of God; to promote and further the organization of State and local federations; to foster intercommunication between

[19] *The Christian City,* June, 1899, p. 100.
[20] Call to a National Conference on Federation of Churches, 1900 (document in Archives of the Federal Council of the Churches of Christ in America).
[21] *The Christian City,* April, 1900, p. 81.

State and local federations and to furnish information regarding the work in every part of the country.[22]

To indicate the support of the Methodist Episcopal Church Frank Mason North quoted a resolution adopted earlier by the National City Evangelization Union:

We firmly believe that the vast and perplexing problems confronting the Christian Church in the cities can be met triumphantly only when the Christians of the various denominations give a practical evidence of the essential oneness of the Church of Christ by unselfish cooperation in federative efforts to reach the unchurched multitudes in the congested centers of our population.

Deploring the "horrible mendicity and mendacity" of many Christian constituents, he pleaded for churches to avoid both underchurching and overchurching by accepting comity agreements in cities and suburbs. Such collaboration, he stressed, did not require union meetings or creeds of agreement. "Theoretically these are nice questions," he remarked sarcastically, "—the exact amount of fervor lost by contact with less emotional brethren in an hour of worship—the precise shade of the theological opinion which entitled another who proves by his work that he has the spirit of Christ, to the fraternal handclasp—but they are incidental, not primary." With such an admonition, it is no wonder that "the question of creed or church union was not contemplated." [23]

This Philadelphia meeting had been made up of "local churches in large measure, not national and church bodies." [24] A year later, however, when the National Federation met in Washington—and was addressed by President Theodore Roosevelt—the members decided that the organization should be composed entirely of official delegates from national church bodies. That decision—and the corollary, to convene this representative body in 1905—stands as an ecumenical milestone in the United States. "In the minds of such men as Dr. Sanford, Frank Mason

[22] John Galbraith in *Zion's Herald*, February 13, 1901.
[23] *Zion's Herald*, February 13, 1901.
[24] Macfarland, *Christian Unity in the Making*, p. 24.

121

North, Charles L. Thompson and their associates, the Federal Council of the Churches of Christ in America was born at that moment, after years of pregnancy and patience. Three more years were, however, to be given in preparation for the proposed conference." [25]

The first ecclesiastical body to take formal action appointing such delegates was the General Conference of the Methodist Episcopal Church, South, meeting at Dallas in May, 1902.[26] Meanwhile, Frank Mason North was named to the interim Committee on Correspondence, along with another Methodist leader, William I. Haven, who worked beside North in many capacities over the years. Pointing out the challenge of such social problems as child labor, divorce, immigration, the saloon, "the social evil," and international arbitration, the official "call" to the major confessional bodies in the United States asserted:

The time is opportune for the extension and strengthening of the principles of Federation. . . . Its basis would not be one of creedal statement or governmental form, but of cooperative work and effort. It is also understood that the organization shall have power only to advise the constituent bodies represented.[27]

Of the Inter-Church Conference on Federation, which met in Carnegie Hall, New York, from November 15-22, 1905, one reporter remarked: "There has never been in this country a gathering where more men of highest rank, lifted there by the Divine Providence, were on the same programme. And, as one delegate observed, 'There was but one speech' . . . 'that all may be one.' " [28] This latter statement was not entirely true. Twenty-nine evangelical bodies, speaking for some eighteen million Protestants, were officially represented. The only major absentees were the Presbyterian Church in the United States and the Missouri Synod and General Council Lutherans. But no invita-

---

[25] *Ibid.*

[26] Sanford, *Church Federation*, p. 157.

[27] *Ibid.*, pp. 29-31. Cf. *The Christian City*, July, 1904; *Methodist Review*, September-October, 1905, etc.

[28] *Central Christian Advocate*, November 29, 1905, p. 5.

tions had been extended to the Mormons, Christian Scientists, Unitarians, Universalists, or "Dowieites" (followers of John Alexander Dowie, a faith healer who, as "Elijah the Restorer," founded a cult in Zion City, Illinois, in 1901). When the question of membership in the proposed Federal Council came up, some speakers urged that the door be "left open" to "our Roman Catholic friends" and to "the very few who are called by His name, but do not fully accept it." But when the votes were taken, they overwhelmingly affirmed a "Trinitarian basis" and inserted the adjective of "*Divine* Lord and Saviour" as the source of "essential oneness," thus effectively excluding the Unitarians (who would have been represented by such able men as Edward Everett Hale, Samuel A. Eliot, and John Long, former secretary of the navy).[29]

Three months earlier President Roosevelt had declined an invitation to participate, in a letter noteworthy for its political utilitarianism:

Indirectly, in addition to the great good it will do here, it is perfectly possible that the movement may have a very considerable effect in the Christianizing of Japan, which I feel to be retarded by the divisions among ourselves and by the failure to recognize the fact that the Christian Church in Japan must of course assume essentially a Japanese national form.[30]

Some other dignitaries cancelled their attendance at the last minute, but speakers at the conference included Associate Justice David J. Brewer of the Supreme Court; John Wanamaker, former postmaster general; James A. Beaver, former governor of Pennsylvania; Presidents Charles Cuthbert Hall of Union Theological Seminary, Woodrow Wilson of Princeton, Henry C. King of Oberlin, William H. P. Faunce of Brown, William J. Tucker of Dartmouth, Joseph W. Mauck of Hillsdale (Michigan); S. Parkes Cadman of Central Congregational Church, Brooklyn; Charles E. Jefferson of Broadway Tabernacle; J. Ross Stevenson of Fifth Avenue Presbyterian Church; Professor Henry van Dyke of

[29] Cf. Sanford, *Church Federation*, pp. 97-100 *et passim*.
[30] Quoted, *ibid.*, p. 41.

Princeton; board secretaries and bishops in abundance—and Frank Mason North, who also served as vice-chairman of the Executive Committee, chairman of the secretaries, and editor of the proceedings.[31] Among presiding officers were M. Linn Bruce, lieutenant governor of New York; William H. Roberts, permanent chairman of the Conference; John R. Mott, general secretary of the World Student Christian Federation; and Washington Gladden, then pastor of First Congregational Church, Columbus, Ohio.

In his address on "The Evangelization of American Cities" (hailed by *Zion's Herald* as "masterly") North stressed that the twentieth century had brought "a new civilization, new in its material basis, in its industry, in its social order, in its intellectual viewpoint, in its religious concepts." [32] Though Christ is the same, he declared, "the atmosphere through which men see Him is new, the life in which He moves is not the life of Galilee. . . . The life of to-day is penetrated everywhere by impulses and by forces which are the unrecognized fruits of the very Gospel which multitudes in this restless age are not unwilling to patronize, to misinterpret or to ignore."

But in the midst of enormous pressures, Frank Mason North always found signs of hope in the church. "Perhaps the most significant," he told this Inter-Church Conference, "is its confident acceptance of its social mission. To-day the Church which does not concern itself with present conditions of life is obsolete." Praising religious agencies for the variety and scope of their institutional concern, he asserted that "they have the same function, to bring Christ to the people in the cities, by building new churches, renewing the old, and by every kind of method reaching the unsaved with the invitation, the warning and the ministration of the Gospel." Here, note, is a trinitarian as well as a triune mission: no lop-sided humanism or even humanitarianism, no shallow optimism, no narrow pietism, but *invitation, warning,* and *ministration.*

Then followed, in some of North's most eloquent prose, a

[31] *Ibid.,* pp. 39 ff., and 47.
[32] *Ibid.,* p. 502; cf. p. 501a.

124

sketch of the metropolitan mission field: the population density, the polyglot immigration, the poverty and vice.

Custom tolerates what conscience condemns, and the custodians of authority often become the promoters of the evil they are appointed to suppress. The ethical sense becomes dull, in trade, in social life, in government, and in the absence of its commands, dishonesty, hypocrisy, and falsehood have their way. In this vitiated social atmosphere lethargy overtakes even a man of good purposes and behind the code of the many the individual conscience hides and gives no sign.

Thus the city becomes for Frank Mason North the purpose of federation. "The dream of a united Church has no field for its actualization nearer or more appealing than our great American cities," he pleaded; "division and conflict here are the betrayal of a sacred trust." Finally, North reaffirmed his faith in cooperative action on the part of Christians:

It is inevitable that as the Churches move forward to their certain conquest of the world, the phases of faith and of practice which survive will prove to be those which now are essentially common to all. . . . The past has proved that the hope of unity is not in the realm of the intellect, in the high altitudes of philosophy, but in the heart, upon the broad plains of human service.

Reported the *Central Christian Advocate:* "Dr. Frank Mason North was vice-president (his paper on 'Cities' was what his statesmanship would lead us to expect—one of the best of the Conference)." [33]

Out of this great convocation came preliminary proposals for a permanent federation or alliance of Protestant churches. It should be "advisory only," with no authority over its constituent groups, no creed, no form of government which would limit the authority of the churches. Yet, as they looked forward to the actual organization in 1908, Christian leaders throughout the world were heartened by what had been done in New York in November of 1905. In a magazine article soon after the conference John R. Mott declared: "I regard the result achieved by the Inter-

[33] November 29, 1905, p. 16.

Church Conference on Federation to be the greatest and most significant accomplished by any religious gathering ever held in North America." [34] And Frank Mason North, calling the meeting an "almost unqualified success," used the symbolic language so often found in his poetry when he summarized it thus: "It was a time, not only for light, but for fire." [35]

---

[34] Quoted in the First Annual Report of the Executive Committee of the Inter-Church Conference on Federation, 1906. Cf. John R. Mott letter to F. M. North, November 27, 1905, ending with the postscript: "I want to congratulate you on your large part in bringing about this glorious result. It has been worth a life. But thank God you have the years in which to realize your objective." (North files).

[35] *The Christian City*, November, 1905.

126

Commemoration Hymn

Thou Lord of Light, across the years
  Thy shining path of love we see;
Bright glows amidst our joys and fears
  The order of our faith in Thee.

The Teacher Thou of those who taught,
  The Master Guide through learning's maze,
The theme of their profoundest thought,
  The object of their reverent praise.

Their hearts interpreted Thy word;
  Through them Thy messages were sent;
Within these walls Thy voice was heard,
  Here wisdom found its sacrament.

We thank Thee for these years of power,
  For stalwart souls, for gentle life,
For men transformed to meet the hour
  Of blasting wrong, of surging strife;

For men who gird the world with flame,
  Who count, for Thee, all things but loss,
Who challenge nations, in Thy name,
  To hear the story of Thy cross.

Yet, beating through our gratitude,
  We feel the pulse of coming days;
Truth stands where it has ever stood;
  New darkness meets its deathless rays;

High courage grant, the outlook broad,
  The strength of joy, the zest for right,
The faith that burns, the sense of God,
  Thy fellowship, Thou Lord of Light.

Semi-Centennial of
Drew Theological Seminary
1917

7

The Social Creed

Touch Thou, O Lord, our waiting hearts with light,
Kindle with holy flame our sacrifice,
Unveil Thy glorious purpose to our sight,
Give clearer vision to our lifted eyes.

The Social Creed owes its direct origin to the Methodist Federation for Social Service. To be sure, there were many springs of refreshing concern, many convergent streams of thought and planning. The writings of Lincoln Steffens and Upton Sinclair, of Henry James, Sr. (*Moralism and Christianity*, 1850) and Richard T. Ely (*Social Aspects of Christianity*, 1889), gave popular backing to a host of early clerical authors.[1]

In the winter of 1906 a group of ministers in Ohio began corresponding about the possibility of forming an organization for the Methodist Episcopal Church similar to the Wesleyan Methodist Union for Social Service in England. Worth M. Tippy was pastor of Epworth Memorial Church in Cleveland; E. Robb Zaring was assistant editor of the *Western Christian Advocate;* Herbert Welch had gone from the Middletown, Connecticut, pastorate previously served by Frank Mason North, to the presidency of Ohio Wesleyan University. After a visit in England during the summer of 1907, Tippy stopped in New York to consult North about the National City Evangelization Union and learned that North had been discussing some such social

---

[1] Josiah Strong (*Our Country*, 1885), A. J. F. Behrends (*Socialism and Christianity*, 1886), Washington Gladden (*Applied Christianity*, 1886), Samuel Lane Loomis (*Modern Cities*, 1887), Julius H. Ward (*The Church in Modern Society*, 1889), Frank Mason North (in *Zion's Herald*, 1891), and many others. Cf. Hopkins, *The Rise of the Social Gospel*, chaps. IV ff., footnotes *et passim.*

service organization with Harry F. Ward, pastor of Union Avenue
Methodist Church in the stockyards of Chicago. As Ward recalled,
"North knew the personnel in the East and really got the group
together." [2] Welch, North, and Tippy met in Cleveland on
September 13, 1907, and issued a call (with the other two
signatures added) for a planning conference in Washington,
D. C.

Twenty-five Methodists, out of approximately fifty ministers
and laymen invited, gathered at Ebbitt House, Washington,
December 3-4, 1907. Frank Mason North opened the meeting as
chairman of the organizing committee, but the group elected
Welch president and Tippy secretary. It was North who actually
moved the establishment of a Methodist Federation for Social
Service. Its "objects" were announced as follows: "to deepen
within the Church the sense of social obligation and opportunity
to study social problems from the Christian point of view, and
to promote social service in the spirit of Jesus Christ." [3] Speaking
on "What Can the Church Do for the Laboring Man?" North
stressed the need for tact and understanding, for mediation and
education. In an address on "Social Evangelism" Ward (variously
cited as "Harry Wanel" and "Harvey F. Ward") declared: "The
teaching of Jesus gave the world a social doctrine that is revo-
lutionizing the world." To celebrate the new organization, the
charter members called on President Roosevelt as guests of Vice-
President Charles W. Fairbanks. Editorializing for *The Christian
City*, Frank Mason North revealed the depths of his own involvement in this embryonic movement:

Back of that meeting are other records—of personal investigations
on both sides of the Atlantic, of heart searching and study of industrial and social conditions, of careful reflection upon the genius and
methods of Methodism, and upon the life needs of the people; records
of private conversations, of group conference, of crystallization of
purpose, of individual agreement upon a common plan, of acts of
venture and earnest counsellings with the Master whose Kingdom it
has been the central aim to promote.

[2] Personal interview, Palisade, N. J., January 23, 1958.
[3] *Western Christian Advocate*, December 18, 1907, pp. 20-21.

It is enough here to say that the outcome has seemed to those who have thus far tried to prepare the way not the result of mere human initiative but rather of the movement of the Divine Spirit in the realm of mind and conscience, giving to individual, half-formed resolves a common basis and a well-harmonized plan.[4]

It may be of interest to summarize some of the more specific aims of the Methodist Federation for Social Service as Ward described them fifty years later—and as he attributed them in large measure to Frank Mason North. The secretary of the New York City Church Extension and Missionary Society saw, according to Ward, that "the initial job was to socialize the church," to make "the church the servant of the community" (a slogan adopted by many local congregations). But North—and presumably his colleagues—felt also that "socializing the church . . . obviously involved socializing of the national departments of the church." This apparently did not mean a revolutionary upheaval in the organizational structure, but a desire to staff the various agencies with socially minded leaders. "The Church was entirely individualistic in its preaching," Ward asserted, and "the boards of missions, education, evangelism, etc. were very seriously limited in their own approach."

To accomplish this goal, "we simply had to change the personnel," Ward maintained, "and the brother who had to go out [i.e., all those who lost their jobs] took it personally." In this process, according to Ward's account, "North was invaluable because he had the contacts with the people. . . . That thing could not have happened without North's broad contacts with the key people." By the same token, however, one can be sure that Frank Mason North was far less ruthless and insensitive and aggressive than this version implies. If he sought, directly or indirectly, to change the personnel of Methodist boards and agencies, it would undoubtedly have been by persuasion and negotiation, not by firing. He probably did agree with Ward, however, that the larger job of "socializing the churches" should not and could not be done through official channels, especially

---

[4] Original manuscript in North's handwriting among his private papers.

those which controlled the funds; hence the establishment of the Federation as an "unofficial" agency of the church.

This is not the place to trace the history of the Methodist Federation for Social Service (later Social Action).[5] From its inception right up to the present time, although always an unofficial organization, it has enlisted some of the ablest leaders and most powerful prophets in the Methodist Church.

Bishop Welch, who served as president of the Federation until 1912 and was succeeded by Francis J. McConnell, recalls fifty years later that Ward had developed radical views in the "stockyard church" and went into the Federation "with a strong bias, as a partisan advocate rather than an impartial judge." "North," he adds, "wasn't of that temper at all. . . . [He had a] thoughtful, judicial mind." [6] And Reinhold Niebuhr comments, "You may well understand that my colleague Harry Ward [together on the Union Theological Seminary faculty for many years] did not see eye to eye with him." [7] Yet North remained on the Executive Committee (later the General Council) until his death in 1935, exercising a restraint, a moderation, a wisdom in the Federation.

With such clearly divergent viewpoints from the outset, it is all the more significant that Welch should give Harry Ward credit for fathering the Social Creed. For many years it was popularly remarked that "Frank Mason North wrote the Social Creed," a half-truth resulting from failure to distinguish between the composition of the *Methodist* Social Creed at the General Conference in May, 1908, and its elaboration and presentation to the Federal Council of Churches in December. Fifty years later I asked Harry Ward point blank, "Who wrote the Social Creed?" Even then, after all the abuse he had received, he did not affirm—or deny—his own central role. Instead he deflected the question: "I never liked the term," Ward said, "any more than I liked the term 'social gospel.' The gospel is both individual and

[5] Cf. Milton John Huber, Jr., *A History of the Methodist Federation for Social Action*, unpublished doctoral dissertation, Boston University, 1949; cf. article with same title, *Zion's Herald*, July 6, 1949, pp. 629 and 635.

[6] Herbert Welch, personal interview, New York, January 21, 1958.

[7] Reinhold Niebuhr, letter to the author, June 4, 1965.

social. The 'creed' was never a creed; it was a statement of principles and actions." [8]

Others have finally agreed that its genesis was something like this. When the General Conference of the Methodist Eiscopal Church met in Baltimore in May, 1908, William M. Balch, pastor of Trinity Church, Lincoln, Nebraska, introduced a resolution asking for a Commission on Social Questions to report to the 1912 General Conference on "What shall the Church do with regard to the Social Problem?" It was suggested that there might be a new department, as the Presbyterians had under Charles Stelzle, or perhaps an official alignment with the new Methodist Federation for Social Service. Recognizing that "the social mission of the church is more than urgent; it is emergent," the Conference voted to refer the matter at once to the Committee on the State of the Church.

For this purpose a subcommittee was appointed, with Levi Gilbert, editor of the *Western Christian Advocate,* as chairman, Balch as secretary. Their initial effort at a resolution was long, abstract, and unsatisfactory, according to Harry Ward. Meanwhile some of the "Young Turks" in the Federation had assembled at the Conference because they hoped to see the adoption of some constructive social resolution and perhaps formal endorsement of their infant organization. In addition to Welch and Ward and Tippy, there was Edgar J. Helms, pastor of Morgan Memorial Church in Boston. North was the only one of the group who was an official delegate to the General Conference.

Welch says at the invitation of Balch, Ward said with or without Balch's request, these leaders of the Methodist Federation sat around a telegraphic pressroom table and drafted a statement on "The Church and Social Problems." According to Ward's own recollection: "I said, 'What's the use? Nobody will pay any attention to anything as long as this [the Balch resolution]. Why not put down a statement of what the Methodist Church stands for?' " As secretary for the group, Ward did just that—on the back of Western Union telegraph blanks.[9] Frank Mason North, involved as a Conference delegate with other committee work, came

---

[8] Personal interview, Palisade, N. J., January 23, 1958.
[9] Huber, *A History of the Methodist Federation for Social Action,* p. 355.

in and out of the Federation session to make occasional suggestions. "That was his contribution to that; it was a group piece of work," Ward insisted.

Years later friends of North insinuated that someone at Union Seminary was trying to claim credit that belonged to the older man. This accusation was as unfair as it was untrue. Ward himself stated unequivocally: "North was the man who put that thing in expanded form through the Federal Council of Churches. I had no hand in that. North did the expanding, put it through, and got it adopted."

Many years later, after his retirement, North in a committee meeting broke out with the comment: "Harry Ward knows who wrote the Social Creed and he hasn't said." Apparently some of North's supporters inferred from this a slur on Ward's integrity. An alternative interpretation, however, based on North's reputation for never seeking fame or credit for himself, could be, in fact, a *denial* of his own exclusive share and an acknowledgment of Ward's secretarial and editorial hand in the Creed, perhaps even a tribute to Ward's modesty. *If* Frank Mason North ever claimed to have produced the Social Creed (and that seems very doubtful), he was, suggested Ward, "thinking and talking of the Social Creed of the *Churches*, with which he had everything to do, and I had nothing to do. . . . The only thing that I was responsible for was the forming of the first draft" of the *Methodist* Social Creed.

Herbert Welch, vigorous and alert well past one hundred, is —since Ward's death at ninety-three in December, 1966—the only living participant in those historic events. In view of his later withdrawal from the Federation, distressed by its one-sided stands, any partisanship on his part would presumably lean toward North. Yet he repeatedly verifies Ward's primary authorship. In his autobiography, *As I Recall My Past Century,* he says of the Social Creed: "Most active and by far most fruitful in suggestion and phrasing was Harry Ward." [10] In personal conversation he declares that Harry Ward's was "the pre-eminently creative mind.

[10] (Nashville: Abingdon Press, 1962), p. 54; cf. "How We Got Our Social Creed," *New Christian Advocate*, April, 1955, pp. 10-14.

. . . He was the man most largely responsible for framing the Social Creed." [11]

Regardless of authorship, Report #5 on "The State of the Church," with its significant section on "The Church and Social Problems" was adopted unanimously by the General Conference on May 30, 1908. One delegate asked that the Methodist Brotherhood be added to a list of organizations "pledged to this sort of service" (such as Sunday schools and the Epworth League) and this was done without objection. The entire report was passed without further comment, *without one word of debate;* in fact, the announcement occupies only twenty column lines in the *Daily Christian Advocate,* including reference to printing the full document in the *Journal.*[12] Such are the inconspicuous ways of history.

The resolution which has come to be known as the Social Creed in Methodism begins with this affirmation: "We believe that in the teachings of the New Testament will be found the ultimate solution of all the problems of our social order. When the spirit of Christ shall pervade the hearts of individuals, and when his law of love to God and man shall dominate human society, then the evils which vex our civilization will disappear." Recognizing "the gravity of the social situation and the responsibility of the Church," it commends those employers who seek to "deal justly and humanely with their employees" and asserts the right and larger benefits of labor organization. It summons its leaders to "fearless but judicious preaching of the teachings of Jesus in their significance for the moral interests of modern society."

At the core of this resolution stand ten specific applications of the gospel to economic life, summarized in "the recognition of the Golden Rule and the mind of Christ as the supreme law of society and the sure remedy for all social ills." This may be liberal and even superficial theology; it hardly sounds like political subversion, as subsequently charged. Because of their

[11] New York, January 21, 1958; cf. letter to the author, August 16, 1961: "Nor can I recall how much North or I or anyone else contributed to the final form of the 'creed.' I am sure only of Ward's special relation to the whole matter."

[12] *Daily Christian Advocate,* Baltimore, June 1, 1908, p. 7; cf. *Journal* General Conference of the Methodist Episcopal Church, 1908, pp. 427 and 545 ff.

importance as a milestone, not only for the Methodist Church, but also for the ecumenical movement and for the social gospel, these ten points are quoted in full:

The Methodist Episcopal Church stands:
For equal rights and complete justice for all men in all stations of life.
For the principle of conciliation and arbitration in industrial dissensions.
For the protection of the worker from dangerous machinery, occupational diseases, injuries, and mortality.
For the abolition of child labor.
For such regulation of the conditions of labor for women as shall safeguard the physical and moral health of the community.
For the suppression of the "sweating system."
For the gradual and reasonable reduction of the hours of labor to the lowest practical point, with work for all; and for that degree of leisure for all which is the condition of the highest human life.
For a release from employment one day in seven.
For a living wage in every industry.
For the highest wage that each industry can afford, and for the most equitable division of the products of industry that can ultimately be devised.

Included with this report the General Conference noted "with satisfaction" the organization of the Methodist Federation for Social Service, approved its objects heartily, and bid it Godspeed in plans for expansion and implementation. In addition it appointed three bishops to the General Council and asked for a memorial at the next General Conference of 1912 dealing with these four questions:

1. What principles and measures of social reform are so evidently righteous and Christian as to demand the specific approval and support of the Church?
2. How can the agencies of the Methodist Episcopal Church be wisely used or altered with a view to promoting the principles and measures thus approved?
3. How may we best cooperate in this behalf with other Christian denominations?
4. How can our courses of ministerial study in seminaries and Con-

ferences be modified with a view to the better preparation of our preachers for efficiency in social reform? [13]

With this mandate Methodism acknowledged and embodied its social responsibility. With this document—and these spokesmen—it contributed its most direct impetus to the ecumenical movement which came to birth that same year.

Exactly six months after the adjournment of the Methodist General Conference in Baltimore, the Federal Council of the Churches of Christ in America convened in Philadelphia for its organizational meeting (December 2-8, 1908). Since the Inter-Church Conference on Federation in New York in 1905, twenty-six of its constituent bodies had adopted the Plan of Federation and four others were immediately enrolled as delegates to the Council. The nearly four hundred participants included most of the great names in American Christianity for that day, representing a total of thirty-three denominations and seventeen million constituents.[14] Frank Mason North, in *The Christian City,* commented immediately thereafter: "The churches of these United States stand toward one another—and, together, toward the nation with its problems, at a vantage point never before occupied. But this is the beginning, not the end." [15]

Attention must be focused here, not on the brilliant array of platform addresses, but on one, not on the scope and structure of the Council, but on a single concern. In addition to serving as vice-chairman of the Committee of Arrangements appointed in 1905, Frank Mason North was also chairman of a committee on "The Church and Modern Industry." His report, a speech which must have lasted nearly an hour, was presented on Friday afternoon, December 4, 1908. Louise Seymour Houghton in *Christian Herald* declared: "The crowning work of the Council was probably that taken with regard to the proper relations of the Church to modern industry." The *Christian Advocate* reported: "The highest point of enthusiasm was reached when Dr. Frank

---

[13] *Journal,* General Conference of the Methodist Episcopal Church, 1908, p. 548.
[14] Cf. Elias B. Sanford, ed., *Federal Council of Churches of Christ in America* (New York: Revell Press, 1909) and Sanford, *Origin and History of the Federal Council.*
[15] December, 1908.

Mason North, of New York, read his paper on 'The Church and Modern Industry.' The reading was attentively followed and at its conclusion the applause was loud and long." [16]

It can be assumed that the statement as a whole was almost entirely the work of the chairman. In the judgment of Reinhold Niebuhr, "He [North] had a remarkable combination of courage and prudence, which enabled him to pilot the creative 'Social Creed' through committee after committee." [17] C. S. Macfarland, in his resumé of the occasion, states: "The report made to the Council by the Committee on the Church and Modern Industry was largely prepared and was presented by Frank Mason North, supported by Mr. Stelzle. It was a classic document, and has hardly been surpassed since that day." [18] Ward's primary role in drafting the original Creed has already been acknowledged. Stelzle, superintendent of the Department of Church and Labor of the Board of Home Missions of the Presbyterian Church in the U.S.A., strongly "supported" the report by arising immediately to say: "The statement presented by Dr. North is the greatest paper on this subject that I have ever heard or read, and if I can say to the workmen of America that the Federal Council really means it it will be the biggest thing that I can say or that I have ever yet said." But Stelzle was not on North's committee, was not even a delegate to the Council, but had been invited to speak "because of his wide experience in social service among laboring men." To North, and probably North alone, belongs the credit for this momentous document—*and* for including in it the ten specific points which Ward, Welch, Tippy, and others had hammered out seven months before.

The hand—and heart—of Frank Mason North can be seen in the opening affirmation: "The Churches of Christ as represented in this Federal Council accept without reserve and assert without apology the supreme authority of Jesus Christ."

Wherever the path in which He leads crosses other highways, whether marked out by the creeds of commerce, the schools of philosophy, the

[16] Both these quotations are taken from undated clippings in North's scrapbook.
[17] Letter to the author, June 4, 1965.
[18] *Christian Unity in the Making*, pp. 42-46.

138

teachers of social theory, the masters of theology, the agitators for reform, the critics of the Church, or the feet of the multitude, His disciples must take all risks and follow Him. Our interpretations of His teaching and purpose are, doubtless, with growing light and new conditions, subject to review and restatement, but no such modification can force or allure the Church to surrender the principle of His absolute authority in the individual heart and in the associated life of men. He charts our way. He commands us.

It is this *personal* religion that distinguishes Frank Mason North's social gospel from that of many of his contemporaries and those who came after him. He believed that "in the teachings of the New Testament will be found the ultimate solution of all the problems of our social order," as "Ward's" statement began, but not as a mere blueprint for moral and economic relationships. He affirmed this confidence *because*, for him, "Christ's mission is not merely to reform society but to save it. He is more than the world's Re-adjuster. He is its Redeemer." Therefore, as the preamble goes on to say, "the Church becomes worthless for its higher purpose when it deals with conditions and forgets character, relieves misery and ignores sin, pleads for justice and undervalues forgiveness."

Whatever comparisons may be made between the church as a social service institution and other welfare agencies (and North had made this comparison himself back in 1891), "there is one contrast which never may be forgotten—the Church stands forever for the two-world theory of life. . . . The Church's doors open upon the common levels of life. They should never be closed. Its windows open toward the skies. Let their light not be darkened." In constant balance throughout this document—and throughout North's life—stands the church as essential to human life and the church "not an end in itself." "The pious and subtle persuasion that the Church absorbs the attention of its Lord and narrows to itself the scope of His grace, is happily a fading belief," he insisted. "The services of the Church have become subordinate to the Church's service to men."

One sentence, at least, strikes horror to critics of the social gospel, those theologians who have inferred man's helplessness

139

from Karl Barth's emphasis on God's omnipotence: "Primarily we are engaged in establishing His Kingdom in these United States." True, there is a shallow liberalism which has been read into this type of language, a presumptuous implication that man can usurp God's function. Neither interpretation seems valid in the larger context of North's theology. His corrective lies in the "two-world theory" already cited. He is always aware that Christians are God's instruments, that doing his will on earth can never be fully "as it is in Heaven." In fact, he said three sentences earlier: "The Kingdom, to establish which the Church is appointed as the representative of Christ, is found not only in the Lord's Prayer but in the Lord's heart."

The church's inevitable, but often shameful, involvement with economic forces in American life the report attributes to the free status of the institution, necessitating private financial support and government as contrasted with establishment in Europe. Furthermore, "at no time have the disadvantages of the sectarian divisions of the Church been more apparent than when the call has come for a common policy or a united utterance" on social issues. North's address then listed "certain indisputable facts which should be candidly stated": (1) "an estrangement between the Church and industrial workers," based often on unfair generalizations from both sides; (2) "a separation between the rich and the cultured and the churches"; (3) "industrial progress has . . . taken the Church unawares"; and (4) "there are many phases of the present industrial conditions in the United States which cry aloud for immediate remedy." Here followed some of the vivid, poignant pictures of city life and evils, descriptions at which North had already proved himself adept. Here, too, appeared a fervent defense of labor's right to organize. As concerned churchmen are saying today about civil rights, North averred in 1908: "It is their right as it is the right of men everywhere, within the law, to combine for common ends. Both Church and society should cease to talk of 'conceding' this right. It exists in the nature of things. We do not confer it. But we welcome its exercise."

In the second half of the document North turned to statements and resolutions. These included such affirmations as the following: the authority of Jesus Christ over social as well as individual life;

140

the acknowledgment that "Christian practice has not always harmonized with Christian principle"; the responsibility for the church to participate, not merely acquiesce, in social change. Passages commending the ethical concern of employers for their workmen, and the increase of arbitration instead of strikes and lockouts, were lifted bodily from the resolution adopted by the Methodist General Conference. But when he came to the Social Creed itself, Frank Mason North had added four clauses which had not been included by Ward and his colleagues at Baltimore:

To us it seems that the churches must stand—. . . .
For the right of all men to the opportunity for self-maintenance, a right ever to be wisely and strongly safeguarded against encroachments of every kind.
For the right of workers to some protection against the hardships often resulting from the swift crises of industrial change. . . .
For suitable provision for the old age of the workers and for those incapacitated by injury.
For the abatement of poverty.[19]

(It is significant to note that the Methodist General Conference of 1912 incorporated these additions into the Creed.)

These were actually statements of principles; the formal recommendations followed:

(1) That the churches more fully recognize, through their pulpits, press and public assemblies, the great work of social reconstruction which is now in progress . . . and the obligation of the churches to supply the spiritual motive and standards. . . .

(2) That . . . in all theological seminaries, and, so far as practicable, in other schools and colleges, there be established, . . . courses in economics, sociology and the social teachings of Jesus, supplemented, wherever possible, by investigation of concrete social fact;

(3) That the churches . . . enter into sympathetic fraternal relations with workingmen . . . by advocating their cause when just . . . and by welcoming them and their families to the uses and privileges of the local churches;

[19] Sanford, *Federal Council*, pp. 238-39.

141

(4) That the Church in general not only aim to socialize its message . . . but also modify its own equipment and procedure in the interest of more democratic administration and larger social activity; that . . . provision be made for the service of the community as well as for the public worship of God; that in its councils of direction workingmen be welcomed and . . . artificial distinctions be rebuked and removed . . . to the end that the workers and the poor . . . may ever find the church as homelike as the union hall, more attractive than the saloon, more tolerant of their aspirations than the political club, more significant of the best which in heart and life they seek than any other organization or institution which claims to open to them opportunity or ventures to offer the incentive to the better life.

(5) That churches and labor be reminded of the historical role which the Church has played in securing a day of rest, inspiring philanthropy, defending the fundamental rights of man, and serving the community.

Finally, the report recommended the establishment of a permanent Commission on the Church and Social Service. When this was done, Frank Mason North was inevitably named as its first chairman. On his committee appeared such giants in the social-gospel movement as Levi Gilbert, Shailer Mathews, J. H. Melish, Walter Rauschenbusch, Charles Stelzle, Josiah Strong, and Herbert Welch.

It was typical of North that he should end his "epoch-making" address with further reference to its source in the gospel of Jesus Christ. "We do not forget," he declared, "that the strength of the Church is not in a program but in a spirit. . . . The Church does not lay the foundations of a social order; it discloses them. They are already laid." In conclusion, he asserted,

Nothing that concerns human life can be alien to the Church of Christ. . . . Once again in the spirit of the Nazarene let it take from the hand of tradition the sacred roll and read so that everywhere the waiting millions may hear: "The spirit of the Lord is upon Me, because He hath anointed Me to preach the Gospel to the poor. He hath sent Me to heal the broken-hearted, to preach deliverance to the captive, and recovering of sight to the blind, to set at liberty them that are bruised, to preach the acceptable year of the Lord" (Luke 4:18-19;

142

cf. Isaiah 61:1-2). May the Church dare to say to the multitudes: "This day is this Scripture fulfilled in your ears."

It is not quite accurate to say, as Macfarland does, that the report was "adopted without dissent or hesitation." [20] One commentator, "like . . . most of you at least . . . profoundly . . . in sympathy with the spirit" of the speech, insisted that theological students need to get practical experience in the labor movement, "not this dandified study of sociology by gentlemen who have never had their nostrils offended on the east side of any great city." Another protested the charge that the churches have failed to reach the laboring people: "If we are to make a specialty of one class of people, let us make a specialty of other classes of people." A third, endorsing the resolution, warned that "workingmen do not want any charity; they do not want to be patronized by you either." Incidentally, when the Social Creed of the Churches was read to a gathering of labor organizations at the Lyric Theater that same weekend, it was "greeted with long-continued applause." [21]

It was greeted with resounding applause by the church press of the nation as well. Said *The Christian Century,* newly acquired and reorganized by Charles Clayton Morrison:

The subject of most commanding interest thus far presented was doubtless the report on the church and modern industry, presented on Friday afternoon by the Rev. Frank Mason North, D.D., of New York. It is a subject with which all thoughtful Christians are now concerning themselves. Dr. North's presentation of it was admirable.[22]

Commented *The Outlook:*

No action of any church body in recent years surpasses in importance the adoption by the Federal Council of Churches of resolutions concerning the relation of the Church to modern industry, in fact, to

[20] *Christian Unity in the Making,* p. 46.

[21] Cf. *Christian Herald,* n.d., and *Christian Advocate,* n.d., December, 1908 (scrapbook clippings).

[22] "Church Federal Council," December 12, 1908; similar language was used by Dr. John Bancroft Devins in *Christian Observer,* n.d., and *Methodist Recorder,* December 19, 1908, so one suspects multiple correspondence.

the whole social order of the day. They may be said to constitute a charter, a bill of rights, which the Protestant Churches of America recognize on behalf not only of those who toil, but also of society.[23]

A Presbyterian journal added its high tribute as follows:

The report was without question the most distinguished paper of the whole congress. It was prepared by Dr. Frank Mason North, an eminent Methodist minister of New York, working with liberal-minded men of other churches who feel the pressure of the social question. They together produced a document of high statesmanship, recognizing that in the modern industrial movement deplorable injustices develop, now on the side of labor and now on the side of capital, but strenuously insisting that in so far as the industrial question is a question of bettering men and making life of more worth to human souls, the church must necessarily support the struggle of the man who has the poorest chance. . . . It might have been expected that a report so positive and outspoken on this particularly precarious question would evoke vehement antagonism. But so just and candid were all its utterances, so high was the plane of human fraternity to which it ascended, that no man had aught to say against it. There was no lack of comment upon the paper; the delegates reviewed it with thorough care, but found nothing to criticise. On the contrary, every voice praised the committee and Dr. North especially for a production so elevated and prophetic.[24]

Thus was the social conscience of American Christianity focused and expressed. Eight years later Elias Sanford, the first corresponding secretary of the Federal Council, described the statement "the influence of which still continues to gain in volume and strength." [25] That has not always been true. Writing forty years after the adoption of the Social Creed, C. S. Macfarland, the next general secretary, referred to the report and the Commission on the Church and Social Service as the center of subsequent attack on the Council "which had caused the loss of thousands of dollars to its income." [26] This reaction is compounded by those

[23] December 19, 1908, pp. 849-50.
[24] "A Federation in Being," *The Interior*, December 17, 1908, p. 1721.
[25] *Origin and History of the Federal Council*, p. 358.
[26] *Christian Unity in the Making*, p. 46.

who villify the Methodist Federation for Social Action and who know the historic ties of personnel and purpose. But Macfarland adds that "in the years immediately following the 1908 meeting it probably saved the nascent Federal Council from possible dissolution and became a rallying point at a moment of threatened disaster." [27]

Despite the survival of antediluvian elements within the church and outside it, history (both recorded judgment and social progress) has vindicated those pioneers of 1908. The numerous amendments and revisions imposed upon the Social Creed (both Methodist and ecumenical) in no way invalidate the Christian concern or the practical wisdom of that day. Frank Mason North would be as scrupulous as Herbert Welch to acknowledge Harry Ward's authorship of the ten articles on labor, and of much of the Methodist resolution on "The Church and Social Problems."

But the Social Creed is vastly more than that. It is the affirmation and the application of the gospel in the workday world. To that conviction and that commitment on the part of the Christian church Frank Mason North contributed in myriad ways. The poet who wrote in 1903 of race and clan and selfish strife, the organizer who in 1907 led the formation of the Methodist Federation for Social Service and encouraged its younger members, the orator who in 1908 placed the practical needs of society in the broader and deeper context of Christian faith, the man of prayer who never forgot that the church "is here to re-present Christ"—that man, at least as much as any other one individual, molded the Social Creed of the Churches. Sixty years—or a hundred years—later it will still be because of Frank Mason North that Christians can sing of the Galilean Carpenter: "We catch the vision of thy tears."

[27] *Ibid.*

The Shadowed Lands

Touch Thou, O Lord, our waiting hearts with light,
  Kindle with holy flame our sacrifice,
Unveil Thy glorious purpose to our sight,
  Give clearer vision to our lifted eyes.

We hear from lands in tumult far away
  The springing tread of multitudes made free;
The nations stir as those who greet the day;
  Around the world rings out the reveille.

Thou seest their toil, though by the world unseen,
  Thou hear'st their cry for help, for daily food.
Challenge Thy people, Lord, to make more keen
  The undefeated quest for brotherhood.

Up from the shadowed lands the murmur swells
  Of broken hearts, of discontent, of strife,
Of faith perverted, quickened hope—it tells
  The multitudes have felt the surge of life.

Hear Thou, O Lord, and teach Thy church to hear;
  To save the suff'ring peoples Thou hast died;
Can we who love Thee fail the cross to bear,
  Since Thou for them and us wast crucified?

Lead on, O glorious Christ, through lands and years.
Our hearts have caught the sounds of victory;
Before our faith the wondrous day appears
When all the world shall love and worship Thee.

Missionary Centenary
1919

8

The Federal Council of Churches

We thank Thee for these years of power,
For stalwart souls, for gentle life,
For men transformed to meet the hour
Of blasting wrong, of surging strife.

"Among the leaders in the Methodist Episcopal Church who aided in the founding of the Federal Council of the Churches of Christ in America no one will question that first place is to be given to Frank Mason North." [1] He had played a conspicuous role in the Open and Institutional Church League, the National Federation of Churches and Christian Workers, the Inter-Church Conference on Federation, and the National City Evangelization Union (which, though Methodist in origin, soon acquired parallels and participants in other denominations). Then, as vice-chairman of the committee of arrangements, he bore major responsibility for the organizational meeting in Philadelphia in 1908.

With his personal courtesy and his professional commitment to the ecumenical ideal, it must have distressed North that, according to a Presbyterian journal of the day, "the worst of the very few sectarian outbursts" in the brand new Federal Council should come from two of his fellow Methodists. Bishop E. E. Hoss, of the Methodist Episcopal Church, South, helped block a resolution favoring "the elimination so far as possible of denominational distinctions" in foreign mission fields, "an ideal to which practically all foreign missionaries are enthusiastically devoted, those

---

[1] Sanford, *Origin and History of the Federal Council*, p. 357.

of the bishop's own church not less than others." [2] And Bishop Thomas B. Neely, of the Methodist Episcopal Church (resident in New Orleans!) reportedly provided "the next most discreditable exhibit of the same spirit" when he upset a resolution designed to assure the Seventh Day Baptists that their conscientious view of the Sabbath was respected even if not shared by the majority. "It is a pleasure to record the conviction that neither of these bishops really represents the sentiment of the church in which he is an officeholder." [3]

Obviously the conference held no animus toward either main branch of Methodism, for it had already elected Bishop E. R. Hendrix, of the Methodist Episcopal Church, South, first president of the Federal Council, and later named Frank Mason North vice-chairman of the Executive Committee and chairman of the Commission on the Church and Social Service for the next quadrennium. If the report on "The Churches and Modern Industry" was one of the highlights of the Council's founding, the Commission on the Church and Social Service proved to be one of its most active, significant, and influential agencies. In fact, one member commented: "The main hope of the Federal Council lies with the Commission on the Church and Social Service. It must go ahead on its own account." [4] Faithfully its chairman presided and prodded, initiated and challenged. When the Executive Committee of the Council met in December, 1909, Frank Mason North was "detained on account of imperative business engagements," but he arrived in time to give his Commission report. It included stress on the workers' right to one day's rest in seven, reasonable hours of labor, and a living wage. In its second year of operation the Commission issued its three-point appeal in behalf of labor, investigated the Bethlehem steel strike (to the dismay of many industrialists), instituted the observance of Labor Sunday on the first Sunday in September, and circulated ten thousand more copies of "The Church and Modern Industry."

[2] *The Interior*, December 17, 1908, p. 1719; cf. Sanford, *Federal Council*, pp. 32-33, *et seq.*

[3] *Ibid.*, although the Neely exchange has not been located in the official report of the meeting, edited by Sanford.

[4] John M. Glenn, quoted in Macfarland, *Christian Unity in the Making*, p. 58.

At its session in January, 1911, the Council's Executive Committee recognized that the Commission on the Church and Social Service faced "a position of large opportunity which is however, not without its embarrassments and its perils."[5] It, therefore, authorized the expenditure of up to five thousand dollars for social service, despite an overall Council deficit, and on May 1, 1911, C. S. Macfarland was hired as secretary for the Commission.

The Commission report the following December expressed concern over northern and southern lynchings, 50 within six months, 2,458 in the preceding twenty-six years, and over the victims of a recent Tennessee coal mine disaster. At this same meeting the names of Harry Ward and Washington Gladden (by then seventy-five years old) were added to the Commission, thus bringing North, Gladden, and Rauschenbusch into official working relationship. Nevertheless, these were lean years for the Council. "Outside the prophetic group responsible for the initiation of the movement, few church leaders were taking it seriously," Macfarland recalls.[6] Most displayed indifference or questioned whether their denominational contributions of a few hundred dollars were warranted. "The emphasis on the social gospel did not kindle the hearts and minds of some denominational leaders. But we had a few men of great faith."

On March 22, 1912, the Executive Committee of the Federal Council approved a letter to the President of the United States which represents perhaps the earliest example of direct "lobbying" or political pressure from the Council:

The Executive Committee of the Federal Council of the Churches of Christ in America, in session assembled at New York City, in behalf of a constituency representing 50,000,000 of the people, believing that in so doing they also represent the public conscience of the Nation, urge that in case of necessity, the President take action to prevent a strike in the mines of the nation.

It is our profound belief that, where interests are involved which affect so seriously the welfare of the whole people, decisions as to

[5] Sanford, *Origin and History of the Federal Council*, p. 297.
[6] *Christian Unity in the Making*, pp. 63-64.

the settlement of such an industrial question, can no longer be left to the limited and classified groups of men immediately involved.[7]

At the second quadrennial meeting of the Federal Council in December, 1912, Frank Mason North was chosen as chairman of the Executive Committee for the coming quadrennium, "a position equal in importance, if not in honor, to the presidency of the Council."[8] Speakers at that session included Professor Shailer Mathews of Chicago, newly elected president of the Council, Walter Rauschenbusch of Rochester Theological Seminary, Edward Steiner of Grinnell College, and both Charles W. Fairbanks, former vice-president of the United States, and Thomas R. Marshall, vice-president-elect.

Although foreign policy at this time gave scant attention to the Turkish situation, American churchmen were concerned for the plight of Armenians in that Moslem land and appealed for governments to "safeguard for all time the interests of Christians in the Ottoman Empire." Retiring President E. R. Hendrix declared: "The Federal Council of the Churches of Christ in America affectionately tender to their fellow Christians under the flags of other nations their sincere sympathies in their peculiar trial during periods of war and upheaval." Specifically, the Council sent fraternal greetings to the churches of China and approved also "a paper requesting the recognition of the Republic of China by the Government of the United States":

Resolved: one, that this Federal Council hereby records its gratitude to God for the wonderful providence which has given to our fellow-Christians in China and the Chinese people a new government which has as its fundamental principles liberty, both civil and religious, equality, enlightenment and progress.

Resolved, two, that we extend to the Christian churches of the new Republic our heartiest congratulations upon the extraordinary opportunity now afforded them to glorify God and serve their nation by helping to lay a foundation of truth and righteousness for the newly established Republic, and that we assure the Christians of

---

[7] Minutes of the Executive Committee, March 22, 1912 (Federal Council archives).

[8] Unmarked clipping in North scrapbook.

China that they have the hearty God-speed and the unceasing prayers of the Christians of the United States of America.

Resolved, three, that this Federal Council respectfully requests the government of the United States to take early action for the recognition by it of the Republic of China, and that the President of the Council be entrusted with this duty associating with himself such other members as he may select.[9]

The Council in session authorized telegrams to the U. S. Senate and House endorsing the Kenyon-Sheppard Inter-State Liquor Shipment Bill (Sen. 4043). It called for the establishment of a Council office in Washington, D. C., as early as feasible. It recommended an increase in the number of Navy chaplains—prophetically? It urged pastors to read (to their people?) the Social Creed, including additional articles on marriage and divorce, education, health, and the liquor traffic. It adopted a program to "present Christ" at the Panama Pacific Exposition scheduled for 1915. Just a year and a half before the outbreak of war in Europe it passed this resolution:

The Council favors the organization of a Church Peace League in America, the annual observance of Peace Sunday by the churches, and the memorializing of the Third Hague Conference in behalf of the establishment of a permanent court of international justice and the adoption of such other measures as shall render war unnecessary and impossible. It calls upon Christian men and women to unite in a demand that the teaching and spirit of Jesus be applied in international relations by our national Congress and Department of State.

One of North's major contributions as chairman of the Executive Committee was the drafting of "A Statement of Principles . . ." for the Federal Council. The subcommittee, which he apparently headed, faced and clarified some of the policies and purposes which are still under debate today. The final report, adopted by the Executive Committee on December 4, 1913, said in part:

[9] *Minutes of the Second Quadrennial Meeting of the Federal Council of the Churches of Christ in America,* Chicago, 1912, pp. 26-27.

The Federal Council . . . is not an individual or voluntary agency or simply an interdenominational fellowship, but it is a body officially constituted by the Churches. Its differentiation from other movements looking towards unity is that it brings together the various denominations for union in service rather than in polity or doctrinal statement. . . .

Its function has been to express the will of its constituent bodies and not to legislate for them. Were this, however, to be construed as precluding the utterance of the voice of the churches upon matters in regard to which the consciousness and the conscience of Christianity are practically unanimous, the Federal Council would be shorn of the power given it by the constituent bodies when they adopted as one of its objects: "To secure a larger combined influence for the churches of Christ in all matters affecting the moral and social condition of the people, so as to promote the application of the law of Christ to every relation of human life."

. . . The autonomy of the constituent bodies is, however, wisely safeguarded. No action by the Federal Council, even though taken . . . by the unanimous vote of the officially constituted delegates of the constituent bodies, can . . . be legally imposed upon those constituent bodies. . . . Such action . . . goes back to the constituent bodies . . . for their action or ratification. . . .

It is, therefore, the function of the Council, not so much to do things, as to get the denominational bodies and the interdenominational movements to do the work of the churches in co-operation. Here its function is not that of overseer or director, but that of an agency for the correlation and the coordination of existing forces and organizations . . . to recommend, give guidance and point out the way.[10]

During this quadrennium, so fateful for world history, Frank Mason North missed only one meeting of the Federal Council Executive Committee, while he was traveling in the Far East. In 1916, when the Executive Committee made its quadrennial report to the full Council, the words of inspiration and affirmation were those of Frank Mason North:

Closer contact has meant clearer focus—focus in which the unities and the diversities have equally been revealed. . . . Fellowship is

[10] "A Statement of Principles Underlying and Guiding the Development and Work of the Federal Council of Churches of Christ in America" (Federal Council Bulletin No. 7, January 15, 1914).

revelation. We are more nearly sure in the mutual examination of our common Christianity where the marks which look like seams in the fabric are but flaws in the weaving. . . . We waive no right or privilege, we break with no sound tradition, we surrender no precious heritage, but we become fixed in the persuasion that the Church has but one inalienable right, the right of finding Christ in the world of today and interpreting Him in all His sacrificial and triumphant power to that world. Perfect agreement in opinion, placid uniformity in expression and method do not appear. It is a waste of energy and time to seek for either. But in this fellowship we have seen the glory [glow?] of sympathy break into the flame of enthusiasm when men of different cults and names have brushed aside tradition and prejudice and found The Christ in one another's hearts. It is not in what we each hold dear that we find our common ground, but in what we each hold most dear. It is not in their history, their traditions, their formulae that the Churches of Christ can be one; it is alone in the Christ Himself.[11]

With such oratory—and such understanding of the ecumenical task—it is not surprising that North was unanimously elected to the presidency of the Federal Council for 1916-20. Twice he declined. For one thing, he felt hesitant as a Methodist to occupy the office which Bishop Hendrix of the Southern Church had held just four years earlier. On the contrary, delegates insisted, his denominational ties would be an asset, for the Methodist Church had missions or conferences in all the warring states, and North himself had foreign contacts already established. When Methodist representatives on the Council begged him to reconsider, he wired the chairman of the Board of Foreign Missions and his associate, S. Earl Taylor. Even with their approval, he accepted only subject to official permission from the Methodist Board. Three weeks after the meeting adjourned North wrote to Macfarland, since 1912 the executive secretary of the Council, expressing his gratitude for time to consider the election and to consult his colleagues. "Thus far no one has advised me not to acquiesce in the judgment of the Council," he wrote in modest

[11] Cf. Macfarland, *Christian Unity in the Making*, pp. 359-60; *Frank Mason North*, pp. 47-48.

reluctance. "At this attitude, I find myself greatly surprised—I cannot deny that it brings the pressure on my own judgment which seems to me practically conclusive." Still he took up the demanding office with the reservation that he would have to withdraw if the task "is beyond my resources of time and thought." [12]

The church press—especially the Methodists—hailed his election jubilantly. The *North-West Christian Advocate* declared: "There is no ecclesiastical position in America that will mean so much for the next four years as this presidency. . . . The Federal Council is Protestantism in action." [13] Speaking of the impending war crisis, the *Central Christian Advocate* editorialized: "When the diplomats meet to decide the issues of the war, in particular when they are debating how to abolish war, then must the voice of the Christianity of this nation be heard. Who shall speak that word? There is no adequate voice but this Federal Council of the Churches. Who must vocalize that council? The president thereof." [14] And the *Christian Advocate* (of New York) claimed, with unseemly pride:

Methodism does a real service to the Federal Council of the Churches in providing it with a president for this quadrennium. . . . We may fairly congratulate ourselves that Methodism possessed the one man who could best serve all the churches. . . . Though his burdens of responsibility will be heavy, they are not beyond his proved capacity for work. And as for honor, well-earned, highly merited and totally unexpected—for by rotation this should have been the year for a Presbyterian president—it is one the highest which can come to any Christian minister. The only emolument is the good will of the brethren and the sense of being a fellowworker with all the churches for the more speedy fulfillment of the universal prayer, "Thy Kingdom come!" [15]

Some of North's "platform" was outlined in a revealing interview conducted soon after the election. Recognizing the new

[12] Letter from F. M. North to C. S. Macfarland, December 30, 1916 (Federal Council archives #119); cf. *Christian Advocate*, December 14, 1916.
[13] December 13, 1916.
[14] December 20, 1916.
[15] December 14, 1916, p. 1638.

Federal Council president as "distinctly a man of vision," the reporter emphasized North's anticipation of a spiritual revival to follow the social revival, which North saw exemplified not only in the Social Creed but also in a war "to make the world safe for democracy." "I am so sure that the Kingdom of God is coming, in places and in ways which we did not recognize twenty-five or thirty years ago," Carlos Hurd quoted North, "and I am so convinced that a larger meaning is being seen in the gospel, and that it is reasserting itself in the world's life, in ways which we once did not recognize, that I must believe a great and wonderful progress is being made." Here is the optimism for which the social-gospel spokesmen are so often criticized today. But others would argue, a half century later, that in spite of wars and depressions and moral revolution there *is* evidence of increasing social concern, there *is* justification for Christian confidence and Christian hope.

With specific reference to the war in Europe, so soon to embroil the United States as well, North told his interviewer: "We must have fraternal relations with the churches in all the now belligerent countries, . . . but we must remember that they will resent an attempt to introduce any directive influence over them." And his comment on the church's role in social action is as pertinent today as it was in 1916:

There are two perils in this kind of work. One is that the more conservative church members, and the more conservative churches, may think we are going outside our proper realm, if we take any action bearing on legislation. And you cannot go very far in industrial work without getting into questions of legislation. . . . The other danger is that the more extreme of the labor leaders will say, "Why don't the churches do something, instead of always talking?" I have always taken the ground that the church has a right, at least, to give active support to legislation that plainly comes within the Decalogue. Legislation insuring one day's rest in seven is in this class, and no church need apologize for supporting legislation of this sort.[16]

Even with such delimitations by the president, the Presbyterian Church in the United States had threatened to withdraw from

[16] Hurd, interview, unmarked clipping in North papers.

the Federal Council at its 1916 meeting, on the ground that speaking for the churches on peace and prohibition was an "improper encroachment upon the sphere of the State." [17]

Less than four months after North's election the United States was at war. The Federal Council of Churches immediately called a special meeting in Washington, May 8-9, 1917: "for prayer and conference; to prepare a suitable message for the hour; to plan and provide for works of mercy; to plan and provide for the moral and religious welfare of the army and navy; to formulate Christian duties relative to conserving the economic, social, moral and spiritual forces of the nation." [18] John R. Mott, Robert E. Speer, and Henry Churchill King were among the principal speakers. Whatever bitterness and fanatical patriotism later marred the spirit of American Churches, Frank Mason North set the tone of the Federal Council in his presidential address:

Never until today has the Christian Church in a free nation, with free institutions, a nation of 100,000,000 of people, an unestablished Church, a free Church in a free state, been called upon to confront the great issues of civilization and of Christian development, and to be tested in its personnel, and in its organization, by questions as great as are before the Church today. . . .

I believe the greatest need of the great American Church today is a realization of the immediate, constant, indwelling presence and power of the personal Christ. I have been profoundly interested in the organization of the Federal Council. I am now profoundly interested that in this widening range of its opportunity and of its service, it may be held just as close to the beating, loving heart of Jesus Christ as ever mystic was held . . . in the ages past, as ever disciple was held when Christ was here upon earth, and that . . . as we go down this land, with these great errands ours, the one presence of which we are conscious is the presence of the Master of Life, the Redeemer of Men, the Liberator of the World, the personal Savior and Friend of all men, our Lord Jesus Christ.

Three days later the Administrative Committee of the Council approved a message on "The Duty of the Church in this Hour

[17] *The Presbyterian* (Richmond), December 27, 1916; cf. earlier protests against President Shailer Mathews' "antitheses of orthodoxy," in Macfarland, *Christian Unity in the Making*, pp. 83-84.

[18] Macfarland, *Christian Unity in the Making*, p. 124.

of National Need." [19] Regretting the tragic necessity of war, and affirming its supreme loyalty to "our divine Lord," the statement pledged to the nation "both support and allegiance in unstinted measure. . . . Since, in spite of every effort, war has come, we are grateful that the ends to which we are committed are such as we can approve: . . . principles of righteousness and the inviolability of faith . . . the right of all the peoples to live their life in freedom and peace." "We enter the war," the document continued, "without haste or passion, not for private or national gain, with no hatred or bitterness against those with whom we contend."

Increasingly the Federal Council extended its organization to meet the multitudinous problems of the war. By May of 1918 its national offices employed a staff of sixty persons. In September, 1917, the General War-Time Commission of the Churches was set up, with Robert E. Speer as chairman, William Adams Brown as secretary, Samuel McCrea Cavert and Eric North as young assistants. Through its Commission on Peace and Arbitration (established in 1911 and later the Commission on International Justice), the Council continued to cooperate with the World Alliance for International Friendship through the Churches. At the end of 1915 C. S. Macfarland had crossed the Atlantic as ambassador from the churches of America to the churches of Europe on both sides of the war. The Commission on Relations with France and Belgium carried on such effective relief work that Herbert Hoover telegraphed in 1917: "The Federal Council has rendered a splendid and greatly needed service. Do not let it wane. It would not, if our American Christians only knew!" [20]

In the midst of such crucial wartime activities the Federal Council did not neglect its many other concerns. Meeting in Cincinnati in December, 1917, the Executive Committee appealed to its constituents:

The times demand, not only new sacrifices, but efforts to conserve all that is good. The danger that the evil consequences of war may

[19] *Ibid.*, pp. 124-28.
[20] Quoted in Macfarland, *Christian Unity in the Making,* p. 131.

overcome the good is serious. We must see that the spiritual influence of the churches and their efforts to ameliorate conditions of human living shall not be diminished. We, therefore, call upon all members of the churches which we represent not to abate in the least their contributions to missions, to their own charities, and to social agencies.

Nor, in the midst of battle, did the president of the Federal Council abandon his vision, his thoughtful perspective, his wise reflection concerning the manifold tasks upon his desk and heart. In an address delivered on February 22, 1918, he soberly examined the nature of the church, its relation to the kingdom of God, and the meaning of true brotherhood. As they represent his profound insight into human experience, they also offer insight for the reader into the man himself.

I remember that when I was in college thinking I wanted to discuss a subject that was worth while and I chose the subject of socialism for one of those horrible things we called "chapel orations". . . . As I come on through my relationship to men in the Church and outside the Church, I have felt that I am in touch with the effects of a tremendous movement in human society, in the minds and the hearts of men, that the Church has never really understood and has never tried to interpret and that we are confronting now in the conditions in Russia . . . and in every nation of Europe . . . and throughout our own land, phenomena in the world of industry, in the expression of men as to their own rights, as to that which is given to them individually as children of God, which the Church has never comprehensively or concretely attempted to understand or to define or to guide.

Even allowing for editorial omissions, these are long, involved, rambling sentences, not typical of Frank Mason North's polished oratory. Rather they carry the mood—and the sincerity—of a man thinking out loud, an old man wrestling with some new thoughts but standing on a foundation of immovable faith. For example, the corresponding secretary of the Methodist Board of Foreign Missions ruminates about whether a sacrificial spirit is exclusively Christian, whether even the Cross does not stand for a universal sense of service.

160

We have found the spirit of sacrifice deepened, clarified, developed, by the revelation of Jesus Christ, but everywhere in the world today is that which was not in the dictionary a dozen or twenty years ago, "altruism", discovered to be a moving power in human life. . . . The Church of Jesus Christ must once more recognize the fact that it has its rights in a person and not in a system of truth or a mode of practice or a type of organization. . . . Let us remember that the belief in God, that a system of theism, to use some theological terms, or a system of deism, a belief in God that doesn't mediate that God through His Son, the Savior of the World, will mean a philosophy and a form of moral life, but it will never, under God's heaven, mean that sacrificial spirit in the Church as the only hope for the salvation of the world.

And the president of the Federal Council of the Churches of Christ in America, looked ahead to the days when these ecumenical and missionary interests would be amalgamated, and when the church would give fresh attention to its unity of faith, an area which he himself had hitherto laid aside for unity of action.

I had hoped that the day would come in the course of these great seething movements of the churches and the peoples, where every church would sit in its own domestic circle, grouped about its own hearthside, and in the quiet—if it can ever get any quiet—take up the question in itself as to whether, after all, the thing it thinks most important and demanding is as essential as it really thought it was; whether the inheritance of the splendid but narrow conscience of our fathers necessarily creates for us a proper barrier between ourselves and Christians of another name; whether, after all, the essentials in which we are all one, if they are really set on fire, may not burn the barriers away and give us a common life in the fellowship of our Lord Jesus Christ.

The Interchurch World Movement, which soared with meteoric splendor in 1918 and fizzled out two years later, proved to be one of the thorniest problems of this period for the Federal Council of Churches and for Frank Mason North personally. Riding the crest of postwar exuberance, it sought to accomplish much of what North was giving his life to: cooperation among the churches and the global spread of Christianity. But it frankly declared its

161

impatience with the gradual, evolutionary methods of the Federal Council and of denominational agencies. Confident of new floods of wealth and philanthropy in the wake of death and destruction, the Interchurch World Movement offered grandiose schemes to revolutionize the Christian enterprise.

North confronted this flamboyant "rival" at a number of different points and always with his customary balance and wisdom. One of his predecessors in the Federal Council presidency remarked that "the only hope for the cooperative movement lies in the absorption of the Council in this movement." [21] However, a careful committee appraisal by those who knew the aims and the struggles of the Council reached the conclusion "that the Interchurch World Movement was not structurally sound, and that its leaders were dazzled by an illusory financial prospect." Apparently most denominational leaders were not convinced that this new venture could effect in one stroke what the Council was trying to do slowly and patiently, by education and persuasion.

But Frank Mason North was drawn more personally and painfully into the arena by the decisions of his colleagues. Arthur B. Moss, who worked closely with him at this period, believes that North was interested and sympathetic toward the movement as a *promotional* undertaking, but apprehensive that it might attempt to *administer* foreign missions on a broad interdenominational basis.[22] Clearly North did not believe that the time had come—if ever—for such joint operation. However in February, 1919, his associate, S. Earl Taylor, wrote to North in Paris:

As I have cabled you, I have been called to lead this Interchurch World Movement. . . . In this event, you will have thrown upon your shoulders the heavy burden of administering our Foreign Board work (with such little help as I am able to give from time to time in counsel and in Board and Committee meetings) and this will come in connection with a greatly increased staff and working budget and also at a time when, as President of the Federal Council of Churches, you ought to be giving much thought and attention to this Inter-

[21] Quoted in Macfarland, *Christian Unity in the Making*, p. 146.
[22] Personal interview, New York, October 12, 1958.

church World Movement which is so closely related to all that you have been planning and dreaming most of your life.[23]

Five months later another associate from Methodist Federation days, Worth M. Tippy, asked to be relieved, at least part time, from his job as secretary of the Federal Council's Commission on the Church and Social Service in order to organize a Department of Industrial Relations for the Interchurch World Movement. Such double "desertion" (as it may well have appeared) produced no perceptible bitterness. "Led by a master-mind in President Frank Mason North," [24] the Federal Council determined to show no hostility toward this rival movement, to cooperate at every possible juncture, but to guard strictly the integrity of the Council by avoiding any semblance of absorption or integration. As chairman of an *ad hoc* committee to discuss organic union between the F.C.C. and the I.W.M., North insisted that such a merger could not be considered constitutionally without reference to all the participating denominations, and that any functional alliance would merely prove an "occasion for confusion and duplication which was to be deplored and avoided." [25] When the Interchurch World Movement collapsed in June, 1920, it left a number of overexpanded budgets and a number of sadder and wiser men.

Immediately at the close of the war the Federal Council's Executive Committee endorsed proposals for a League of Nations—and for collecting signatures of support through the churches, with a National Day of Prayer. On behalf of a specially appointed commission, Frank Mason North as president (in Europe to study postwar needs and opportunities for Methodist work) and James I. Vance of Nashville as chairman of the executive committee traveled to Paris early in 1919 to present these resolutions to the Peace Council meeting there. The Declaration adopted on December 12, 1918, said in part:

The time has come to organize the world for truth and right, justice and humanity. To this end as Christians we urge the establishment

[23] February 24, 1919 (Methodist Board of Missions correspondence files).
[24] Macfarland, *Christian Unity in the Making*, p. 151; cf. pp. 177-78.
[25] *Ibid.*, pp. 167-68.

of a League of Free Nations at the coming Peace Conference. Such a League is not a mere political expedient; it is rather the political expression of the Kingdom of God on earth. . . .

The world is now so small, the life of nations so intertwined, the mastery of nature's titanic forces so complete, and the power of selfish, economic or nationalistic groups to enslave whole peoples and to bring tragedy to the entire world so dangerous, that the re-establishment of the old world-order of irresponsible states must become intolerable. We must have a governed world in which the security and rights of each shall rest upon the combined strength of all. Humanity must be organized on a basis of justice and fair-dealing. The law of brotherhood must supersede the law of the jungle.

A League to attain these results must be democratic in spirit and in form. It must be capable of continuous adjustment to the advancing life of separate nations and also of the world. It must be directed by the enlightened conscience of mankind.

The Church has much to give and much to gain. . . . What is the Kingdom of God, if it be not the triumph of God's will in the affairs of men . . . ? And what is this vision of a world-federation of humanity organized on a basis of justice and fair-dealing, for the effective and impartial maintenance of peace, if it be not an international manifestation of the Kingdom of God?

The Church can give a spirit of goodwill, without which no League of Nations can endure. . . . The Church can give the driving power of Faith, without which no great ideal can be realized. . . . The Church has much to gain. Its message will encounter less opposition from selfish nationalism. Its missionary enterprise will prosper as never before, freed from the blight of unChristian conduct of the nations of Christendom. The Church will, moreover, recover its international character and consciousness.

We call upon all Christians and upon all believers in God and lovers of man, to work and pray with whole souls, that out of the ashes of the old civilization may rise the fair outlines of a new world, based on the Christ ideal of justice, cooperation, brotherhood and service.

While they were in Europe, these officials of the Federal Council engaged in a survey of rehabilitation needs in devastated areas of France and Italy. North and Macfarland were made Chevaliers of the French Legion of Honor, in appreciation for the Council's relief work during the war; later, at the full Council meeting of 1920, North was made an Officer of Public Instruction by France and an Officer of the Royal Order of George I by Greece. At this session Frank Mason North, two days short of his seventieth birthday, relinquished his presidency to another great statesman in the missionary movement, Robert E. Speer. The spirit and the direction of his valedictory were typical. Rejecting "the lure of reminiscence," he said: "The backward glance belongs to leisure, not to action . . . better the mood of the starting post than that of the goal. These have been years of experiment and discipline—now for the race!" North listed the assets of the Federal Council as he had found them in twelve years of intimate association: (1) a high estimate of personality, in which oneness of faith and logic of action overcome most differences; (2) a self-testing by three sins of mind and will which Christ condemned: intolerance (aggressive or indifferent), intellectual pride (or Pharisaism), covetousness (grasp of power); (3) values of denominational life recognized, not denied or ignored ("*The good of all must come not by the negation but by the affirmation of the values of each*"); (4) the essential oneness of the churches affirmed in the charter, yet aware that "it [the Council] has received no mandate from its constituents to promote organic union or a common creedal statement."

Nevertheless, the retiring President went on:

If the churches federate, it is that the world may be better and hear the good tidings. If organic union should be accomplished, it is not an end in itself, the peoples for whom Christ died, stretch in multitudes far beyond it. Our sickles are near at hand. We shape and sharpen them. Yonder are the whitened fields. Our Master cares not less for harvest than for sickles. Never can we measure the meaning of the church until we share His thought of the Kingdom.

Always, North continued, there have been men who thought the Kingdom more than a dream, though as a dream it has shaped the course of history. In all religions and even mythology there appears the "deathless confidence that some day, somewhere, there shall be a reign of righteousness, a realm of content"; imagine the Bible or Christ or prophet without the Kingdom.

165

Deny to patriarch, lawgiver, captain, seer, the forward look, the conception of escape from evil, of rectification from wrong, of realization of hope, of permanence of righteousness, of completeness of individual and community life, and the book would become a book of dread. Rob the conversation of our Lord of its reference to the Kingdom, blot out its ideals and its promises, mutilate the Lord's Prayer, and cancel the parables, assume His pledge of its coming to have been unspoken, or its inspiration to the men who heard Him to have been a passing emotion, even though the Cross remains, the gospel loses its gladness, and its tidings bring not great joy to all people. For a Savior means not only forgiveness but life. Redemption is more than deliverance, it is power. . . . There is no gospel without its Kingdom, no complete Savior from sin who does not become a King in righteousness.

This was North's answer to critics of the social gospel, to "crisis theologians" just emerging on the horizon.

It is eminently fitting that this last year of North's administration should have included a giant step forward toward his lifetime goal; namely, the official endorsement of a delegation to take part in an ecumenical conference in Geneva, "a world conference of church bodies to consider the urgent practical tasks of Christian life and service and the possibilities of world-wide cooperation in testimony and action."

The man who worked most closely with Frank Mason North in the Federal Council of Churches did not always see eye-to-eye with him. The general secretary differed sharply with the Executive Committee chairman, later the president, on various questions, especially on postwar church policies in Europe (see pp. 207-9). When Macfarland complained about North's using Methodist stationery for Federal Council business, the president explained soothingly that he had been doing some dictaphone work in his office, where there was not enough Council paper on hand, but now "we have sufficient stationery here and will see that this matter is rectified." [26] In another letter North reprimanded Macfarland sharply for being in France, engaged in a host of peripheral matters, instead of doing his job as

[26] Letter to C. S. Macfarland, August 7, 1919 (Federal Council Archives #119).

secretary of the Federal Council of Churches. "It will not be a matter of choice from this time on," the president warned, "that I absolutely decline to assume any executive responsibilities in connection with the administration of the Federal Council, excepting in so far as my position as president may involve them. The actual executive functions must rest where they are placed by our Constitution and by our procedure." [27] To this Macfarland penciled a reply on the back for his stenographer's transcription:

After you and I have an hour together, you will feel differently (and better) about some things. All we need is patience with (each other and) every body else and also that every body else should have patience with us. I am asking Miss C to secure a real conference for at least an hour. It will be well worth it—at least to

Yours faithfully

No wonder Macfarland's history of the Council appears cool or even curt in some of his references to North.

It is all the more significant—and a tribute to both men—that he ends his definitive book, *Christian Unity in the Making*, with a lengthy quotation from North, preceded by this testimony: "Were the writer called upon to name the man whose vision and action best characterized the spirit of the advisers to the staff, his instinctive choice would be Frank Mason North." [28]

[27] Letter to C. S. Macfarland, October, 21, 1919 (#134 in Federal Council Archives #119).
[28] P. 359.

A Missionary Commission Hymn

With Thee, our Master and our Lord,
  We greet this wondrous day;
The gates swing open at Thy word,
  The paths stretch far away.
The way we take is known to Thee,
  Thy footprints there we trace;
Oh, grant us now that we may see
  The radiance of Thy face.

We little bring; our gift is small,
  Yet all we are is Thine;
Ourselves we give, our life, our all;
  Thy life in ours enshrine.
Oh, lead us forth in ardor bright,
  Enkindled from above;
O Christ, reveal in heaven's own light
  The challenge of Thy love.

Afar the troubled lands await
  The rescue from distress,
The gentleness that makes Thee great,
  Thy healing tenderness.
To meet the world's unmeasured loss,
  Its sin, its woe, its strife,
Send out the glory of Thy cross,
  Thou Master of our life.

Together still: e'en though we part,
  Our life is one in prayer;
Our hearts are ever where Thou art,
  And Thou art everywhere.
About the world Thy servants stand;
  With them one song we sing,—
Thy conquering love in every land,
  Thy triumph, Christ, our King!

Commission Service of the
Woman's Foreign Missionary Society
1925

9

In Methodist Conference

Their hearts interpreted Thy word;
Through them Thy messages were sent;
Within these walls Thy voice was heard,
Here wisdom found its sacrament.

For all his depth of ecumenical concern, Frank Mason North was—as he himself expressed it—a "born Methodist" with two generations on one side and on the other "undisguised and active loyalty." [1] He was ordained to the Methodist ministry in 1873 and served pastoral appointments for nineteen years, administrative offices for thirty-two more. There were those within the church and outside, then as now, who wondered—"how, being rather keen myself about individual freedom, I can endure being tied up in a hierarchy, how being of a democratic spirit, I can be content to work in even a well articulated organization which I cannot control." [2] By the age of seventy-five North had formulated his answers.

Although he was not uncritical, Frank Mason North believed in the message and the method of the Methodist Episcopal Church. "The message was and is 'good news'," he affirmed, "—the very best news that ever came into the world. The ruling motive, as I conceived it, was not its protection, but its circulation." North's Arminian theology will be discussed in a subsequent chapter. It was always a missionary faith. "It is [the church's] business to do its

---

[1] North, "Why I Am A Methodist," *The Forum,* July, 1926.
[2] *Ibid.,* p. 77; cf. pp. 71-82 for quotations following.

part to see that no man anywhere, in our favored homeland or in the remotest corner of the globe, is denied his chance to hear and to understand the message of the Gospel."

To his death, North remained convinced that the Methodist Episcopal system provided the most effective tradition and framework within which to fulfill this task. In structure, he recognized, Methodism is "not a pure democracy. Just as surely it is not an autocracy." The bishops, he pointed out, are not a third order of clergy, but they have authority "which can be, but rarely is, misused," while "the ministry is made by the people." Or, to sum it up in another way: "Within this organization there is freedom. Order is essential to smooth operation. . . . Methodism has bones as well as arteries and nerves. There is a frame as well as circulation and feeling."

But North paid tribute to many other aspects of the Methodist program. "I like a church which deals with the child not as alien, but as one of the family," he commented. He praised the church's concern for education, the position of women, and total abstinence. He rejoiced that it was "sensitive to the disasters, the distress, the injustices, and the inequities of the social and industrial order." He held that the church should believe in the nation and serve it, yet never lose a "vision and conviction as to its world task." At the same time he acknowledged that his own denomination "has failures enough for wholesale humiliation and self-discipline, and it is eager to meet the new day." In the last decade of his long and fruitful life, Frank Mason North could affirm with sincerity what he had demonstrated with devotion: "The history, the essential doctrines, the ideals, the worldwideness, the fellowship, the adaptiveness, the glow, the courage, and the efficiency,—in a word, the message and the method of the Methodist Episcopal Church hold me both in conviction and service."

As recorded in chapter 2, North served six urban or rural pastorates in the New York Annual Conference between 1873 and 1887. Then, convinced of a real opportunity in his college community, he accepted the appointment after the regular conference session. Moving to Middletown meant transferring not only to Connecticut but to the New York East Annual Conference, where his distinguished career began to flower. Arthur B. Moss, a younger associate in the Conference and in the Board of Foreign Missions, recalls: "He did not often speak . . . or seek the Conference floor . . . rarely got up on his own initiative . . . generally only on being asked to speak, or on a missionary issue where he felt direct responsibility." [3] In General Conference and Annual Conference North often introduced resolutions and memorials from committees on which he served but seldom took part in debate. For this reason it is difficult, if not impossible, to identify specific ideas or statements as coming from North. As Moss adds, many committee reports "in phrasing and emphasis would have had his close personal supervision" even though he did not always present them himself.

In other words, North's unquestioned leadership was largely exercised behind the scenes, in quiet personal influence. Lynn Harold Hough, former dean of Drew Theological Seminary, wrote, for example: "When I became most active in the New York East Conference Dr. North was a grand old man regarded with the highest appreciation by all of us." [4] And he added in conversation that any evaluation of North's Conference activities would have to rest on more than ascribed documents, since North always wanted to let other people have their say in formulating resolutions, reports, and the like.[5]

North's active participation in Conference affairs began with his chairmanship of the Committee on the Relation of the Church to Socialism (later The Church and Social Problems). That report, adopted in 1892, has been reviewed as part of the background to the Social Creed (see chapter 4). However, it was not acted upon by the General Conference of that year and was therefore renewed, with minor revisions, in successive quadrennia. The report of 1896 proved to be an almost equally historic document. Since North had proposed the appointment of the committee the preceding year, his own name had been modestly omitted and had to be added by subsequent vote. With him were associated the original committee of 1891-92 (Bradford P. Ray-

[3] Personal interview, New York, October 12, 1958.
[4] Letter to the author, April 23, 1957.
[5] Personal interview, New York, January 24, 1958.

mond, Joseph Pullman, William North Rice, John Rhey Thompson), plus Samuel L. Beiler, B. F. Kidder, and Herbert Welch.

Although rejoicing that "on the whole the economic and social condition of humanity is improving," the document deplored the fact that working people still looked on the church as "in alliance with the wealthy and the powerful and indifferent to the condition of the poor." It affirmed the right of private property with the emphatic assertion, "There must be no toleration for communistic theories," but hastened to add that this did not mean rejection of all measures proposed under the "vague and elastic name of socialism." Liberty, it said, must be limited for the good of society, particularly in such areas as public utilities and industrial exploitation under the "sweating system." Specifically, "the right of laborers to associate, and the right of the individual laborer to act as an individual, are equally sacred."

In a plea for more Christian business ethics, the resolution declared that "no business is legitimate which does not promote the welfare of society," and property ownership, it maintained, involves not only rights but duties which are *owed* to the weak and poor and ignorant. It reiterated earlier attacks on the pew system and plutocracy (government by the rich and powerful) within the churches, and called for institutional services and more extensive study of sociology by members and ministers. "It is, indeed, true," the report concluded, "that the Church is not a political organization. It works directly, not upon society at large, but upon individuals. . . . Yet it must never be forgotten that beyond this primary aim lies the ulterior aim of establishing a kingdom of heaven—a new social order wherein righteousness shall be the universal law." [6]

Despite his obvious leadership in social concerns, Frank Mason North did not remain consistently and steadily on that—or any other—committee. Apparently it was customary during this time for the New York East Annual Conference, at least, to rotate its committee memberships—and not for the younger men only. North served briefly on the Committee for Evangelistic Work, on the Board of Education, and on the Board of Examiners, later

[6] *Minutes*, New York East Annual Conference, 1896, pp. 89-93.

Ministerial Training (testing candidates specifically in Isaiah and the Gospels). Forty years later the Conference Memoir recalled: "He was especially solicitous that no candidate should be admitted to our ranks who had not a real experience of and a clear conviction about the saving grace of Jesus Christ. Any uncertainty in this respect grieved him." [7]

North was a Conference trustee from 1903 to 1935, president of the board from 1926 to 1933 (and was given a bouquet of roses on his retirement from that office!). He was president of the Endowment Fund Commission from 1906 to 1917, presumably resigning because of Federal Council and other responsibilities. Numerous other committees drew on his wisdom and dedication from time to time. For example, in 1907 alone he was appointed to special committees to study "possible recognition" of Orders of the Old Catholic Church (a theological issue), National Arbitration and the Peace Congress (a political problem), and the Income of Pastors or "a minimum living wage for ministers" (a financial matter).

The trust and esteem of his colleagues shines through the *Minutes* and *Journals* in little inconspicuous ways. Beginning in 1896, there were very few of the next thirty-five years when North was not asked by the presiding bishop to take the chair during one or more sessions of the Conference. The year after his election as corresponding secretary of the Board of Foreign Missions brought no direct mention of his new office, but the Annual Conference mission report commented that "never before in the work of Foreign Missions were intelligence, zeal, wisdom in method, economy in administration, and emphasis of the most important principles, more marked than at present." [8] In 1914 his Conference colleagues wished him official Godspeed as he was "soon to make a visit to foreign mission fields." Referring to the presidency of the Federal Council of Churches, W. D. Beach said in 1917: "We hereby congratulate F. Mason North upon his election, and express our sense of the honor which has come to Methodism and this Conference through his election." [9]

[7] *Journal*, New York East Annual Conference, 1936, p. 798.
[8] *Minutes*, New York East Annual Conference, 1913.
[9] *Minutes*, New York East Annual Conference, 1917, p. 33.

More personally—and therefore more significantly—one of his very young colleagues recalls how North entrusted the editing of a report on world peace to two junior members of the Conference, and how Charles Noble, dean at Syracuse University "remarked about the time and trust given a couple of youngsters by such a VIP as FMN." But Loyd Worley, throughout his lifetime an active leader of the Methodist Federation for Social Service, adds this revealing comment:

In Social Service circles I suppose I was one of the "Young Turks" who always wished to go faster and further in pronouncements. Many times since have I wished that the counsel of FMN had prevailed— urging us to be ahead of the crowd, but not so far ahead as to lose contact. He was regular in attending committee meetings—always well informed—always urging that our pronouncements carry a Christian motivation. Needless to say he always had the respect of the most radical among us.[10]

In 1928, when "The City Hymn" was twenty-five years old, a Memorial to General Conference requested a supplementary collection of hymns on social service, brotherhood, and international goodwill to be inserted in *The Methodist Hymnal*, which, "aside from Dr. North's unsurpassed 'Where Cross the Crowded Ways of Life,' is sadly lacking in the hymns and tunes through which to give expression to these contemporary notes of Christian emphasis." In 1930 the Conference sang his relatively new hymn, "The Waking World." In 1933 Bishop Francis J. McConnell, who had been associated with him since the early days of the Methodist Federation, called attention to North's sixty years in the ministry, which were hailed by a standing greeting. And in 1935, as if with some premonition that this would be his last session, the Conference voted that the Social Service Report for 1936 should include "recognition of the work of F. M. North in the field of Social Service," [11] and Bishop Titus Lowe called on North to give the final benediction.

A significant tribute to his sagacity and fairness lay in his frequent appointment to judicial courts and committees of in-

[10] Letter to the author, July 24, 1965.
[11] *Journal*, New York East Annual Conference, 1935, p. 422.

quiry. As early as 1897 he was assigned to a "morals case" in the Conference but asked to be excused. In 1901 he served on a committee to phrase the reasons why the New York East Conference should reject political charges against George Reed, president of Dickinson College. In 1910 he presided over a committee to examine the transfer of a colleague to another denomination—coming to the conclusion that the procedure had been inconsiderate and improper but that no offense to the Conference or the Methodist Church had been intended. In 1926 he visited a Connecticut church to help ascertain whether the congregation had misused funds in supporting a community or interdenominational parish; again the decision was: technically— yes; deliberately—no.

The most famous judicial action in the New York East Annual Conference was the "heresy trial" of Borden Parker Bowne, professor of philosophy at Boston University. In 1904 G. A. Cooke of the New England Conference filed charges against Bowne which were originally "recognized and entertained without reading." J. M. Buckley, editor of the *Christian Advocate,* and the most outstanding member of the New York East Conference, was appointed to conduct the defense; F. M. North was named as chairman of a "Select Number" (fifteen others) to try the case. Two days later he reported "that the Select Number, by unanimous vote taken by ballot, find and decide that of the five specifications none are sustained, and that the charges are not sustained." [12]

An hour later a new set of charges was filed by Cooke. Although Buckley moved that Cooke had forfeited any right to a hearing by releasing his accusations to the press, the bishop appointed another committee in order to safeguard "the spiritual and temporal business of our Church." These three new men, ordered to report speedily, did just that, in a few minutes reaching the "unanimous opinion that there is nothing in the charges presented demanding the consideration of the Conference, and, therefore, respectfully move that the said charges be not entertained." Four years later Cooke, by then in the Troy Conference, brought

[12]*Minutes,* New York East Annual Conference, 1904, p. 25.

presumably punitive charges against Buckley ("Nothing derogatory to the moral or ministerial character of J. M. Buckley was
presented during the investigation.") and renewed his accusations against Bowne for "Defamation of Character . . . Intimida-
tion . . . Hypocrisy." The Conference refused, by unanimous
rising vote, to entertain the charges. Whatever perverted motivation lay behind these attacks—and they were so embarrassing
to all concerned that no official records of the hearings can be
found—the Conference protected its integrity by conducting a
trial under the judicious direction of Frank Mason North.

For the chairman of this "Select Number" had carefully studied
similar cases—and the issues and attitudes involved. Writing
"Concerning Methodism" in *The Evangelist,* a Presbyterian magazine, North had discussed the "heresy trial" of H. G. Mitchell,
professor of Old Testament at Boston Theological Seminary,
four years earlier. "The advantage of associating common sense
with courage in the defense of orthodoxy was never more conspic-
uously shown," he had declared. "Were the relative values of
wisdom and valor more accurately judged, quixotic attacks upon
theological wind mills would surely be less frequent." He then
proceeded to list considerations which should be given weight.
First, the personal character of the supposed heretic; in this case
his "personal faith is undimmed. . . . He shows no confusion
where conscience is involved. . . . He certainly has the Spirit of
Christ." Second, the peculiar method of attack used; "whoever
planned the manoevres . . . the firing line was occupied by a
platoon of boys, who seemed unused to arms and scant of
ammunition." Third, "a far larger question was involved than
the teaching of one theological professor," presumably the climate
and reaction of the church as a whole, especially the Board of
Bishops who heard the case.

You say quite truly, "The Bishops are, without exception, conservative men." But that rather over-worked word, "conservative," should
not in this case be misconstrued. For among the Bishops of the Methodist Church are some whose conservatism is that of breadth not that
of narrowness of view. . . . Many of these Bishops are broad-minded
men, not only skilled in affairs but sympathetic with all that is most

178

vital in human life and thought. . . . They rejoice in the growth of intellectual freedom in the ministry, and while swift to condemn departures from the essentials of the faith are slow to conclude that thinking is harmful or that honest research is not one of the prerogatives of a manly ministry.[13]

Somewhat ironically, the Board of Bishops refused, five years later, to endorse Professor Mitchell. But North's philosophy was already clearly on record when he was chosen to supervise the investigation of another distinguished teacher, Borden P. Bowne. And his comments on the quixotic attacks of inexperienced boys might readily have applied to G. A. Cooke.

Quite obviously Frank Mason North had a sense of political strategy and an awareness of public opinion. No false pietism prevented him from using the instruments of secular society. Very often it was he, rising to his full dignity on the Conference floor and using his resonant voice, who recommended the wider circulation of resolutions and Conference actions. For example, in 1923 he moved that a special report on International Relations be forwarded to the Federal Council of Churches (as well as the President, the Secretary of State, and the senators of Connecticut and New York). And at the age of eighty-two, when most men have lost their progressive enthusiasm, Frank Mason North joined with five colleagues to introduce a resolution of praise for Franklin D. Roosevelt. Two and a half months after the inauguration the Conference voted its "hearty congratulations for his faith, courage, and spirit, since he has been elected to the Presidency, in lifting the morale of this country and of the world by the measures which he has initiated, and the addresses which he has delivered to the people of the United States and to the rulers of the world." Acknowledging that there were differing opinions as to the necessity of certain actions (presumably the repeal of prohibition, for one), the New York East churchmen promised to "pray for his continued vision and his good health." [14]

Few Methodist ministers have ever been so faithful in their

---

[13] North, "Concerning Methodism," *The Evangelist*, July, 1900, pp. 5-6.
[14] *Journal*, New York East Annual Conference, 1933, p. 25.

connectional responsibilities over so long a period of time as Frank Mason North. According to the records, he missed only two sessions of the New York East Conference in forty-eight years, 1913 and 1915. At the latter time he was in Europe completing an eight-months' circuit of the globe. On at least three occasions he arrived at Annual Conference late, "detained by official engagements" (two of these during World War I and his Federal Council presidency) rather than by illness. Although personal comparisons are always invidious, it is not surprising that at his death the president and secretary of the Conference Board of Trustees, both occupying positions which North himself had held for many years, should record "our affection and admiration for one who was for so long our most distinguished member." [15]

North's first attendance at a Methodist General Conference apparently took place in 1888, as a correspondent for *Christian Union*.[16] Among the issues on which he commented was the exclusion of women from General Conference, including Frances E. Willard, whom John Greenleaf Whittier had recently called the "noblest woman of her time." "The policy [of the 1888 General Conference as a whole]," North observed, "has been conservatively progressive." That phrase may well have been an apt description of himself.

In 1900 and 1904 the New York East Annual Conference elected Frank Mason North as a reserve delegate to General Conference, but there is no evidence that he attended. In 1908 he was the sixth clerical delegate (out of seven from his Conference) at the historic session in Baltimore when the Social Creed was first adopted. It was North, in fact, who presented the Memorial "from Herbert Welch and twenty-nine others recommending that the attention of pastors be called to certain movements for social progress." [17] The document was referred to the Committee on the State of the Church, of which he was not a member. He did serve, however, as chairman of the Committee

[15] *Frank Mason North*, p. 59.
[16] *Christian Union*, April-June, 1888, *passim*.
[17] *Journal*, General Conference of the Methodist Episcopal Church, 1908, p. 310.

on Home Missions and Church Extension, and on the Committee on Temporal Economy (polity and structure). In presenting the report of the National City Evangelization Union, he was introduced to the Conference as "the efficient and gifted secretary of the Church Extension Society of New York."

Despite this prominence as a "freshman" representative in 1908, North was not reelected to General Conference in 1912—although he was chosen as the first reserve delegate. Reminiscing about their early Conference associations, Bishop Herbert Welch explained that "there were at that time in these Annual Conferences two antagonistic groups, and North was definitely identified with one of these groups." This may have meant only that North belonged among the "independents," unwilling to "play politics" for his own advancement, or to compromise his convictions for the sake of popularity. "The division, however, was real, and doubtless affected such matters." [18]

Certainly North's disgust at ecclesiastical ambition had been bluntly affirmed years earlier. Commenting on the General Conference of 1888, where five bishops had been elected out of fifty candidates, he added: "A severe rebuke has been administered to the tendency to office-seeking by intrigue." [19] Just before that session he had reported:

that a number of men well known in the Church are carefully learning by heart I Tim. 3:1 (RV) . . . and that the Church is urging the next clause . . . "without reproach". For it has passed into current statement that there is a strong disrelish for any candidate who "has claims" or who shows any industry in advancing them. This may be easily believed when once it is understood how absolutely selfishness must disqualify any man from exercising the delicate function of so high an office.[20]

Arthur B. Moss, a colleague in the New York East Conference and in the Board of Foreign Missions, writes: "I could not think of Dr. North as having been personally ambitious for, or even interested in, the episcopacy. The strict limitations of action

[18] Letter to the author, May 4, 1959.
[19] *Christian Union*, May 31, 1888.
[20] *Christian Union*, April 26, 1888.

inherent therein were fully known to him, and he would have been galled by them." [21]

In spite of North's modesty—and his aversion to political maneuvering—there were many in the church who considered him well fitted for highest office. As early as 1903 a letter in the *Central Christian Advocate* remarked that "the work of Dr. North in connection with the society has impressed not a few that he possesses good episcopal qualifications." [22] At the 1908 General Conference "he had votes for Bishop, but withdrew his name after the second ballot," Welch recalls.[23] At the General Conference of 1912, where he was not a delegate, North ran strong for fifteen ballots, although he never polled more than 182 votes toward over 500 needed. Two years later, following his visit to the Orient, a missionary wrote: "One of the Korean missionaries is for nominating Dr. North as our next Bishop, and I second the nomination. He unites practical ability with spiritual power and is a thorough Christian gentleman." [24] Even in 1916, at the age of sixty-five, North received 56 votes on the opening ballot at General Conference—and must have rejoiced at the subsequent election of his long-time friend, Herbert Welch, and the renewed episcopal appointment of his co-secretary in the Board of Foreign Missions, William F. Oldham.

North went to Springfield, Massachusetts, in 1924 as the second clerical delegate from the New York East Annual Conference. At seventy-three years of age, he withdrew his name from the balloting for the Board of Foreign Missions (as did four others, leaving still a field of ten candidates), although the *California Christian Advocate* (June 19, 1924) declared that North would have been reelected. The General Conference added a directive, however, that the Board of Foreign Missions be "authorized to utilize the accumulated knowledge and experience of Doctor North and to make it available for the work of the Board by appointing him to a consulting position with such title and such compensation as may best serve the interests of our Foreign

[21] Letter to the author, January 30, 1966.
[22] December 23, 1903, p. 24.
[23] Letter to the author, August 16, 1961.
[24] F. Herron Smith, letter to supporting church, n.d. (Board of Missions files).

Mission work." It also ordered the preparation and publication of "a fitting action concerning the distinguished service rendered by the Rev. Frank Mason North in these extraordinary years of world conflict and missionary opportunity and achievement." [25]

At this session North signed his name (along with such others as Brenton Badley, Ralph W. Sockman, and G. Bromley Oxnam) to a resolution presented by E. Stanley Jones and adopted by the Conference. It read in part:

Whereas, The problems that grow out of race are the most acute and potentially the most dangerous of existing world problems; and,

Whereas, Jesus Christ our Master stands for the oneness of our humanity and the equal worth of every human soul, regardless of race, birth, or color; . . . and,

Whereas, the most outstanding obstacles to the coming of the kingdom of God among the nations of the earth are these national and racial arrogancies; . . .

We repudiate as unchristian and untrue the idea that certain races are born to inherent and fixed superiority and rulership, while others are born to inherent and fixed inferiority and subordination. We stand for the life of open opportunity for all.[26]

Another significant report appeared over the signatures of Frank Mason North and Titus Lowe, along with that of Theodore S. Henderson, chairman of the Committee on Policy and Work in Europe. Urging "war against war," it suggested that "this is the time for holding steady. Now we must help. To-morrow or the day after we can construct." Then, avowing the desire of the church to avoid political involvements, it asserted in conclusion:

If in Italy or in any other land we should be forced to accept the theory that a democracy and a dictatorship are identical we might need to surrender our task to others. If to maintain our work in Russia it should become necessary not only to obey the Soviet government but, against conscience, to adopt or advocate its principles, our energy and our resources would need to be invested elsewhere. . . .

[25] *Journal,* General Conference of the Methodist Episcopal Church, 1924, p. 398.
[26] *Ibid.,* p. 295.

We avoid, always, entangling alliances with government and if we must on principle rebel, we also must withdraw.[27]

In an obvious gesture of affection and appreciation, the New York East Annual Conference elected North as its sixth clerical delegate again in 1928, though by this time he had retired from all official positions and had passed his seventy-seventh birthday.

"In a great centralized organization like the Methodist Episcopal Church it is easier to name the leaders of aggressive action than those of progressive thought." These words open an article on "Progressive Religious Leaders: The Methodist Episcopal Church" in 1890.[28] The writer, presumably North, refers to the previous General Conference as having spent a month on organization and not one hour on doctrine. In naming several college presidents and professors, he adds: "Others, who might be leaders, become, by the demands of their office, executives only, while it goes without saying that, though the editors of the official paper have a wide hearing, their individual freedom is so modified by the necessity of conservatism that personal leadership is seldom possible."

Some readers may conclude that Frank Mason North fell into the trap which he described so vividly in his younger days. Certainly he produced no systematic statement of faith to place alongside Richard Ely's *Social Aspects of Christianity* or Rauschenbusch's *Christianity and the Social Crisis*. Perhaps each man makes his choice—or is chosen—for the executive role or the intellectual one. It is significant, of course, that North, despite all his administrative positions, is known—if at all today—for a deeply moving bit of poetry.

At the same time Frank Mason North can be put in no restrictive categories. With all his commitment to the functional institution, he would defend this aspect of his life—and the life of the church—only if it contributed to a creative encounter with his Lord.

[27] *Ibid.,* p. 1709.
[28] *Christian Union,* January 30, 1890, p. 74.

When we cease to treat Methodism as a mechanism and understand that it is a life, the question of "making it succeed" will be outdated. Whatever adjustments may be important in the external appliances of Methodism in New York City, the real increase of its scope and sway will depend upon its receiving the more abundant life which comes neither from men nor from measures, but from Christ the life giver. [29]

This was his faith and hope for the church to which he so vigorously devoted his life. In his locus of purpose, in his breadth of service, Frank Mason North was a statesman, not a bureaucrat. He was an organization man who was always on the move. For him, as he put it at the end of his career, "Methodism is a stream, not an inland sea." [30]

[29] "New York Letter by Knickerbocker," *Central Christian Advocate*, November 15, 1893.

[30] "Why I Am a Methodist," p. 76.

Francis Asbury

The Statue in Drew Forest

From out the stern, heroic past
  Rides forth into our softer day
    A stalwart, mystic soul;
So long as sun and shadow last
  That fell upon his rugged way
    His fame will onward roll.

Across the nation's restless years
  He marked the trails which now we tread,
    Secure and unafraid;
The challenges which stir men's fears,
  The sinking heart, the pallid dread
    Still left him undismayed.

They watched him with a strange surprise—
  The sombre garb, the quiet word,
    And in his hand the Book;
They saw within his patient eyes
  The kindling glory of his Lord,
    The far, immortal look.

Our forest welcomes now his form,
  Erect, forthlooking, hero, seer,
    A chevalier of God;

In summer's heat, in winter's storm
  He rides, a mighty leader here,
    This prophet of the road.

Each soul is still a pioneer,
  Still mind must venture, still the art
    Of serving have its test;
The frontiers of the faith are here;
  Give us, O God, the singing heart
    In life's undaunted quest.

We crave the gifts of simpler days,
  The culture of the wilderness,
    The wisdom of the wood,
The courage of the lonely ways,
  The brooding thought, love's eagerness,
    The grace of hardihood.

O Master of his life and ours,
  Thou art the Light, Thou art the Force!
    The conquest is with Thee;
Reveal to us the mystic powers,
  The stalwart strength, the secret source
    Of winning ministry.

The softer day, the harder task!
  A wider world! Come from above,
    Set faith and hope aflame!
Command us forth, O Christ, we ask,
  With burning heart, with deathless love,
    Victorious in Thy name.

Madison, New Jersey
1926

10

"Nations in Thy Heart"

For us his narrow stretch of shore
Has widened to a hundred lands;
The isles are waiting evermore,
Strange peoples plead with eager hands.

"The first followers of our Lord were known by two
names. They were disciples—learners; they were apostles—messengers. Each man came under two distinct obligations, the duty
to hear and the duty to go. No one was truly Christian who
neglected either of these two functions." [1] This conviction of
Frank Mason North permeated his entire ministry. From his
early pastorates, where he reserved one Sunday each March—at
least—"to scrutinize the terms of our Great Commission," through
his distinguished service on the sidewalks of New York and as
correspondent for the *Christian Advocate, Christian Union,*
and other publications, North had demonstrated his interest in the
still wider mission of the church. Because of his outstanding
service in the New York City Church Extension and Missionary
Society, North received the second highest vote at the General
Conference of 1908 for the position of corresponding secretary
in the Board of *Home* Missions and Church Extension. And he
had served on the Board of Managers of the Missionary Society
from 1897 to 1904, on the Board of Foreign Missions from 1904
to 1912.

Nevertheless it surprised many when this "city missionary"
was chosen in May of 1912 for leadership in the overseas work of

[1] "A New Apostolic Age" (undated manuscript among North's papers).

189

the church. The incumbent corresponding secretary, S. Earl
Taylor, and the world-famous bishop from Southeast Asia,
William F. Oldham, were elected to the triumvirate on the first
ballot with over 400 votes each. But Frank Mason North, who
had placed fourth with 231 votes, vaulted to election on the
second ballot with 2 more than the 355 votes needed.[2] Said
Bishop Frederick B. Newell at North's memorial service:

> No city could bound the achievements of such a man as this. It was
> inevitable that the Church would recognize him as a citizen of the
> world and, in respect for his world citizenship, he was elected as
> Corresponding Secretary to the Board of Foreign Missions in 1912.
> . . . So the mind which felt the need of our great city enlarged until it
> took into its consciousness the need of the world. The love which he
> bore to Negroes, Italians, Scandinavians, other Europeans, and Ori-
> entals in New York City, turned itself in happy service toward these
> same peoples in Europe, Africa, and in Asia. For half a generation he
> lifted high the Cross of Christ to the peoples of the world, and saw
> millions of people in many mission fields, come seeking the Christian
> Church. . . . For most men that time of life is but a few short years
> before retirement, but for him it was the beginning of his greatest
> work.[3]

Between 1904 and 1906 the Missionary Society had been reorganized as the Board of Foreign Missions of the Methodist
Episcopal Church. One of North's most significant contributions
proved to be the introduction of area secretaries,[4] young men
from the field who may have been assigned initially to promotion,
to the Centenary Program, or to the Interchurch World Movement, but who moved—before North's retirement—into administration of certain geographical regions. Among these were future
bishops (Edwin F. Lee of Malaysia, Ralph Ward of China) and
career executives (such as Ralph Diffendorfer, Arthur B. Moss,
Thomas Donohugh, and Harry Farmer).

In the revised constitution for the Board, adopted at the 1912
General Conference, the duties of the secretaries were defined

[2] *Daily Christian Advocate*, May 25, 1912, p. 659 and May 27, 1912, p. 672.
[3] *Frank Mason North*, pp. 56-57.
[4] Arthur B. Moss, personal interview, New York, October 12, 1958.

as follows: conducting correspondence, furnishing the church with missionary intelligence, supervising the foreign missionary work of the church, and promoting the general interests of the cause by correspondence and travel. And the by-laws went on to add: "They shall advocate the cause of foreign missions at such Annual Conferences and in such churches and conventions as their judgment may dictate and the Board approve. They shall keep a vigilant eye upon all the affairs of the Board and especially upon all its missions." [5]

How faithfully Frank Mason North fulfilled this task the present chapter can barely suggest. In the initial division of labor Taylor was assigned administrative duties for the "home base"; Oldham for India, Malaysia, the Philippines, South America, and Mexico; North for Africa, China, Japan, Korea, and Europe. Through the tumultuous years ahead, however, changing circumstances and personnel, coupled with inherent abilities and interests, laid increasing responsibilities on North. In 1916 Bishop Oldham resumed episcopal functions, this time for Latin America, and in 1919 Taylor withdrew temporarily to devote his full energies to the Interchurch World Movement. As a junior colleague, Arthur B. Moss commented: "I have always marvelled at how he [North] completed so much work so well. . . . He was just about a master in every field . . . a great administrator and a great inspirational man." Without "a marked degree of supremacy in any one field," he handled all fields and all types of work well. [6] In a memorial tribute the editor of the *Christian Advocate* described how North undertook his new job:

He read books, records, correspondence; he sought the acquaintance of veteran missionaries; he established closer relations with the other mission boards of America, studying their methods and promoting union and co-operation at home and abroad; he modernized the methods of selecting and testing candidates; he devoted himself with success to building up endowments for retired workers. No captain of industry ever gave himself with more complete devotion to the direction of a vast business concern than this Christian minister gave

[5] *Annual Report*, Board of Foreign Missions, Methodist Episcopal Church, 1912.
[6] Personal interview, New York, October 12, 1958.

to the King's business of carrying the Gospel, its teaching and its loving ministry, to those who needed it most.[7]

One of the administrative procedures which concerned him most was the difficulty of contact and clearance between the Board and the bishops and other workers on the field. Cables were slow, air travel nonexistent. But the issue went beyond that of communication to that of authority. More than once a missionary had been sent out for a specific job, only to find it filled by the time he arrived. Unwise actions "out yonder" often gave North genuine pain, and as early as 1913 he wrote to his colleague, Bishop Oldham: "Such individual initiative as that of the Bishops . . . and perhaps others in the past should be replaced by a well reasoned basis for action which the General Committee, the Board and back of them the church should adopt and work upon." [8] Thus Moss declared forty-five years later: "His effort to define areas of division between bishops and Conferences on the field and the Board here was one of his constant problems." [9] Without criticizing any individuals, Bishop Herbert Welch cited this same tension from the opposite side. Bishops, he said, should be representatives of the Board, but were more often treated as if their sole function was to make appointments, some of which were already set in New York. We "felt always as if we were on the outside looking in," he complained.[10] Thus sincere differences in policies and points of view could arise even between old and trusted friends.

North was equally committed to efficiency with democracy, responsibility with cooperation, at headquarters. By his second year in office he was handing out assignments to cover one secretary's absence, or calling for firm and courageous decisions in time of crisis. Yet this was no dictatorship. North insisted that proposals should be "sold to the staff as a whole" before going to the Board for action, but *if* the plan was rejected by the staff it was not to be mentioned in the Board. In other words, there

[7] James R. Joy, "Dr. Frank Mason North—His Missionary Passion," in *Frank Mason North*, pp. 33-34.

[8] Letter to W. F. Oldham, July 23, 1913 (Board of Missions files).

[9] Personal interview, October 12, 1958.

[10] Personal interview, January 21, 1958.

was to be no "minority opposition," no going behind the staff to individual members of the Board for support of defeated measures. "He'd look at you and you'd squirm like a fool. . . . It was that teamwork in the entire proposition," Moss recollects.

Neither clearly established policies nor the respect and loyalty which North invariably displayed toward his associates prevented sharp divergencies of opinion. But these were always tempered with courtesy and charity. North's judgments clashed often with those of S. Earl Taylor, for example. North could recognize and admire the broad sweep of Taylor's mind and the penchant for vast and visionary planning which finally took him from the Board of Foreign Missions to the Interchurch World Movement, yet doubt with equal sincerity whether Taylor could ever handle the administrative details of the missionary program. Similarly, when the treasurer, George Fowles, introduced before the General Conference of 1924 a proposal for drastic reorganization of the Board of Foreign Missions, North felt disappointed and hurt because he fully acknowledged Fowles' preeminence in finance but regarded him as unqualified to criticize field administration. Yet in all such issues—

Whatever his own personal feelings might be with regard to a particular liking for one field over another, or for an individual, he never let those interfere with his own judgment as to the value of the matter under consideration. . . . He would back up a matter that was not his own particular interest just as fully as one he was vitally interested in.[11]

The years 1912-24 were critical ones for the Board on financial as well as political fronts. When North first began journalistic coverage of the General Missionary Committee, he reported a total income in 1892 of $1,257,372.92, in addition to World Service and Freedmen's Aid Society, and Bishop Taylor's Self-Supporting Missions in South America—and looked toward an annual goal of $2,000,000, still less than $1 per member.[12] Twenty years later, when North assumed responsibility, the total

[11] Arthur B. Moss, personal interview, October 12, 1958.
[12] "What the Methodists Are Doing?" *Christian Union*, November 26, 1892.

193

income from conference sources (not counting annuities) was only $1,046,113.51, with disbursements $1,128,598.31.[13] The picture was not quite as dismal as these figures suggest. Reviewing the first year of the Board under its new administration, the associate editor of *Zion's Herald* denied charges of "an avalanche of debt. . . . Nothing of the kind exists." He explained that the Board did borrow each year between $350,000 and $600,000 for operating expenses, but most of this was repaid as gifts from the churches came in.[14]

Nevertheless, these were obviously lean years. Arthur Moss commented, in his personal reminiscences of North, that "he always had a desire to judge a problem in view of its human factors and not just in terms of buildings and investments." For example, when North was serving on the Board but not as its executive, he raised strong objections to Dr. Adna B. Leonard's suggestion that missionary salaries should be reduced *pro rata* in order to make up the operating deficit. First, North insisted, this "places the demand for heroism at the wrong point"; the Church needs greater self-denial from those who have stayed at home, not those who have gone abroad; it should seek to awaken sleeping congregations here rather than to exact greater sacrifices from missionaries. Second, such a retrenchment abroad would tend to emphasize distinctions which have been gradually dying.

The sooner we escape from the artificial sentiment which reckons other lands, as it formerly regarded remote parts of our own, as missionary territory to which embassies are to be sent, and recognize them as part of the commonwealth of the world, for which we bear a given responsibility no different in kind from that which rests upon us for our own nation, the more rapid will be the mobilization of the forces which are to conquer the world for Christ.[15]

This represents but one of the guiding principles which Frank Mason North brought to the Board of Foreign Missions, prin-

[13] *Annual Report,* Board of Missions, Methodist Episcopal Church, 1912.
[14] E. C. E. Dorion, "The Board of Foreign Missions," *Zion's Herald,* November 19, 1913, p. 1477.
[15] "Comments on Dr. Leonard's Proposed New Departure" (undated memorandum).

ciples which sound almost half a century ahead of their times. In another undated manuscript he spoke of "how swiftly and inevitably discipleship moves the true followers of Christ to become the man *sent*—the apostle. . . . The characteristic figure of our generation is not the anchorite, nor the ecclesiastic, nor the controversialist, but the missionary—the man with a mission." [16] The opening sentence of his editorial in *The Christian City* (as reorganized in 1897) proclaimed North's missionary commitment as follows: "The belief in the Divinity of our Lord is no more distinctly an essential element in the fundamental conception of the Christian church than is the spirit of ministration." He went on to explain this "new concept" in graphic terms:

Men who have begun with no conscious call save to declare the holiness of the Lord have found themselves intensely occupied ere long with building up a highway, bridging streams, leveling mountains, draining morasses, gathering out the stone. John Wesley, starting as an evangelist, soon became a promoter of education and a philanthropist. . . . General Booth . . . inaugurated an army of invasion and very quickly found it necessary to establish also an army of occupation. . . . The picture of the man with the Bible standing on a sandy shore beneath a solitary palm tree, preaching to a little group of unclothed savages, has given place to photographs of groups of children from orphanages and schools, and of medical missionaries in their dispensaries, and of colleges, hospitals, and havens of refuge.[17]

With this reinterpretation of the missionary task had come—a decade before North's vocational involvement—a plea for the centrality of mission in the life of the church. Speaking for nine professors from eight seminaries of five denominations, he wrote:

We are of the opinion that some earnest efforts should be made to secure more time on the seminary curricula for instruction in the whole subject of missions; that its Biblical, historical, philosophical, practical, and personal aspects should be carefully and extensively set before seminary students, to the end that their affections may be roused and that their minds may be educated to broad and thorough

[16] "A New Apostolic Age."
[17] "The New Era of Church Work in the City of New York," January, 1897, pp. 1-2.

knowledge of the missionary spirit of Christianity and of the development of missions in the past and the present claim of missions upon
the ministry and upon all the churches of our Lord.[18]

Thus Frank Mason North brought to the worldwide enterprise a
wisdom, a maturity, a statesmanship, which few others without
direct previous participation could have commanded. At the end
of his first full year in office an editor in attendance at the Board
meeting reported: "One of the best reviews of the work that the
General Committee has listened to in years was made by Secretary
North. His discrimination, his appreciation of fine racial and
religious distinctions, and his grasp of the details of the work,
brought illumination and inspiration." [19]

Early in 1914 North began making plans for a tour of his
Asian territory. Little did he dream that the outbreak of war in
Europe—and on the rim of Asia as well—would force delays and
disruptions in the schedule, though no serious dangers or dele-
tions. He was accompanied by his son, Eric, his long-time friend,
William I. Haven (on official business as general secretary of the
American Bible Society), Mrs. Haven, and their daughter, Gladys,
who later became Mrs. Eric North. In announcing the trip North
explained:

In several of the fields problems of major importance are to be studied.
. . . Projects for union in educational and medical work have created
new programs for the church. Race conflicts and material ambitions
are challenging the missionary forces to larger enterprise. The work
of the Methodist Board of Foreign Missions which is found at practically all of the world's strategic centers each year grows in importance and significance. It is believed by the Board that consultations on the field between a representative of the administration and
the missionary leaders and workers will increase efficiency and resources.[20]

With the news of war in Europe the party's Pacific sailing was
delayed ten days. North took the opportunity, the day before their

[18] Editorial Notes, *The Christian City,* July, 1897, p. 205.
[19] E. C. E. Dorion, *Zion's Herald,* November 19, 1913, p. 1477.
[20] Handwritten memorandum, n.d. (Board of Missions files).

departure from San Francisco, to send to S. Earl Taylor a letter
for his wife—"only in case I sh'd not come back. Further it must
be destroyed if for any reason she in person cannot receive it. I
beg you will not think me unduly serious. . . . In spite of horrid
and inexcusable war we count God still in His world—and the
Gospel still in action." [21] In a separate letter to his two associates
he recommended that an official representative of the Board
should be stationed on the West Coast for the cultivation of
money and missionaries. And he did not fail to add a typical
word of appreciation: "I am most grateful for your constant
consideration during these past 2 years of arduous work and I
pray that God may keep you both safe and ever guide and guard
you. With assurances of deep affection, Your colleague, Frank
Mason North." [22]

The travelers arrived in Japan on September 7, and after a
quick visit to Korea North wrote from the Imperial Hotel in
Tokyo to the General Committee of the Board:

The work everywhere is undermanned. The results of the investments
of the past are everywhere. The increase in membership in the North
China Conference last year was twenty per cent. The impulse toward
evangelistic work in Japan and Korea grows stronger. Larger provision must be made for both the evangelistic and the educational
work. . . . The missionaries understand the possible meaning of this
horrible European war. The whole East is inquiring—"Why does not
the Gospel you preach keep your Christian nations from fighting?" [23]

To his colleagues in the office he directed an even more plaintive
appeal. "My heart is sore at the meagre provisions," he wrote.
"How I am to endure all around the world I do not know." Then,
after listing a number of items which he believed deserving of
extra financial appropriations, he begged: "Do the best you can
for these fields. They are white!" [24] A few weeks later he wrote
to Thomas Donohugh, then in the personnel office: "The *best*

[21] August 23, 1914 (Board of Missions files).
[22] Letter to Taylor and Oldham, August 23, 1914 (Board of Missions files).
[23] September 30, 1914 (Board of Missions files).
[24] Letter to S. Earl Taylor from Tokyo, Japan, September 30, 1914 (Board of
Missions files).

men only for Japan! There must be some with fervent hearts and evangelistic purpose. Some of the finest I have met here." [25]

Japan represented one of the significant challenges for the church because here in 1907, for the first time anywhere in the world, three major branches of Methodism had united to form the Japan Methodist Church. Then—as now!—many church people found in such organic union an excuse to reduce their support. In his very first annual report to the Board North had felt impelled to say: "A marked and growing sentiment is the conviction that the organization of the Methodist Church of Japan, so far from relieving the home churches of responsibilities really offers larger opportunities for service, and that the withdrawal of resources and influence by the home boards would be a distinct break in the hitherto successful policy." [26] At the same time, however, he had taken the occasion to endorse the principle of comity, or territorial division of certain fields among various denominations. "Methodist forces . . . believe that the assignment of different sections of the country to the various existing missions, with accompanying responsibility for the evangelization of the respective areas, affords a definite advantage in the orderly and successful evangelization of the empire." [27] With such farsighted ecumenical statesmanship, it is little wonder that after North's visit in the fall of 1914 Bishop Harris, the general superintendent for Japan and Korea, wrote as follows:

The patience and thoroughness with which every mission problem was heard, together with the very evident desire to acquaint himself with the Mission's viewpoint, made for Dr. North a place in the sympathies and created pleasant memories in the minds of all our number which will not soon be forgotten.

In China, although church union was far away, many proposals were afoot for the merger of particular schools and colleges. In his first annual report quoted above North had affirmed: "To these plans for union educational work the Methodist Church

[25] From Tokyo, Japan, Cctober 23, 1914 (Board of Missions files).
[26] *Annual Report,* Board of Foreign Missions, Methodist Episcopal Church, 1912, pp. 52-53.
[27] *Ibid.*

is definitely and without reluctance committed, and as rapidly as
resources may be secured will take its share in the larger enterprise."[28] Perry O. Hanson, one of the great Methodist missionaries, whose career in China extended even into the
Communist period of the 1950's, writes:

I remember Dr. Frank Mason North very well as he was not only my
Secretary but he visited us in China. . . . It happened that when he
got to Taian my School Boys could sing his Hymn 562 and that
pleased him greatly. Strange how it happened that the boys were prepared to sing that song just at that time! ! ! . . . Dr. North was very
patient with me as I pressed the building of a school in Taian.[29]

Apparently Mr. Hanson "pressed" convincingly, for North's next
letter to the home office remarked on how vital schools were in
that great land and added of Taian in particular: "This is a
base which should be strengthened."[30] As the group moved
southward, North reviewed his weeks in Japan, Korea, and North
China, and challenged the Board to provide "no less attention
to the educational projects, and better system there, but a larger
consideration and a larger investment in the aggressive evangelistic work."

At the end of November Dr. E. C. Perkins, a colorful and
dedicated missionary physician, ordered Frank Mason North
down the Yangtze River from Kiukiang to Shanghai with what
the corresponding secretary dismissed as a "heavy cold." He did
admit, however, that "these modern physicians have impressions
which one cannot with propriety gainsay," and the fact that he
spent some weeks in the hospital and then in convalescence,
chafing at the delay, indicates that it was severely threatening
pneumonia. Even two months later, nearing Ceylon, he remarked
again: "I must have given the doctors and my friends quite a
start in Shanghai—but as a matter of fact I believe I am in perfect
condition—Except that Lat. 6 is different from Lat. 41.50." How-

[28] *Ibid.*, p. 52.
[29] Letter to the author, June 19, 1961 (an error in number, for North's Hymns
#423 and #549 were included in the 1908 *Hymnal*; #562 in the 1935 *Hymnal*
"The world's astir!" was not written until 1917).
[30] Letter to S. Earl Taylor, en route to Nanking, China, November 20, 1914
(Board of Missions files).

ever, he added at that time: "I have reached the conclusion that this kind of travel . . . puts the anatomy and the rest of the system to one of the severest of tests. Travel one can provide for— but travel plus work—and adjustments to prepared programs—is something not set down in the guide books." [31]

Since Southern and Southeast Asia belonged technically in Bishop Oldham's administrative field, North was careful to send full reports from his visit there—which Oldham had urged him to make. Of the Philippines he wrote:

My interest in this vast island work has been greatly quickened. . . . Instead of lamenting over their large church with its indebtedness, I urged putting the property to effective and varied use as an institutional—or socialized church—which, of course, means the right man to do it and some money to help it on.[32]

In Malaya, on the other hand, he found that "the present pressure comes on the educational program. The Bp. feels that some embarrassment has arisen because the plan was not indigenous— or at least had not been worked out on the field itself and that certain mental adjustments are difficult on that account."

Along with his statesmanlike vision and comprehension of vast movements and policies, Frank Mason North was always alert to small details. In Singapore, for example, he found that the first issue of the new Board publication, *World Outlook,* had arrived badly torn in the mails; in at least two subsequent letters he instructed the New York office that heavier wrapping would have to be used for overseas copies. He further recommended that the Board provide photographic equipment to missionaries who could take good pictures. "The man on the field," he realized, "if he have the ability and the commission, can get what the visitors can never find."

North also encountered another perennial problem, still present even in days of rapid communication; namely, the difficulties of accurate accounting by missionaries and nationals without

---

[31] Letter to S. Earl Taylor, "nearing Colombo," February 12, 1915 (Board of Missions files).

[32] Letter to W. F. Oldham, February 12, 1915 (Board of Missions files).

training in finance. Here again the secretary's genuine concern
for persons transcended his emphasis on efficiency.

In this [new accounting system] as in the other instance we should
have the consenting cooperation of the men on the field, many of
whom I find to be very effective accountants after their kind. Our chief
strength, so far as the field forces are concerned, lies in their conviction that we are efficient *and considerate*. We must not lose this asset.
Better slow changes than those which seem to impose new burdens or
unjustified methods upon the treasurers and committees.[33]

The leisure on shipboard in mid-February and again in March
gave North and his party not only physical recuperation, but a
chance to catch up with their own impressions and evaluations of
the manifold work they had seen. In retrospect he formulated
advice concerning the purchase of property in Foochow, repay-
ment of advance appropriations to the Philippines, a printing
press in Madras and a hostel in Delhi, the need for a clear policy
on home visits by the overseas bishops. "I like talking better
than writing," North commented with a note of frustration, ". . .
but how shall I ever gather up the observations into conclusions
and recommendations!" Exactly a month later he wrote from the
Red Sea to "My dear Colleagues" as follows:

With these quiet days from Bombay to Port Said comes not only a
review of my pilgrimage but a keen sense of my failures. . . . The
schedule has been so crowded at each station and the physical and
mental weariness has been so great that any well-reasoned discussion
appeared to be quite out of the question.[34]

Nevertheless he was looking forward eagerly to a meeting in Cairo
with the distinguished missionary, Samuel Zwemer, to assess the
Muslim situation and "our North Africa and Jerusalem interests."
As he neared the Mediterranean, North wrestled with the
decision as to whether to try to get to London. On one hand, he
was frankly tired and genuinely anxious about having left his
New York office responsibilities on other people for so long. Yet

[33] Letter to S. Earl Taylor, February 12, 1915 (Board of Missions files).
[34] March 12, 1915 (Board of Missions files).

conversations in Peking, Foochow, and Chengtu in regard to institutional mergers had convinced him that first-hand consultations with executives of the London Missionary Society and the Church Missionary Society in England would be highly desirable, though not absolutely necessary. As for the danger in the submarine zone around Britain, he wrote candidly: "I would not hesitate for myself—if a duty were involved—but in view of the judgment so strongly expressed by some before I came away, there might be objections to one incurring needless risk in whose journey the Board is making so large an investment of money and time." As he surveyed the long journey from the serene setting of the Red Sea, he offered this sober summary:

I am profoundly impressed with the strength of our foundations, the enterprise and wisdom of the men of the past, and the high level of character and efficiency of the men of the present. Ours is one of the greatest schemes of world enterprise now extant. My one fear is my own inability to make clear what it all means.[35]

Back at his desk, Frank Mason North picked up the multitudinous strands of administration. One of his problems was to continue far beyond his term of service, through several structural reorganizations, until 1964: namely, relationships with the Women's Foreign Missionary Society. Learning before his world tour that the women were planning a five-year program of cultivation leading up to their Silver Jubilee in 1919, which would coincide with the Centennial of American Methodist Missions, North wrote to Taylor in Switzerland: "I have given much thought to the question of a possible combination with them [the ladies], and the fact that they are laying out a program for the last 4 years of our century adds some emphasis to my own thought . . . that it might be a good idea for us to extend our plans so as to include a culminating period for our own centennial." [36] Eight years later he replied to a memo from his son, then working for the Board: "Note the desire and tendency toward closer identification of our women's groups in the con-

[35] Ibid.
[36] May 28, 1914 (Board of Missions files).

sideration of missy [sic] policy—but without modification of their present status of detachment from Board's organization." [37]

As the scope of Methodist mission activities expanded, Frank Mason North sought to organize and systematize the work of administration. One of the unresolved issues proved to be the William Taylor Self-Supporting Missions. Bishop Taylor, evangelist extraordinary to five continents, had enlivened the church with one of the most colorful careers in the nineteenth century. Elected from India to be bishop of Africa, he left his most permanent institutional legacy in South America. Here—and elsewhere—he had established schools and churches whose teachers and pastors (sometimes both simultaneously) were expected to earn their own support from the local community. As early as 1886, while still in the pastorate, North had commented, appreciatively but critically, on the extension of this policy to Africa:

William Taylor, whose missionary labors in every continent are among the most successful and inspiring in the annals of Christian work—is establishing upon what he calls the Pauline method, self-supporting missions. . . . He gathered together a band of missionaries, men, women, and children—44 in all—and less than a year ago set out with them, censured, laughed at, admired, and followed by the hopes and fears and prayers of the friends of himself and his cause, to enter the Dark Continent. . . .

Bishop Taylor's peculiar view concerning self-supporting missions not only gives to his present experiment the claim upon general attention to which heroism always has a right, but presents to the Church distinctly a new departure, whose outcome is of the intensest interest. If missionaries ought to be conveyed to the field by the gifts of the Church, and then left to the mercy or otherwise of the populations they seek to convert, a great change must come over both the spirit and the method of the Church's benevolence.[38]

Some thirty-six years later, now responsible for the policies and procedures of the Methodist Board of Foreign Missions, North

[37] Notation on memorandum from Eric M. North, 1922 (Board of Missions files).
[38] *Christian Union*, c. 1886 (unmarked clipping in Board of Missions files).

apparently remained unconvinced that the church was ready for Taylor's unconventional methods. Scattered across Africa and on other continents were stations and personnel operating under the banner of American Methodism but not integrated into the program of the Board of Foreign Missions. Thus North responded to a memorandum from his Africa secretary:

In its initiation and for years the individualistic ideals and methods of Bishop Taylor dominated our work. Neither the church nor our Board was intelligently shaping policy. Commendation for Bp. Taylor for inextinguishable enthusiasm but not for well ordered plan. He was coerced by his own self-support theory and our Board inherited his unwise and incomplete work.[39]

The Methodist Centenary Fund, launched at the close of World War I, proved to be one of the greatest opportunities and one of the greatest crises in the life of the church. It was designed to honor the hundred years of consecrated service which Methodists had rendered around the world since Frank Mason North's grandfather, Thomas Mason, had joined with Nathan Bangs and others to form The Missionary and Bible Society on April 5, 1819. It was also designed to augment the resources for a great program of postwar rehabilitation and expansion. North himself listed some of the specific objects as follows: relief needs of approximately $600,000 in Europe; building and equipping of three hospitals and missionary houses in Africa; new schools and evangelistic programs in Japan and Korea; training institutes for mass movements and village work in India; "adequate participation of the Methodist Episcopal Church in the 4 great union universities in China," plus hospitals, an episcopal residence, literature, and a school in Shanghai for missionary children. "We did not know it, but the Centenary was timed to meet the most serious financial crisis our Missionary Society and its Successor, the Board of Foreign Missions, have ever known," North confessed.[40]

The preliminary momentum of the Centenary accomplished great things. The Board debt was liquidated, the number of new

---

[39] Memorandum to Thomas Donohugh, May 1, 1922 (Board of Missions files).
[40] "A Direct Word For Those Who Want To Know," Department of Education, Centenary Observation Committee, March 1, 1920.

missionaries increased from seventy-five to a hundred, the Centenary funds for the year ending October 31, 1919, brought in 175% more than the total mission income for the previous year. As North put it graphically: "The Centenary is filling the channels, is pouring water on the wheels, is putting in the foundations and lifting the walls, and everywhere valiant, devoted, patient missionaries are finding their dreams coming true." The committee hoped for over five million dollars more in 1920, for this "new constructive program which will give among the peoples of the world a plan of action for the Gospel of our Lord for a thousand years." It was a time of projecting—a time of dreaming, in the best sense of the word. While faithful workers at home solicited pledges across the home church, faithful workers abroad drafted blueprints and surveys for larger evangelism and new institutions, "in everything, a stronger staff, greater efficiency, higher ideals." "Christendom in its history since the first century has not known a greater movement," North wrote enthusiastically. "Under its sweep the foreign mission enterprise for the Methodist Church ceases to be a venture and becomes a program."

Then came the deluge. With the collapse of postwar prosperity appeared a more critical collapse of American concern for the rest of the world, evidenced by the rejection of the League of Nations and the Versailles Treaty. Millions of dollars' worth of pledges to the Centenary Fund remained unpaid. Halford E. Luccock, then a young journalist with the Board of Missions, called it "one of the most embarrassing conditions that ever confronted its [the church's] benevolent work." [41] By 1923 contributions had dropped over a million dollars below the annual giving the year before, a sum equal to the entire Board of Missions budget for China, Japan, Korea, and Rhodesia, *or* for India, Burma, Malaysia, the Philippines, Netherlands Indies, and Sumatra. In May alone of that year the deficit was equivalent to total financial operations in South America and France, or to *all* Negro work under the Board of Home Missions.

Frank Mason North said very little. He had not himself been directly involved in the money-raising at home. But he had been

[41] Draft article, June 15, 1923 (Board of Missions files).

205

intimately engaged with the bishops and missionaries and nationals abroad in dreaming great dreams and devising great programs. Just before the annual meeting of the Board of Missions in 1921 he had written to India: "My hope does not wither, nor my faith grow dim." [42] Indeed the Centenary should not be dismissed as a failure. The "Memorial Minute" adopted by the Executive Committee of the Board of Missions after North's death registered the conviction that the Centenary "literally influenced the viewpoint of a thousand missionaries in more than forty mission fields. It changed the mental attitude of many of our people concerning the need and opportunity of the Church." It raised more than twenty million dollars and sent 632 missionaries and 17 bishops to foreign fields between 1918 and 1922. It helped create "the miracle of a new day in the glorious missionary enterprise, educational, social, political, and religious, of the Methodist Church." [43]

Such a long perspective must have been extremely hard for the executive who had to cancel vital projects, close schools, withdraw missionaries—and to make these agonizing decisions at a time when S. Earl Taylor was on leave with the still more disastrous Interchurch World Movement or in ill health and partial working capacity with the Board. One of the most sensitive tributes ever paid to North came during this period—doubly precious because it originated in a critically affected field and because it appeared at the moment of emotional need instead of after the subject's death. Brenton T. Badley, second-generation missionary, who was to be elected a bishop in 1924, wrote in *The Indian Witness* under the title "Frank Mason North—Beloved":

In this emergency Dr. North proved himself again to be one of the strong men of American Methodism. . . . Only to the few has he voiced his heartbreak at having to send messages to the field that hopes of the past had not been wholly fulfilled and that caution and curtailment were necessary. . . .

In it all, Dr. North thinks of us, not as *agents* of the Board, but as men and women, and his own friends. I have seen him, bearing almost

[42] Quoted in *The Indian Witness*, March 23, 1921.
[43] *Frank Mason North*, pp. 42-43.

indescribable responsibilities, and surrounded by an overwhelming amount of work, stop and give invaluable hours to the personal problems or needs of any one out of hundreds of missionaries who might have come to consult him. He is as great of heart, as he is of mind and soul. Frank Mason North, we all love you! [44]

One of the few areas of tension which arose between North's position as president of the Federal Council of Churches and his role as corresponding secretary of the Board of Foreign Missions of the Methodist Episcopal Church involved the place of Methodism in postwar Europe.

In his very first annual report to the Board North had voiced the conviction that "those in charge of the administration greatly desire the development of a common ground of sympathy and understanding between the forces of the Methodist Episcopal Church and the other Protestant bodies at work on the Continent." [45] A year later he said:

Protestant Europe should not be treated as missionary ground. What we ought to do is to recognize in these churches in Switzerland, Germany, Sweden and these other lands, allies of the home church . . . so that our brethren there shall not be placed upon the basis of being beneficiaries of people in this land. Something should be done to give them a better standing among their own people than is now possible.[46]

As corresponding secretary for Europe, North was of course concerned for the strengthening of the Methodist Church there. What distressed him in the confusion of postwar inspection trips, relief missions, and fraternal delegations was the growing suspicion that the "old-line" state churches were attempting to squeeze out newer sects (including Methodism) and that the executive secretary of the Federal Council of Churches, C. S. Macfarland, was a party to this move. Rumors of remarks by Macfarland as critical of Methodists had reached North, who wrote fully and frankly and sharply:

[44] March 23, 1921.
[45] *Annual Report*, Board of Foreign Missions, Methodist Episcopal Church, 1912.
[46] "The Board of Foreign Missions," *Zion's Herald*, November 19, 1913, p. 1477.

Convinced as I am of the opportunity of cooperation in promoting the material and spiritual welfare of the Protestant forces in France, as represented by those historic churches, I hold that there is no field more definitely open for the warm-hearted service of other religious forces—and especially American forces—than France. And the Church and the Board with which I am connected will not feel that it is necessary to confine their activities to the channels already provided. I have shown my sympathy with the purpose for the cooperative effort. I think I shall venture to ask that you, as representing the united effort, will show your attitude by not depreciating the Methodist effort in this matter, which, if it can be controlled and properly developed [from Methodist Churches in Switzerland and Italy] will bring as powerful a stimulus to the Protestant churches of France by neighborship as the United Committee can by an overseas direction.

You are quoted as having said . . . "We were after Methodists in this meeting. The fact is, they went into France without consulting anybody." I wonder if you said that, or whether that expresses any part of your motive in holding the meeting? . . .

The organized Methodist Episcopal Church in France is a Protestant body which should be recognized by any assembly which aims to be inclusive of the organized Protestant forces. If there is any reason in the Constitution of the Assembly which makes this impossible, it should be shown and action should be taken accordingly. . . . I hope that the French brethren will not force the issue of the proper ecclesiastical and legal standing of the Methodist Episcopal Church in France. It would be a very serious comment upon a branch of the Church which quite as much as any other has put itself in line to forward the interests of French Protestantism. We can rest under the criticism of faulty methods and try to better them. We will not rest under the imputation of assuming to be a Church when we are not one. Yours cordially.[47]

Despite subsequent exchanges of courteous correspondence —and the termination of North's office in the Federal Council in 1920—the issue continued to smolder. Three years later the Methodist Board secretary sent to Macfarland a letter of protest over an article by Dr. Frederick Lynch referring with contempt to Methodists and Baptists as "interlopers" in countries where

[47] October 25, 1919 (Federal Council Archives #119).

Lutheranism was the state religion. "This, from a man identified as he is in our cooperative programs here, seems to many of us to require explanation before we commit ourselves to further efforts of cooperation which include him, and perchance others who think as he does. Action upon the further appropriation of the Federal Council has been jeopardized and perhaps entirely thwarted," North warned in an unprecedented tone. Referring again to the situation in France, he added bluntly, "This influence, subtle or open, as it might be, is traced to yourself." [48] Macfarland subsequently characterized the action of the Lutheran Bureau of Publicity as "a gross violation of our principles of comity," but the extant correspondence reveals no denial or apology.

Frank Mason North was too big a man to let personal differences of opinion obstruct the work of the church. But his loyalties to both the Methodist Board of Foreign Missions and the Federal Council of Churches ran so deep that a divergence of interests pained him acutely. He had insisted, when he accepted the Council presidency, that he could not let it overburden his time or energy committed to the Methodist Board. But when the conflict involved policy decisions as well as relationships with the Council staff, he made his position clear and forthright:

Perhaps I ought to say that I have less heart in this task than is usual to me in matters of this kind. . . . If the clear-cut propositions that we are making and the plans which we have laid are subject to review in the way and in the spirit which I have noted here, and which perhaps prevails overseas, I think I shall feel impelled not only not to write messages but not to continue my effort fairly to represent both the Federal Council and our own denominational interests. At the present time there is only one of these situations that I can modify by withdrawal from active participation. You know well which one that is.[49]

This concern for the worldwide interests of Methodism in no way diluted North's commitment to ecumenical cooperation.

[48] July 11, 1922 (Federal Council files).
[49] Letter to C. S. Macfarland, October 21, 1919 (#134 in Federal Council Archives #119).

Having attended the famous Edinburgh Missionary Conference of 1910, he became subsequently a member of the Continuation Committee and chaired the drafting committee for the Constitution of the International Missionary Council, adopted at Lake Mohonk, New York, in October, 1921. "With great clarity," says William Richey Hogg, "he helped all to understand what were then assumed to be necessary limitations upon the powers and functions of the council." [50] J. H. Oldham, ecumenical pioneer and still honorary president of the World Council of Churches, credits "such great ecclesiastical statesmen as . . . Dr. Frank Mason North" with the increasing emphasis on church boards of missions rather than the independent missionary societies of the past.[51] "The only bodies entitled to determine missionary policy," says the original Constitution, "are the missionary societies and boards, or the churches which they represent, and the churches in the mission field"—this last phrase a far-sighted and broad-minded inclusion.

Other provisions had international, tactical, and theological implications. For example, two out of three representatives from Japan, China, and India should be nationals; "co-operation shall be sought with other national missionary organizations . . . not at present participating in the International Missionary Council, whenever conditions make such co-operation possible"; and "the successful working of the International Missionary Council is entirely dependent on the gift from God of the spirit of fellowship, mutual understanding, and desire to cooperate." [52] In a personal tribute J. H. Oldham writes of North:

He was one of the three or four people from whom I learned most in my early days; and who contributed most to the lines on which the International Missionary Council developed. . . . Dr. North was an outstanding example of the best type of churchmanship; and in many long conversations with him I drew deeply on his stores of wisdom. . . . I look back on Dr. North as one of the formative influences in my

[50] *Ecumenical Foundations* (New York: Harper & Brothers, 1952), p. 410.
[51] "Reflections on Edinburgh, 1910," *Religion in Life*, Summer, 1960.
[52] *Minutes*, International Missionary Council, Lake Mohonk, N. Y., 1921, pp. 29-35.

life and outlook; and . . . I had the highest respect for his judgment and wisdom.[53]

Despite the editorial guess (see page 182) that he would have been reelected corresponding secretary of the Board of Foreign Missions, even at the age of seventy-three, Frank Mason North withdrew his name at the General Conference of 1924. One of his associates, Thomas Donohugh, suggests that "he did not feel he could work successfully with Diff [Ralph E. Diffendorfer], who campaigned on the idea that Dr. North was responsible for the debt of some $4,000,000, which was due to the falling off of gifts from the church each year and not from expenditures above appropriations." [54] Certainly North recognized that the retirement age of seventy-two for bishops ought in fairness to apply to Board secretaries as well. Whatever his reasons, North retired, to be succeeded by Diffendorfer and John R. Edwards, but was given the post of secretary counsel for the next four years.[55]

In accordance with General Conference directives, a special committee on Recognition of the Services of Dr. Frank Mason North (consisting of E. S. Tipple, D. G. Downey, and Ralph W. Sockman) paid this tribute before the Executive Committee of the Board: "Dr. North has had the missionary heart, the missionary passion from the beginning of his ministry in 1873. . . . For . . . decades he stood 'where cross the crowded ways of life,' and prayed, and pioneered, and toiled for the countless multitudes 'in haunts of wretchedness and need.' " [56]

[53] Letter to the author, November 29, 1960.
[54] Letter to the author, July 21, 1958.
[55] *Annual Report,* Board of Foreign Missions, Methodist Episcopal Church, 1924, p. 8.
[56] Report of the Committee on Recognition of the Services of Dr. F. M. North to the Executive Committee, Board of Foreign Missions, June 19, 1924 (Board of Missions files).

The Waking World

O Master of the waking world,
Who hast the nations in Thy heart,—
The heart that bled and broke to send
God's love to earth's remotest part,—
Show us anew in Calvary
The wondrous power that makes men free.

On every side the walls are down,
The gates swing wide in every land,
The restless tribes and races feel
The pressure of Thy piercéd hand;
Thy way is in the sea and air,
Thy world is open everywhere.

We hear the throb of surging life,
The clank of chains, the curse of greed,
The moan of pain, the futile cries
Of superstition's cruel creed;
The peoples hunger for Thee, Lord,
The isles are waiting for Thy word.

Thy witness in the souls of men,
Thy Spirit's ceaseless, brooding power,
In lands where shadows hide the light,
Await a new creative hour.

O mighty God, set us aflame
To show the glories of Thy name.

O Church of God! Awake! Awake!
The waking world is calling thee.
Lift up thine eyes! Hear thou once more
The challenge of humanity!
O Christ, we come! Our all we bring,
To serve our world and Thee, Our King.

1927

11

"Fellowships of Life and Thought"

No human life was ever blessed
With human love more rich and rare;
But never finds my heart its peace,
Unless Thyself art there.

According to a publicity folder for the Board of Foreign
Missions, the duties of the corresponding secretaries "stretch from
selecting a picture bride for a lonely missionary man to signing
Thank-You letters for million dollar gifts, neither of which they
have done often enough to form a habit." [1] Items in the files
during North's tenure reveal almost as wide a range of problems:
the price of galvanized steel pipe goes up five percent; a missionary
daughter just out of college deliberately gets herself arrested as a
suspected prostitute in the hope of writing a "human interest"
study which will win her a newspaper job; it is "most important"
to get government clearance for a new college in Singapore; a
pastor in the mid-west requests funds to inspect mission work in
Europe and North Africa. To this last appeal North, though
recognizing the dangerous precedent, inquires the exact amount
needed and whether a good case can be made, adding: "Let him
know that we are *personally* sympathetic with him and his
proposal." [2]

This response is typical of the senior secretary. Behind the
reserve, behind the dignity, lay a sensitive concern for every
individual in his worldwide parish. To be sure, there were

[1] N.d. (Board of Missions files).
[2] Memorandum, January 12, 1921 (Board of Missions files).

215

occasional instances when his receptivity was unrecognized or ignored. Frank Mason North sounded both hurt and indignant when one missionary submitted through a junior staff officer a series of anonymous questions about salary and withdrawal from the field. "So far as I am officially concerned it should be known to all our missionaries," North wrote, "that no problem personal or general is considered unworthy of full and, if necessary, extended consideration. If the seeker for information will write me—even though he may need to do so confidentially—I shall be glad to give information and interpretation to the best of my ability."

On the whole, few executives have filled the "father role" more warmly and effectively. Few have won such genuine affection from their junior colleagues. A first-term missionary to China told Frank Mason North: "I . . . have taken the liberty of writing as frankly and freely as though I were not writing to the Board secretary." [3] And at a later date he expressed his gratitude and trust as follows:

I had expected that with the appointment of an associate secretary for the China field we could not look for any more of your personal letters that have meant so much to some of us. How happily disappointed do I find myself. Little else can be so encouraging as the assurance that you, with your very heavy burdens and involved problems, appreciate the relatively petty difficulties that seem such mountains to us young fellows in this field.[4]

The corresponding secretary, thirty-eight years older, replied on different occasions with a rare combination of camaraderie and understanding: "I have been rather looking for one of your refreshing letters. Probably you are penalizing me for not having been more prompt in answering those you have already sent." [5] "You will have had quite sufficient advice [in regard to a new assignment], I do not doubt. I shall not attempt to add to your burdens in that direction." [6] To a senior missionary North wrote

---

[3] Carleton Lacy, letter to F. M. North, October 3, 1917 (Board of Missions files).
[4] Ibid., September 26, 1919 (Board of Missions files).
[5] Letter to Carleton Lacy, July 27, 1917 (Board of Missions files).
[6] Letter to Carleton Lacy, October 15, 1918 (Board of Missions files).

whimsically: "I trust you will not let your work get on your nerves. I am trying my best to keep my work on the outside of that important part of my anatomy." [7]

Frank Mason North, as an office associate recollects, was "an administrative genius" with a "capacious memory" for correspondence, reading, and conversations with missionaries—a file-card or "IBM memory" which could "pop up" the right data at the right moment.[8] But he also possessed what another subordinate and successor termed "the biggest heart of any man I ever knew." [9] His official correspondence sounds, for the most part, formal and businesslike. Even his closest friends and colleagues were addressed with titles, in conversations as well as memoranda. Notes were signed *F.M.N.* or occasionally *N.*, other communications by surname and initials or full name. This was partly the practice of the times, partly a measure of the respect North's seniority and wisdom engendered, but partly a characteristic of the man himself—like "Päter" from his children. One junior staff member recalls him as "in presence, in speech, in his approach to people . . . 'a gentleman of the old school'. . . . He was kindly, thoughtful, and every simple remark seemed to have come from the heart of an oration. He was 'Churchillian' in speech—and I take it that goes back to Macaulay." [10]

Yet time and time again North's compassionate concern breaks through the routine, and the human being is recognized as far more important than any rules—or any budgets. Quite naturally, many of the missionary problems involved financial hardships. For a young man in Japan, unable to afford a vacation, the corresponding secretary wrote: "1. He should not spend the summer in Tokyo. 2. His deficit runs about $400-450 per annum. Will his share of the [cost of living] bonus equal that? 3. If not, we should find some way to relieve him. 4. If there is no other recourse, I can send him a little extra. Prompt action is needed. N." [11] In another "hardship case" where the area secretary had reported, "I fail to see why these children should receive special con-

[7] Letter to W. H. Lacy, October 27, 1915 (Board of Missions files).

[8] Arthur B. Moss, personal interview, October 12, 1958.

[9] Frederick B. Newell, personal interview, April 1, 1959.

[10] William W. Reid, letter to the author, June 12, 1965.

[11] Memorandum to Arthur B. Moss, May 31, 1921 (Board of Missions files).

sideration that is not granted to the children of other missionaries," North had penciled: "Correct.—N." But mercy always tempered his justice, and he added this postscript: "If further distress appears let me know and I may be able to help from special funds." [12] Again, when currency exchange problems in the Belgian Congo had led to shortages and overdrafts North ordered:

This situation should be at once remedied. 1. Whatever our usual program for exchanges, there is every reason why we should vary it or scrap it if it is putting our missionaries on a bread and water diet. Let us *at once* find a way. 2. Delays due to lack of proper communication of information between treasurer's department and foreign secretaries should be avoided. This may call for consultation and correction.[13]

Nor was such concern reserved for the missionaries alone. Despite the need for general, undesignated funds, he recognized the natural inclination on the part of many contributors to maintain a personal and preferential relationship to specific projects. "My own judgment," he wrote, "is that these special gifts, where there is the slightest unwillingness on the part of the donor to transfer them, should be held to their original purpose. The question of regular credit seems to me less important than the maintenance of our honorable relations with those who have specific desires in the matter of giving." [14]

Of course, the Board of Foreign Missions stands always ready to relieve emergency needs in time of catastrophe, but this fact was seldom more evident than following the disastrous earthquake in Japan in 1923. Frank Mason North happened to be on a trip to the West Coast, but his son and other staff members in New York kept him fully appraised of reports as they came in. On September 24 Bishop Welch had cabled: "Property losses latest estimate six hundred forty thousand immediate need, twenty five thousand additional." [15] Three days later North was informed by telegram that the earthquake fund to date totaled

[12] Memorandum to Arthur B. Moss, c. January 17, 1920 (Board of Missions files).

[13] Memorandum to Thomas Donohugh, August 31, 1920 (Board of Missions files).

[14] Memorandum to Mr. Morrow, January 17, 1918 (Board of Missions files).

[15] Eric M. North telegram to F. M. North in Denver, September 24, 1923 (Board of Missions files).

thirty thousand four hundred two dollars.[16] As he journeyed across the country—to Chicago and Denver and Los Angeles—he found that "churches here plan offerings";[17] no doubt he helped stimulate generous responses. But the money was dispatched without waiting for the emergency appeal to bear fruit. An unsigned letter from Aoyama Gakuin, in one of the most severely devastated areas, is a tribute not only to the Board machinery, but also to the compassion and efficiency of Frank Mason North:

I want to tell you how splendidly the Office in New York . . . stood by us through our disaster. They began to send us money before we could get any word at all to them—and before any money had come from the Churches to send. And they . . . did not leave a way untried to reach us with their help in those dark days. Long before any other Mission here had received any word or money from America— our Board had succeeded in getting funds through to *us*. Those repeated cables from New York lifted up our hearts—as though God had sent an angel down from Heaven to help us. All our Methodists in America ought to know not only how generously but with what efficient skill our Board in New York got relief through to us out here in our dire need. Even now I cannot think about it—cannot write about it without tears in my eyes. . . . The dearest word in the Japanese language now is Ah-may-ree-ka! The heart of all Japan is wide open to you across the sea in gratitude and admiration.[18]

Although a distinct personnel office developed gradually in the Board of Foreign Missions during North's tenure, the corresponding secretary took a direct hand in appraising candidates and showed himself deeply sensitive to missionary motivations. When one associate recommended that recruitment programs at Epworth League Institutes for youth should make it clear "that no person should go into the work for any other purpose than that he or she believes it to be the call of God," North replied: "I enter into this heartily and if you will secure the names I will

[16] G. M. Thomson telegram to F. M. North in Los Angeles, September 27, 1923 (Board of Missions files).
[17] Telegram to Eric M. North from Chicago, September 25, 1923 (Board of Missions files).
[18] Unsigned letter (probably Charles Iglehart) to the Methodist Church in Maplewood, N. J., September 21, 1923 (Board of Missions files).

write the letter." [19] But on many occasions he deferred gracefully and gratefully to the judgment of others. To one junior staff member he wrote, in regard to a candidate for a journalistic post:

1. The fact that P. H. [Paul Hutchinson, later well known as editor of *The Christian Century*] believes in him and feels that he can work with him is a great point.
2. For myself, left alone to judge, I w'd not select him.
3. I am open to conviction and as it was left to me, I think, for decision, I would like to see you about him. N.[20]

Not infrequently the corresponding secretary recognized unusual promise in a young missionary and saw the necessity for latitude and unconventional treatment. For example, Charles S. Braden, noted authority on world religions, author, and teacher at Northwestern University, began his career as a missionary in Bolivia and Chile. Of him the South America secretary reported to North:

He shows the spirit of a real missionary. Mr. Braden will stick to his job, I think, and if he does will become one of the outstanding men in Latin America. I asked ——— what he thought of Braden's theological views, and he said the only trouble was that he was apt to boast of his advanced views with a view to frightening some of the brethren, which he succeeded in doing in the case of the Presbyterians.[21]

The Board executive was neither shocked nor critical. "After all," he jotted at the foot of the note, "are there not some radical changes needed to meet Braden's contentions?"

Similarly, E. Stanley Jones, world-famous evangelist, recalls with gratitude North's willingness to make Board policy flexible and adaptable. When the Y.M.C.A. of India wanted to employ Jones on an interdenominational basis for work among the educated classes, "the reply of Dr. Frank Mason North, the secretary was: 'No, but we will do the same thing. We will keep

[19] Memorandum to James H. Lewis, May 17, 1921 (Board of Missions files).
[20] Memorandum, October 31, 1921 (Board of Missions files).
[21] Harry Farmer, memorandum to F. M. North, October 18, 1921 (Board of Missions files).

Stanley Jones as a Methodist missionary, but we will pay his salary and traveling and lend him to the whole situation in India to do an evangelistic work among all the missions.' " Eventually Jones's field of witness became the entire world, and he took care of his own travel expenses while continuing to draw the salary of a Methodist missionary. "I am certainly not a good organization man," the world-famous preacher and lecturer admits, but "the organization has held me by letting me be free. This is to its credit. For the organization has shown that it is resilient, adaptable, and can follow the leadings and drives of the Spirit." [22] E. Stanley Jones made reference in this published statement to the Board and the bishops of the Methodist Episcopal Church, but in private correspondence he added a further personal tribute: "It was a statesmanlike thing to do and Dr. North pointed out with pardonable pride his part in it." [23]

Frank Mason North's protegés—and his problems—were not always the dramatic—or successful—kind. Sometimes his role was one of encouragement and discovery. In reply to a report from Angola, North commented on an unknown young missionary: "The man has a *mind*—and knows not only how to *observe,* but how to think—and to state a case." Suggesting that copies of the letter—dealing with agricultural machinery!—be prepared for the entire Executive Committee "both to prove that we have intelligence on the field and to show the nature of the operation as a missionary enterprise," North added with genuine surprise: "Where did we find him?" [24]

Sometimes, on the other hand, the corresponding secretary had to be firm but gentle. In regard to a man who had left one field and accepted another post without Board approval: "Whether ———— should remain upon our list as a missy [*sic*] for whom we are responsible is quite a question. To be impartial—he should *not* be." [25] Concerning a doctor who, after thirty-eight

[22] Letter of January 16, 1959, quoted in "Methodist of the Year," *World Outlook,* April, 1959, p. 162.
[23] Letter to the author, June 29, 1959; cf. F. M. North memorandum to Thomas Donohugh, October 14, 1921 (Board of Missions files).
[24] Memorandum to Thomas Donohugh, February 21, 1921 (Board of Missions files).
[25] Memorandum, March 2, 1920 (Board of Missions files).

years of service, was using funds at his own discretion instead of according to designation: "We must adjust for a change without break of sympathy or relations." [26] And to a missionary impatient over delays in appointing his youngest son to the field: "Some times it seems a good while to bring things into line, but if we keep at them and our hearts are right and our prayers are not too sluggish, and we keep our eyes open for the resources, and our minds open for the plan, God manages to use these dull tools in doing his work. Is it not so?" [27]

Sometimes, in fact, it was necessary to be firm and impossible to be gentle. The memorial statement from the Executive Committee of the Federal Council, read and probably written by North's long-time associate, C. S. Macfarland, said: "Often severe, at times to the point of censuring, he loved even when he chastened. His criticism went deep, but left no lasting wound or scar. He had his failings, but they 'leaned to virtue's side.' " [28] Once in a while North was provoked into blunt scorn—within the confines of interoffice memoranda. "If Brother M——— is not exaggerating—and we have proof of it—I think I should take it up with him diplomatically." [29] In regard to a woman requesting a special grant from the Board: "This may be a proper settlement. The earlier statements did not locate the blame in just this way. The 'victim' seems to have been singularly persistent in permitting herself to be victimized." [30] Or with, for North, quite uncommon hopelessness: "I fear that ——— ought never to have gone and that it is a waste of time to try to make him a success." [31]

When one of the area secretaries submitted a "sob story" about the immediate need (from emergency funds?) for a new home for a Korean district superintendent because there was a liquor establishment on one side of his residence and a "disorderly house" on the other, North replied sagely: "This has an Emergency look, but it really is a property investment and must, I

[26] Memorandum, October 9, 1918 (Board of Missions files).
[27] Letter to W. H. Lacy, May 17, 1917 (Board of Missions files).
[28] In *Frank Mason North*, p. 49.
[29] Memorandum to Thomas Donohugh, September 21, 1921 (Board of Missions files).
[30] Memorandum, September 20, 1920 (Board of Missions files).
[31] Memorandum, June 19, 1922 (Board of Missions files).

think, be so treated." [32] Then, more gently, for another dissatisfied worker, North recommended: "He should go to work in his job with the devoted men who are giving their lives to the subsoiling in Christian education in China and to take the higher and the lower together as Providence may open the way." [33]

In the corresponding secretary's relation to his subordinates, two emphases come through clearly. One is the demand for accurate and detailed information. "This is a most important matter, and we must have clear understanding as to the antecedent facts" (December 27, 1922). "We must go into this situation thoroly. N." (July 15, 1922). "How about prices? . . . Have conditions modified?" (January 29, 1921). "I find it impracticable to decide these rather important items by memo. . . . Your advice!" (January 29, 1921). When the medical secretary, discussing missionary breakdowns, reported that the Baptists required two years of successful executive experience to watch for lack of self-restraint or overzealousness, North replied: "This is worthy of careful consideration. Does the Baptist board show fewer breaks than we do? How can two years of such experience be secured? By the candidate? By the Board?" [34]

The other conspicuous element in North's dealing with his associates is a tension between an autocratic tendency to run the entire mission operation single-handedly and a sincere respect and trust toward his colleague and staff. After W. F. Oldham had been reassigned as bishop in Buenos Aires and S. Earl Taylor devoted most of his time to the Centenary and then to the Interchurch World Movement, North—at seventy—carried the administrative burden almost alone. Taylor had urged the appointment of area secretaries, and North eventually agreed, but one of the first of these, Thomas Donohugh, recalls that for the work in Africa "he [North] was rather reluctant to turn it over. In fact he was not very keen on sharing work as he had a remarkable grasp on all the fields and once told me that if he had been able he would have carried it all himself." [35] Another junior colleague

[32] Memorandum to Arthur B. Moss, November 18, 1922 (Board of Missions files).

[33] Letter to Thomas Donohugh from Pocono Manor, Pa., August 16, 1916 (Board of Missions files).

[34] Memorandum to J. G. Vaughan, 1924 (Board of Missions files).

[35] Letter to the author, July 21, 1958.

comments that "in many ways, Dr. North was a 'lone' administrator; his Board had confidence in him; I think it very seldom 'directed' him, but rather trusted and followed him." [36]

This confidence North, in turn, extended to his staff, who acknowledged his unquestioned wisdom, experience, and authority. In their respective spheres he trusted them with a large measure of freedom and responsibility, but there was never any doubt that final and crucial decisions lay solely in his hands. "You have written wisely and I think it would be best not for me to intervene at this time. . . . I will leave it to you at this stage" (August 16, 1916). Declining to intrude in certain correspondence, "let me know if there is any snag and I will join you in trying to remove it" (October 2, 1920). After commending other points in a draft letter, "I would think it unwise. . . . Perhaps you will confer with me about this before sending the letter" (June 8, 1918). "If you think my note sounds querulous, or in any way unsatisfactory, either modify it or answer the note yourself, leaving me to take the matter up with Brother M——— at some other time" (May 2, 1924). "In writing it will be well to remember that practically nothing remains long 'confidential'. Say little, say it straight, stand by it!" (June 26, 1924).

Such assorted office memoranda give occasional clues to significant Board policy, as well as to personal relationships. In response to a letter recommending that mission architecture should "appeal to the people of India . . . and meet their ideals, rather than duplicate European or American types of bungalows and churches, which are the product of the thinking of the missionary rather than of the Indian himself," North scrawled in the margin the single word: "Surely!" [37] When an area secretary complained that one or two individuals were dominating the finance committee in Rhodesia, North agreed to putting all the missionaries on the committee unless distances would make action difficult. "However that would be better than absolutism," he concluded.[38] Again, in regard to unilateral decision-making in the field: "It is

[36] William W. Reid, letter to the author, June 12, 1965, p. 2.

[37] Memorandum to Thomas Donohugh, December 16, 1921 (Board of Missions files).

[38] Memorandum to Thomas Donohugh, December 8, 1920 (Board of Missions files).

not sound for it ignores the fact that the work is one and that we here are partners at least" (July 20, 1922). When the medical secretary proposed putting on the Medical Advisory Board some "non-evangelical" doctors, including the prominent Jewish superintendent of Mt. Sinai Hospital, North replied:

1. There is no prohibitive objection.
2. On the other hand, this is definitely a Christian and missionary proposition—are there not enough Christian physicians who have not only the scientific and the philanthropic interest but the spiritual interest to fill out the number?
3. Personally I sh'd hope so. N.[39]

After fifty years there are few associates, even among North's younger friends, who have vivid personal recollections or anecdotes to report. Since he was seventy years of age when most of his junior colleagues joined the Board staff or most of the surviving missionaries first knew him, it is quite understandable that they should have a picture of a staid and portly "gentleman of the old school" whose very bearing—as well as fame and position—inspired awe and deference. As one of these young missionaries, later an area secretary, put it: "He appeared to my fairly youthful eyes as a veritable giant among men and I profited much from the infrequent and brief contacts with him."

But Frank Cartwright went on to reminisce about how the corresponding secretary took him, as a young candidate for service in China, to have lunch at "Billy, the Oysterman's, a onetime popular eatery among the gourmets. There I had for the first time in my life creamed clams on toast as recommended by Dr. North." The occasion ended less happily, for Cartwright chose milk to drink instead of coffee on a hot day and "learned for me raw milk and shell fish are a deadly mixture. It ruined a ball game later in the day." [40] Whether the ball game, too, was to have been with his Board secretary, he did not say. It could have been, for J. H. Oldham, the great British ecumenical statesman, looks back over forty years to this little incident in 1921:

[39] Memorandum to J. G. Vaughan, June 10, 1922 (Board of Missions files).
[40] Letter to the author, May 17, 1957.

The one detail that happens to remain alive in my memory is a train journey with him when we returned from the meeting of the I.M.C. at Lake Mohonk to New York. John R. Mott had exerted his powerful influence to obtain tickets for Dr. J. H. Ritson and me for the final of the base ball competition between two New York teams. I had never seen a base ball match, and during the train journey Dr. North instructed me in the niceties of the game, in which he was evidently an expert. Unfortunately, when we reached New York rain had begun to fall, and continued through the afternoon, and the game was not played.[41]

If personal anecdotes outside the family have been hard to find, the Victorian formality of North's correspondence reveals little of the humor that lay beneath the surface—or even very little of the personal. Even family letters during North's journey around the world contained few comments on the places he visited, or references to scenic views or tourist sights or strange cultures. Yet correspondence addressed *to* Frank Mason North, now in the library of Drew University, reads almost like a Who's Who of his day: Katherine Lee Bates, S. Parkes Cadman, Theodore Dreiser, Edward Everett Hale, Adolf Keller, Thomas H. Lamont, William T. Manning, Shailer Mathews, John R. Mott, Jacob A. Riis, Walter Rauschenbusch, John D. Rockefeller, Jr., Isabella Thoburn, Mary E. Wooley, Thomas Tiplady, and many others.

Quite obviously he himself was quick with notes of congratulation or commendation or condolence. Tyler Dennett, then in the political science department at Princeton, responding to the first category, adds: "I shall always treasure my association with you and shall hope to attain some of your moderation" (May 16, 1934). J. R. Dwyer confesses, of North's encouragement after a heart attack: "When disposed to depression of spirit then come words from you to lighten my darkness. . . . Then your words revived hope" (March 15, 1934). Jacob Riis, accepting an invitation to speak, admits: "I like of all things to dip enthusiastically out of the well of Methodist fervor that never runs dry. . . . I should like [my son] to catch some of the same infection" (March 20, 1896).

[41] Letter to the author, November 29, 1960.

226

John R. Mott, appointed by President Woodrow Wilson as United States Commissioner to Russia in the midst of the first Revolution, turns to North for support (though North presumably wrote first): "In view of the dangers and serious difficulties attending this mission, as well as the boundless opportunity it affords to witness for Christ, to apply His guiding principles and to further the plans of His Kingdom, I crave, more than I can express, your help in intercession. I know you will not fail me" (May 16, 1917). And Halford Luccock, in his own inimitable style, acknowledges North's comment on his new book and goes on to say: "You *do* have some divine qualities—slow to anger— long suffering and plenteous in mercy! . . . As the one who had much to do with my entering the Methodist ministry—you will be somewhat encouraged"—apparently at the news that Luccock would be "using the word God—right out loud and in a firm voice several times" in a series of projected lectures (May 4, 1934).

Very, very seldom did the underlying whimsy or sly amusement creep into North's letters. When he started on a vacation trip in the summer of 1913, he reported his departure from New York with some relish: "To reach the office and then West 42nd Street leaving the Aldine at 3:27 and due to arrive at 3:45 is going some. I had 1½ minutes to spare.—Success was due to a good taxi driver and the kindly inattention of 'cops'!" [42] Perhaps the very escape from office routine, or the excitement of travel, served to relax North's reserve, for the same letter to "Dr. Taylor" included other wry comments. On the unwelcome interference of a distinguished retired bishop he remarked: "The unconscious or conscious cerebrations of the public official who is at present unassigned to any diocese are a menace and a peril and an unmitigated nuisance—not he—but the cerebrations." And on some program which was meeting objections from a group in Philadelphia: "Some way must be found of persuading them that we wish they would not join and then quite likely they will."

No records could ever convey the infinite variety of kindly, thoughtful acts which Frank Mason North performed quietly and inconspicuously. He was as deeply interested in the personal

[42] Letter to S. Earl Taylor, July 27, 1913 (Board of Missions files).

problems of a file clerk or a shipping room boy as of a missionary or an executive—and usually managed to find discreet ways of helping. Often he would draw on special funds or his own resources to relieve a critical need. At other times, without embarrassment or apology, he would turn to his wealthy friends (e.g., the manufacturer of Welch's grape juice) so that a departing missionary might find an unexpected sewing machine added to his baggage, or a college student discover his bank account augmented.

Perhaps this depth of involvement in the problems of other people is best illustrated by the story of Julius F. Hecker, Ph.D., a German pastor at the Church of All Nations and a member of the New York East Annual Conference. Resigning his post in New York in the midst of World War I, Hecker set off to work among Russian prisoners of war in Austria, bearing expressions of esteem from North and others in America.[43] From the ship Hecker wrote: "I am safely on board and before the pilot drops us to our fate, I wish once more to express my gratitude to you for your sincere fatherly interest in me and my family." [44] Mrs. Hecker, daughter of a president of the Methodist Theological Seminary in Frankfurt, was to join him later.

In the summer of 1921, as work among prisoners and refugees tapered off, Frank Mason North asked him to make a quiet examination and report of conditions inside Russia, "at my personal request—not as a formal representative of our Board. There will be no special publicity given as to the nature of your errand." [45] That fall Hecker managed to get into Russia from Berlin, but not before meeting considerable difficulty from American officials in Germany. "It is true that I disagreed with the Allied policy of military intervention and the blockade of Russia," he admitted to North,[46] but so deeply did he resent the accusation of being a "Bolshevist sympathizer" and the implicit denial of citizenship in refusing him a travel permit that he wrote directly to Secretary of State Charles Evans Hughes.

[43] Cf. *Journal*, New York East Annual Conference, 1916, pp. 28-29; 1917, p. 18; *et cetera*.

[44] Letter to F. M. North (Board of Missions files).

[45] Letter to Julius Hecker, July 2, 1921 (Board of Missions files).

[46] Letter, October 24, 1921 (Board of Missions files).

For a while long and vivid letters came through from Soviet Russia. Hecker traveled through famine areas and "valleys of death," spent nights in appalling refugee trains, and entitled his report of a month's journey "In the Wake of Death and Horror." Despite the relief program of American Quakers, he said, "the need for more help is imperative to check the horrible mortality from famine and typhus." For this he advocated a four-point program: (1) increase gifts to relief agencies; (2) grant credit to the Soviet government for the purchase of grain; (3) help the government reestablish railroads to provide essential transportation of food; (4) —

Finally, fear not to deal with the Soviet Government. It is the only government Russia has or could have for some time to come. It is firmly established and knows its own mind. Most of its leaders are strong, energetic men and whether one likes their ideas or not, they are sincere and honest. This impression everyone gets who stays long enough in the country, no matter how prejudiced he was against the Soviets and the Communists.[47]

Even the *New York Times* took note of this report in a feature story written by Halford Luccock. It quoted from Hecker's account of the cold and disease in refugee camps, the hunger and typhus on trains (which sometimes took two to four months to reach their destination), the famine conditions which "exceed anything people in this country can imagine and rival those of any of the great famines of world history." [48]

That same year North reported to the executive secretary of the Federal Council of Churches that Hecker had got to Moscow and the Volga region. "He has such relations with leaders in the Government and outside of it that he seems to have no difficulty in approaching the persons and the communities unapproachable by others. I am inclined to think that any organized approach must be abandoned for a time." [49] Hecker seems to have paid a brief visit to the United States in 1924 and to have planned

[47] Hecker, "In the Wake of Death and Horror," December 12, 1921, to January 10, 1922 (Board of Missions files).
[48] March 26, 1922.
[49] Letter to C. S. Macfarland, May 22, 1922 (Federal Council Archives).

another in 1926, when his correspondence abruptly ceased. According to Frederick B. Newell's recollections, however, he became somehow involved in the Trotsky revolt (?) and disappeared about 1925. When, years later, a committee in the New York East Conference suggested removing his name from the rolls, North protested indignantly: "Until you hear that he is dead, you keep his name on the conference roll. . . . You ought to be proud of him." And he gave the same emphatic instructions as one of his last words to Bishop Newell, then with the New York City Society: "Fred, as long as you live, until you hear that this man is dead, don't you take his name off." [50]

Nothing further was ever heard from Julius F. Hecker himself. His sister in Brooklyn had no word on which to hold—or collect—his insurance policy. Finally in 1958 Bishop Newell visited a sister of Mrs. Hecker in Berlin. She had just received her first letter from her sister in Irkutsk, Siberia, where apparently the Heckers and their five daughters had been sent as political prisoners. By this time Mrs. Hecker wrote: "Generally speaking we are all right and contented, although we live far from one another. Alice, Marcella and Olga live in Moscow, the other two and I here in Siberia. *Good Julius is unfortunately no longer among us; he succumbed to circumstances in 1943.*" [51] As Bishop Newell concluded his part of this tale, he commented soberly: "There are not many men who ever walked this earth who would do for a little German school teacher what Frank Mason North did for Julius Hecker."

As a matter of fact, this episode constituted but one dramatic strand in the network of personal loyalty and sympathetic service woven through the life of Frank Mason North. For Bishop Newell's tribute drew on twenty years of friendship in the New York East Annual Conference as well as successive responsibility in the New York City Society. North, he recollects, "had an uncanny way of knowing what was right to do about some poor person who had nothing in the world. . . . He cared, to the extent that he really shared his life with people like that."

[50] Frederick B. Newell, personal interview, April 1, 1959.
[51] Mrs. Julius Hecker, English translation of letter to Mrs. Ernest Scholz, from Irkutsk, U.S.S.R., November 10, 1957.

O Wondrous Child

O Wondrous Child! The lowing kine
Have never gazed on face like Thine;
The light of stars was never shed
On cradle like Thy manger bed;
The wise have found no greater joy
Than comes from Thee, Thou Blessèd Boy

Do now the rugged shepherds press
Their worship on Thy helplessness?
Thou dost not in Thy weakness cry,
Hushed by Thy mother's lullaby;
Yet earth is bringing Thee surprise,
The wonder deepens in Thine eyes.

The mysteries of Thy life begin
Here in this stable of an inn;
The paths Thy tender feet must tread
Reach out from this, Thy humble bed;
Thy outstretched hand, so soft, so wee,
Must know the cross's agony.

O Wondrous Child! Where angels sing,
Where wise men richest treasures bring,
Where shepherds worship, can there be
A place at Thy nativity
For us whose hearts in eager quest
Are seeking joy and peace and rest?

The love of God which lived in Thee
Was nurtured at Thy mother's knee;
Thy kinship with the world of men
Was deepened, stirred, and strengthened then;
We, too, come near Thee. Wilt Thou take
The lives we give for Thy dear sake?

'Tis joy to have the joy Thou hast,
'Tis peace when sin and shame are past,
Tis love to have Thee in the heart,
'Tis power to know the Christ Thou art.
O Wondrous Child! our Light, our Guide,
We worship Thee this Christmastide.

1927

12

"With Minstrel Heart"

We hear from lands in tumult far away
The springing tread of multitudes made free;
The nations stir as those who greet the day;
Around the world rings out the reveille.

For every Christian who can name even one of Frank
Mason North's offices or positions, a score would identify him as
the author of "The City Hymn" ("Where Cross the Crowded
Ways of Life"). For half a century it has appeared in practically
every denominational or union or private hymnal in the English-
speaking world, and in China, India, Japan, and several European
countries as well. It has been called "the most famous city-centered
hymn of the twentieth century," [1] or, more extravagantly, the
greatest hymn in more than a hundred years. Christians of every
theological stripe have sung it—and prayed it—for more than
sixty years and will continue to do so for generations to come.

Although few people could name any other verse which North
wrote, he shared with Henry Hallam Tweedy alone among living
poets the distinction of having three hymns in *The Methodist
Hymnal* of 1935, the year of his death. In a literal sense these
represented three outstanding phases of his career: "Where Cross
the Crowded Ways of Life" (1903) from his city service; "The
World's Astir!" (1917) which reflected the enthusiasm of his own
student days and his lifelong commitment to youth and education; "O Master of the Waking World" (1927) at the close of his
world mission. Add to these "Jesus, the Calm That Fills My

---

[1] W. W. Reid, "Frank Mason North Centennial," *Zion's Herald*, December 6, 1950.

Breast" (1884) from his pastoral ministry, and we have the principal perspectives of his life in poetry.

Frank Mason North was not a musician. As his son recalls, "He may have started violin as a boy but certainly never got anywhere with it. Occasionally he sat at the piano and played with a sensitive touch but entirely by ear." During one meeting at Carnegie Hall North ventured—to the consternation of his wife—to pitch the singing of "Crown Him with Many Crowns" when the organ failed, but "it was *quite all right*. He had sung the hymn too often and was too aware of vocal music to slip here." [2] He did study some hymnology but made no pretense of creating music to go with his verse. Sometimes he wrote his meter to fit a tune he especially liked; sometimes a musician composed for his poetry, as Karl P. Harrington of Wesleyan (co-editor of the 1905 *Hymnal*) did for "O Morning Land of College Days." More often an established tune was borrowed by North or someone else and became an inseparable part of the hymn: *Waratah* by Moses S. Cross ("Jesus, the Calm That Fills My Breast"), Henry Cutler's *All Saints New* ("The Son of God Goes Forth to War"), for "The Student Hymn"; John Dykes' *Melita* ("Eternal Father, Strong to Save") for "The Waking World"; and Beethoven's theme (from William Gardiner's Sacred Melodies) for "The City Hymn."

In 1931, four years before he died, Frank Mason North gathered together fifteen of his best-loved poems and published them in a little book entitled *Hymns and Other Verses* for distribution to his many friends as a Christmas gift from Mrs. North and himself. These ranged in date from 1884 to the Wesleyan centennial in 1931. It can be assumed that this printed collection represented the final form in which he wished these poems preserved, for some had undergone drastic revision since their original composition or publication. In a few cases earlier manuscripts supply accurate clues as to the initial version; here a word or phrase has been changed, there entire stanzas omitted. In some instances, alas, no original copies have been discovered, and no information about their sources, no comments or interpretations from the author himself.

[2] Eric M. North, memorandum, September 22, 1965, p. 8.

Two poems date from North's brief visit in 1884 to Magnolia, Massachusetts, where he and Louise McCoy confirmed and re-affirmed their love, although her mother was still adamant. "The Life of Trust" (p. 7, more commonly known by its opening line, "Jesus, the calm fills my breast") was written overnight that summer (after a dinner conversation about John Wesley's "Jesus, thou source of calm repose") and first published in the *Christian Advocate* the following year.[3] This hymn has been a favorite with many missionaries around the world. Reminiscing about his associations in the Board of Foreign Missions, Thomas Donohugh wrote:

Dr. North was a delightful man to work with, always considerate and courteous. He was one of the finest Christian gentlemen I ever knew and it was a privilege to work with him. I asked him once why he did not write a hymn on this theme and he called my attention to the one in the older hymnal beginning "Jesus, the calm which fills my breast" which to my horror was omitted from the present edition when many far inferior ones were included.[4]

As recently as 1965 a retired missionary who served under North fifty years earlier told this writer that he had petitioned the new (1966) hymnal committee to include "Jesus, the calm" because he regarded it as one of the finest.

Looking Seaward" (p. 15), on the other hand, has been drastically rewritten and rearranged from a 1922 version (which presumably followed substantially the original of 1884). The original fourth, fifth, and sixth stanzas, ultimately omitted, read as follows:

> What if an unexhausted hand
> Has planted there the deathless trees,
> Where hills of light in radiant splendor stand
> And droop their silent shadows on the sailless seas!
>
> What if along each pebbled stream
> The stones the murmuring water laves

[3] February 19, 1885.
[4] Letter to the author, July 21, 1958.

> Are gems beyond the fancy's wildest dream
> And pearls uncounted hide beneath the crystal waves!

> What if in isles of fadeless green
> Grow fruits no other gardens bear,
> And over level plains, 'neath skies serene
> Sweep, surge on surge, the golden waves of harvest rare!

If the language sounds overly lush to modern ears, too "purple" for publication in 1931, it may have sounded somewhat extravagant to the poet himself when he reworked the lines in 1922. Stanza seven (now stanza four) originally read as follows:

> This land-locked harbor, still and pent
> Within a narrow edge of shore,
> Calms not my spirit's restless discontent,
> Unmeasured spheres and spaces eager to explore.

The next two stanzas received significant revisions from their initial phraseology:

> The search of my unaided sight
> Discovers not the chartless ways;
> Not on this side that line of curving light
> Bloom richest buds of peace or shine the perfect days.

> Ah! Master Mind—out on Thy sea
> I send my thoughts in earnest quest
> Of lands afar, in realms known but to Thee;
> Guide my frail ships through wrack and gloom to
>   harbors blest.

The concluding stanza has also been omitted:

> And as I wait upon the sands,
> May many a golden argosy
> Come back with treasure from the unseen lands
> To fill Time's meagre hours with Thy eternity.

Or (in the 1922 rendition):

> And as I wait here on the sands,
> May many a golden argosy

Bring treasures from the far-off spirits lands
To fill Time's waiting hours with Thy eternity.

The specific changes may indicate less about North's developing sense of poetry than about the fluctuations in cultural taste. They do suggest a great deal, however, about a man with the keenness of mind and the humility of heart to rewrite his youthful verses during his seventies and eighties.

"Chastened," which was written in 1885 and published in *Christian Union* in 1888, offers no alternate text (pp. 29-30). Some readers will say it is because the original gem was already polished in suffering and sparkling with tears. "My Lord, My Life" (p. 45) is undated and unidentified in the 1931 collection; perhaps North himself had forgotten just when or where it was written. Yet his son considers it, "of all his verse, most significant of his inner character." [5] Dating from his pastorate at Middletown in 1891, "O Morning Land of College Days" (pp. 67-68) has been sung, lustily and loyally, by generations of Wesleyan students, none more devoted than Frank Mason North.

For over a decade the poet's pen lay still. Perhaps the pressures of a new administrative job were too great. Perhaps the faith and fire were being poured so unreservedly into addresses and articles and sermons that little leisure remained for the contemplative task of poetry. Then Caleb T. Winchester, professor of English literature at Wesleyan University and one of the editors of the revised Methodist hymnal (1905), challenged North to write a missionary hymn. It was not a new idea. In 1897 an anonymous writer—presumably Frank Mason North—had commented wistfully:

Professor George Adam Smith finds in hymn collections no hymn referring to city missions at all comparable with "Greenland's Icy Mountains" on foreign missions. It is quite true. Perhaps the subject is too nearby and sordid for verse. Heber wrote his famous hymn without having seen Greenland, and several years before he reached Calcutta. Our chief hope for a great city missionary hymn is in some hillside poet who knows his theme only from a safe distance.[6]

[5] Eric M. North, memorandum, September 22, 1965, p. 10.
[6] "Side Lights," *The Christian City*, July, 1897.

No "hillside poet" responded to the summons; no Christian spokesman knew the city better than Frank Mason North. Under Winchester's urging, North admitted, "I wrote what was in my thought and feeling." The result was "A Prayer for the Multitudes" (pp. 85-86), first published in *The Christian City* in June, 1903. The old Methodist Building at 150 Fifth Avenue, which housed both the New York City Society and the Board of Foreign Missions, stood only three blocks from the bustling thoroughfare of 23rd Street, in those days more nearly the center of the city than 42nd Street is today. "Where cross the crowded ways of life" more visibly than at that corner in 1903? "Where sound the cries of race and clan" more audibly? Years later North told an interviewer that he kept asking himself two questions, out of the acute problems of city mission work: "What is the Lord going to do with all these people? What is the Lord going to do to us if we don't do something for them?"

Some of the verses came with a flash and needed no reworking. Others his wife, sensitive and artistic herself, discussed and criticized and helped develop. Many of the ideas and phrases had been employed in previous speeches and sermons. A decade earlier North had written of the "surging crowds of our great cities." In an article on the "Forward Movement in Cities" he had explained the movement as an instrument through which Christ's disciples "will catch the meaning of his tears and move forward to find for him the wayward children of Jerusalem." [7]

Among the notes and jottings now bound and preserved in the library of Drew University may be found six full versions of "The City Hymn" in the process of composition, and nine scraps of couplets or partial stanzas. For example:

Above the noise of busy (human) strife,
Above the clash of race (tribe) and clan,
Where crowds the wretchedness of life,
We hear Thy voice, O son of Man.

Where cross the (weary) ways of weary feet
(On helpless, hopeless thresholds thronged),

[7] *Northern Christian Advocate*, December 20, 1893.

"WITH MINSTREL HEART"

Where throng the shadows of our fears
    (Where throng the feet of vice and greed),
Where sin and sorrow hopeless meet,
We catch the vision of Thy tears.

The helpless poor, the child of want,
    (For tender childhood's outstretched hands)
The man of ill requited toil,
    (For beggared blindness, burdened toil)
The wasted soul, the beggar gaunt,
From these Thou never didst recoil.

Today and yesterday the same
The multitudes Thy heart still move
    (Thou canst our wretchedness remove);
The cup of water in Thy name
Still holds the freshness of Thy love.

Send comfort to the comfortless,
    (For in each wronged and sullen heart)
Let healing come to hearts of pain
    (Where toil is honest and in vain);
Thy messengers of gladness bless
And tread the city streets again.

O Son of Man, we hear Thy voice
In hush of heart, in public ways;
We make Thy ministry our choice
And consecrate to Thee our days.

This intimate glimpse of the poetic mind and heart at work gives added value to the finished product. No wonder Bishop Newell could say at the memorial service: "To be introduced to his poetry is to find that thing which will live after his records as minister and secretary have passed away. Into them he put the things we did not see about him." [8]

For purists, musical or political, the setting of North's most famous hymn has posed some problems. North himself had tried *Linwood* (No. 496 in the 1905 hymnal), *Welton* (No. 322, 1905)

[8] *Frank Mason North*, p. 58.

and *Ernan* (No. 292 in the 1935 hymnal) before he settled on *Germany.* When the "slightly eccentric" William Gardiner included the tune in his 1815 collection, he remarked of its origin: "It is somewhere in the works of Beethoven, but where I cannot point out." [9] No other musicians or historians have been able to locate it either, although *The Methodist Hymnal* of 1905 trustingly attributes it to Ludwig von Beethoven. In the midst of World War I a correspondent from Illinois suggested in the *Christian Advocate* that the designation of the tune as *Germany* created an unfavorable reaction among some congregations and should therefore be changed. The alternatives proposed were *Beethoven* (of dubious accuracy as indicated above) or *Belgium*— on the ground that Beethoven's grandfather had been born in Belgium and that North's stirring words fitted appropriately the bleeding condition of wartime Belgium.[10] Of North's reaction to such prejudice we have no record.

Too late North discovered one flaw in the use of his popular poem as a congregational hymn. The last two stanzas comprise a single sentence, and the verbs fall in the fifth rather than the sixth. Thus, when pastors call impatiently for "the first three and the last stanza" or some similar combination, they are singing an amputated verse with neither subject nor predicate. This practice used to make North furious, and, though he sometimes remarked disgustedly that he should have known better than to write the poem that way, he did think people could sing the first two and the last two stanzas if they had to cut. At least that would make some sense and, even more important, would include the true subject of the hymn, the Master himself.

Despite this minor handicap, praise continued to shower upon the poem and its social significance. Says Edward S. Ninde in *The Story of the American Hymn:* "Nothing in the hymnody of the Christian Church voices more appealingly the yearning of the Master after the thronging multitudes and the human response to that yearning, nothing more truly expresses the ardent spirit of social service which is animating the church in this new age than

[9] "Hymn of the Month," *Together,* February, 1964, p. 60; cf. photo feature, *Together,* October, 1962, pp. 36-44.
[10] August 22, 1918, p. 1066.

these noble stanzas." [11] An undated clipping about 1921 remarks, somewhat ambiguously:

During the sixteen years in which the Methodist Hymnal has been in use, one hymn has risen and grown and become greatly beloved as probably no other in the collection. We refer to No. 423, "Where cross the crowded ways of life." It is the hymn of the city, and with the increasing trend of massed city life, hymn makers should, like Jesus, keep their eyes on the multitude. It is the hymn of brotherhood, and never was there more insistent demand for this. It is the hymn of social unrest, on which we are at present fed up [?]. It is the hymn of womanhood and childhood, who, in the days gone by, had all too little consideration.

To all these tributes and many more Frank Mason North remained characteristically modest. W. C. Barclay recalls that the author described the poem's popularity and translation into many tongues as "significant not as to the quality of the hymn itself but as to the fact that it is an expression of that tremendous movement of the soul of the gospel in our times which demands that the follower of Christ must make the interests of the people his own and must find the heart of the world's need if he is in any real way to represent his Master among men." Halford Luccock, that winsome exponent of the gospel in literature, who worked intimately with North in the New York East Annual Conference and in the Board of Foreign Missions, has spoken of the "great social awakening and literary expression in the United States [at that time as] the most promising thing in America in a hundred years." [12] Specifically he cited the first publication of Rauschenbusch, the poetry of Harriet Munro, Vachel Lindsay, and Carl Sandburg. "The fiddles are tuning up all over America," he quoted an unknown source. In 1916 North himself commented: "I have written other verses, some of them unpublished and most of them unremembered. Perhaps these ["The City Hymn"] were more received because they came at a time when the growing social consciousness of the church felt the need for some such expression."

[11] (New York: The Abingdon Press, 1921), p. 383.
[12] Letter to the author, June 17, 1958.

Most Christians would acclaim some quality more profound and more lasting than a mood of history. "A Prayer for the Multitudes" sketches the tragedy of the city in words as vivid as they are concise. More than that, it puts the priority and the power with the Son of man, the responsibility with the sons of men to learn his love. Despite some critics of the social gospel, this hymn affirms in unmistakable claims that the City of God is not built by men, but it will come from above only when they have followed in the steps of the Master. In later years North said simply: "This hymn has but one mission in the world, and that is to help men of all races and conditions better to understand the person and meaning of Jesus Christ." [13]

Again more than a decade elapsed before Frank Mason North composed another poem deemed worthy of subsequent printing. He himself has commented: "Through the years I had written much, even occasional verses, but no hymn for fourteen years." [14] Then, in 1917, in the midst of World War I and the burdens of the Federal Council of Churches, came "The Students' Hymn" (pp. 111-12) and the "Commemoration Hymn" (pp. 127-28) for the semi-centennial of Drew Theological Seminary.

The latter was one of North's "occasional verses" composed on request. When he replied to President Squiers' invitation to speak at the centennial observance (Why ask "an old humdrum like me"?), he enclosed a copy of "Thou Lord of Light," written "one mid-August Sunday afternoon (August 9, 1917). But in one of the very rare letters signed "Mason" he said of the seven short stanzas: "I beg you not to feel that they need to be used." [15] Yet the hymn shines with the same balanced perspective, the same joyous confidence, that mark his finest poetry. There is the tribute to Christian teachers for whom "the subject of their deepest thought" (later changed to "the theme of their profoundest thought") was the Lord of Light, the Master Guide. There is the awareness of Drew alumni, "who gird the world with flame." And there is the forward-looking faith that "Thy truth must stand

[13] Cynthia Pearl Maus, *Christ and the Fine Arts* (New York: Harper & Brothers, 1938), p. 739.
[14] Robert Guy McCutchan, *Our Hymnody* (Nashville: Abingdon Press, 1937), p. 532.
[15] September 9, 1917 (Drew Library archives).

where it has stood; new darkness waits its deathless rays" (as the original version ran). Here was a minstrel approaching his allotted three-score-years-and-ten, yet singing in the midst of new world darkness about "the outlook broad . . . the faith that burns."

"The Students' Hymn" (pp. 111-12) ("The world's astir!") is better known because it found a place in the 1935 *Hymnal*. North recounts that Dr. Abram W. Harris, corresponding secretary of the Board of Education, had asked him to compose a "Children's Day" hymn for young people. When North was pastor in Middletown, Harris had been an instructor at Wesleyan (note again the "old school" ties) and "my delightful Sunday School Superintendent." Even deeper and earlier lay the memory that Charles Carter North had helped initiate Children's Day in 1866. So once more, while war rocked the world, Charles North's son assured youth then and far into the future that "the clouds of storm have melted into light, . . . now brightens dawn toward golden day; the earth is full of song."

The third hymn included in *The Methodist Hymnal*, 1935 was composed in late 1927 as "The Waking World" (pp. 213-14), but it had two similar predecessors which North preserved independently: "The Shadowed Lands" (pp. 147-48) for the Missionary Centenary of 1919, and "A Missionary Commission Hymn" (pp. 169-70) for the Woman's Foreign Missionary Society in 1925. The first of these had one line of particular interest which North later changed. Stanza two originally began: "We hear far down the future's widening way." North himself must have realized, or someone pointed out to him, its close parallel to a much older phrase by his friend and colleague and social gospel preacher, Washington Gladden, written back in 1879: "In Truth that sends a shining ray Far down the future's broadening way." In any event, North's final version reads: "We hear from lands in tumult far away."

Again, with "The Waking World," Frank Mason North was responding to a personal appeal from a friend. Dr. Henry H. Meyer wanted to provide a "world service emphasis" for *The Church School Journal* (January, 1928). North's comment was typical:

My unrelenting interest in the Missionary Movement refused to let me excuse myself. I was in constant touch with men and women who were giving their lives to the "work of missions,"—who was I, that I should not at least try to put into verse what was in their hearts, and mine, and, if the verse could be sung, so much the better. The task was not simple; this hymn was the result.[16]

Frank Mason North had relative leisure by this time in his life, but he was seventy-seven years old, an age when few men are still writing great poetry. That same year of 1927 also produced "O Wondrous Child" (pp. 231-32), a Christmas hymn published on the cover of the *Christian Advocate* for January 5, 1928, almost simultaneously with "The Waking World." It is said that at a 1926 Christmas party for office workers in the Board of Foreign Missions (which North still attended after his retirement), Bishop L. B. Wilson challenged him to write a hymn for foreign missions. Perhaps both poems grew from the same episode, but it was "O Wondrous Child" which was sung at the succeeding party on December 23, 1927, to the tune *St. Petersburg* (by Bortniansky).

The previous year North had composed "Francis Asbury" (pp. 187-88) for the unveiling of the Asbury statue in Drew Forest. It was a narrowly topical poem, and yet it employed a different verse form with the same smooth precision of his earlier work. Some of the phrases and themes were familiar: "the challenges which stir men's fear . . . the kindling glory . . . the lonely ways, the brooding thought . . . set faith and hope aflame!" But the spirit of the man in his last decade can be found in a profoundly characteristic note. Like most of the others, the poem moves from description to commitment to challenge, a progression made conspicuous here by three adjectives: "the sinking heart . . . the singing heart . . . the burning heart."

The latest of the poems collected and printed by North was "Wesleyan University, 1831-1931" (pp. 249-50), a prayer for the centennial of the college. It is more traditional, more pedestrian in language and form than some of the others, but it follows the pattern of retrospect and prospect. At eighty the poet declares:

---

[16] McCutchan, *Our Hymnody*, p. 466.

"Another century meets our sight; Oh, lead us still, Thou Lord of light."

But this was not Frank Mason North's last published verse. In 1932 the Methodist Episcopal Church celebrated the centennial of its first foreign missionary, Melville B. Cox, who sailed from Norfolk, Virginia, on November 1, 1832, and died in Liberia on July 21, 1833. Thomas Donohugh, then executive secretary for Africa in the Board of Missions, asked Frank Mason North to compose an "Anniversary Hymn" (pp. 269-70), which was sung at the General Conference on May 8, 1932, and at the Norfolk Centennial Celebration in November [17] (to the tune of *St. Catherine*). As poetry, these verses repeated a common meter and somewhat trite phrases: "we honor here . . . down the century . . . grant us the power . . . to show the glory of the Cross. . . . the isles are waiting evermore . . . a restless age . . . thy halting Church inspire." In its printed form it contained several typographical errors, notably the mistaken capitalizing of "his" when referring to Cox rather than God or Christ.

But as a testament of faith, by a missionary statesman in his eighty-second year, this hymn shares with others a common grandeur. Still the familiar metaphor of the kindled flame, still the invariable shift from historic past to future challenge. In a very real sense, what the old poet wrote about the young missionary applied supremely to his own career: his radiant faith, his sacrifice, "his ardent zeal to tell abroad the grace of Christ, the love of God." Truly his narrow stretch of metropolitan shore had widened to a hundred lands—and his denominational witness had contributed directly to the ecumenical movement. But most of all, perhaps, his devotion and his creative gifts had helped "the halting Church inspire with life and love, with faith—with fire."

A year later Charles F. Eggleston, chairman of the Methodist Episcopal Commission on Sesquicentennial Celebration of Organization of Methodist Episcopal Church [sic], wrote North about plans for a historical pageant, a musical festival, and other churchwide observances. "Naturally the program would not be

[17] "Carry Christ to Africa" (Norfolk: Committee on Historical Pamphlet, 1932), p. 29; cf. Thomas Donohugh, personal letter to the author, July 21, 1958.

complete without a commemorative hymn," he said, "and we are turning to you as the one most capable to bless us with a spiritual hymn message." [18] Apparently in his reply North suggested several possibilities, for Eggleston agreed that an ode "would give a far better chance to commemorate some of the stirring events and also some of the names of our early leaders . . . Asbury, Lee, Garrettson, and the other founders of our Church." [19]

Apparently, also, North stipulated that he must have time "to mull over the theme, . . . to let it germinate," and that until the muse inspired a satisfactory composition no publicity should be given to his assignment.[20] When the sesquicentennial poem was finished, however, it made no explicit reference to the heroes of early Methodism. Textual critics may deplore the overworked form and language, the tired reference to "some stalwart souls," the strained imagery of bowed and kneeling spirits. They will recognize in this last published verse the familiar metaphor of "the sacred flame." Yet as Methodism commences its third century in America, every Conference would do well to ask the poet's rhetorical questions and offer the poet's commemorative prayer:

> Within their counsels can there be
> A world-wide Church's destiny?
> Will here they make a valid plan
> To search the world for every man?
> They did their part! God grant that we
> May now fulfil their prophecy! [21]

This, then, was Frank Mason North, the poet. Less than three months before his death, he wrote to the editor of *Our Hymnody,* "I am not a hymn writer, as that term is ordinarily used." One wonders what criteria he would "ordinarily" apply: sheer quantity, the composition of music as well as verse, stereotype language? When an interviewer in 1916 suggested that to have written "Where Cross the Crowded Ways of Life" was a greater honor

[18] Letter to F. M. North, March 7, 1933 (in North files).
[19] Letter to F. M. North, March 30, 1933 (in North files).
[20] Charles F. Eggleston, letter to F. M. North, April 24, 1933 (in North files).
[21] "The Christmas Conference, 1784," *Zion's Herald,* September 26, 1934, p. 913.

than being president of the Federal Council of Churches, North agreed simply: "I would rather be the author of a hymn that lives than to be the holder of any official position. A hymn may have an influence that goes on and on."

Halford Luccock has expressed the same feeling in a far more intimate recollection of North:

One day he said to me in a wondering and somewhat wistful tone, that it was strange. He said, "I have lived a long and active life of many things as pastor, secretary of City Mission work in the greatest city in the world, director of Foreign Missions all over the earth, and I will be remembered for only what I did one afternoon in all the 50 years of my working life, that is writing a few lines of a poem 'Where Cross the Crowded Ways of Life.' " [22]

In truth, the people called Methodists may not know who led the New York City Church Extension and Missionary Society, or the National City Evangelization Union, or the Board of Foreign Missions. Christians in America may forget who introduced the Social Creed of the Churches or who guided the Federal Council through its formative and its critical war years. But the people of God will continue to sing the inspired words of Frank Mason North:

> O Master, from the mountain side
> Make haste to heal these hearts of pain;
> Among these restless throngs abide,
> O tread the city's streets again;
>
> Till sons of men shall learn Thy love,
> And follow where Thy feet have trod;
> Till glorious from Thy heaven above
> Shall come the City of our God.

[22] Letter to the author, June 17, 1958.

Wesleyan University, 1831-1931

Here stand we at the century's crest;
  Shine Thou upon us, Lord of light;
Out from the ways that Thou hast blest
  New paths are broadening to our sight;
The strength for larger life we find
  In Thee alone, O Master Mind.

We thank Thee for the former days,
  For treasures which the years have brought;
Our songs of gratitude we raise
  For fellowships of life and thought,
For men with heart and spirit free
  Who, seeking truth, were seeking Thee.

With beauty Thou hast touched these walls
  Which here are lifted toward Thy skies;
Thy voice is heard within these halls,
  The guide to nature's mysteries;
Here, bringing guesses of the mind,
  Men listen, till Thy thoughts they find.

This hill of light from age to age
  Will thrill with tread of ardent youth;
Keep, Lord, unstained its heritage,
  Its love of right, its search for truth,
Its eagerness to know Thy plan
  In star, in atom, and in man.

Accept, Eternal God, our praise;
  Hear us in this, our deepest prayer:
May scholarship Thy altars raise;
  May learning serve Thee everywhere!
Another century meets our sight;
  Oh, lead us still, Thou Lord of light.

Centennial of Wesleyan University
1931

13

"The Undefeated Quest"

Accept, Eternal God, our praise;
Hear us in this, our deepest prayer:
May scholarship Thy altars raise;
May learning serve Thee everywhere!

One cannot follow the manifold ministry of Frank Mason North without finding constant evidence of the faith by which he lived. His words from the pulpit and the platform proclaimed it. His verses sang it. His tireless devotion to the restless throngs, on urban thresholds and on waiting isles, witnessed to it. It is time now to try to summarize the doctrines which were central in his work. That is no easy task, for North himself often evaded it. In its final tribute the Executive Committee of the Federal Council of Churches declared: "While Dr. North was not a systematic theologian, he knew what and whom he had believed." Tracing his faith as often through his hymns as through his sermons, the memorial added: "His theology was that of the revelation of the Father in the face of Jesus Christ." [1]

There may be at least three reasons why North was reluctant to spend much time on systematic theology. In the first place, it implied a reliance upon reason above faith, a presumptuous pretense to understand divine mysteries. "Christianity is a religion of facts," he asserted in the opening sentence of one pulpit message (December 6, 1890). But these are facts of history and of human experience. They need not be—nay, cannot be—in-

[1] *Frank Mason North*, p. 48.

251

terpreted—or turned into metaphysical riddles. In one of his earliest sermons he spoke of the manifestations of God's saving grace but confessed: "I do not propose an answer. That which is finite can not understand that which is infinite"—any more than a child can comprehend an intricate scientific experiment or a profound philosophical thought. "In everything essential to man's salvation—the great end of all revelation—He has made every-thing plain. . . . Shame on you—to spend your life and energies in quibbling over wh. may be hard to understand" (May 11, 1873).

A second reason for theological tolerance is the freedom essential to personal faith. "No man binds himself to proclaim all his private opinions, and the wise teacher discriminates between the speculative and the essential in religious thought. . . . Every man must answer to his own conscience when he finds himself pressing near, in his thinking, to the assumed limits of the creed to which he has consented." [2] Although occasionally regretting the fact that "we have not a theologian in the church whose best book would command a sale of 500 copies outside of the communion," [3] North regarded this as evidence that the basic tenets of Methodism are clear and open. "The Church is content with its statement of dogmatic truth," he asserted.

The allurements of a new theology are not felt, because a satisfactory solution of the questions in discussion enters into the very basis of the Church's belief . . . every man thinking freely and having room to think, but without that sense of irritation against an unwelcome creed which fosters intellectual rebellion, and with rebellion creates also leaders. . . . Methodism, with its doctrine of Free Grace and its appeal to *all men* to repent, was in its very beginning a sociological force.[4]

This last statement points to the third facet of North's attitude toward theological speculation; namely, that it often diverts a Christian from active service, from neighbor love. After a decade of preaching the young pastor finally approached what might be

[2] "Methodism and 'Progressive Orthodoxy'," *Christian Union*, 1890.
[3] "Who Are the Leaders?" *Zion's Herald*, May 28, 1890.
[4] "Progressive Religious Leaders: The Methodist Episcopal Church" (By a Methodist") , *Christian Union*, January 30, 1890.

labeled a "social gospel" sermon. Using the text, "who went about doing good" (Acts 10:38), he appealed for philanthropy, for a genuine alleviation of human need, for rejection of an other-worldly concept of salvation. "Neither *charity* nor *education* can do the good they might," he affirmed—with more emphatic underlining than usual—"because theology stands in the way. *The entire THEORY of the church is antagonistic to any con-centrated or consistent scheme for raising the earthly condition of the suffering masses."* It is Christ, not prayer and contempla-tion, he concluded, that will lead to any "earnest care for the present welfare of our fellowmen" (May 14, 1882).

All three of these criticisms of theological dogmatism are implicit in a paragraph from his article on "Why I Am a Meth-odist," one of his frankest and most personal testimonies, written in his seventy-sixth year. There North declared:

As a matter of fact, we suspect that most Methodists are both funda-mentalist and modernist. They are less interested in the tiltyard of controversy, than in the broad highway of service. They observe with interest the present virulent epidemic of intolerance. The liberals have it in as dangerous a form as the standpatters. The Methodist Church is largely, though not entirely, free from the infection.[5]

But Frank Mason North had a firm theological position, which he proudly affirmed on many occasions. He himself identified it as Wesleyan Arminianism. This creed, he said in 1890, "has never ceased to antagonize the Calvinism which has incurred the enmity of the thinking world by its doctrine of election and its inevitable self-contradictions about infants and the heathen." [6] Thirty-six years later he recalled that among his "pastoral friends" a Baptist (Alonzo Parker) had labeled him a "pedobaptist" and a Presbyterian (Will R. Terrett) considered him "Arminian or, worse, as he believed, a Pelagian." By that time North had come to the conclusion that Calvinism and Arminianism are "two phases of one unshaken truth," but he still reiterated his belief in human freedom by declaring that "the 'whosover' doctrine in

---

[5] P. 79.
[6] "Methodism and 'Progressive Orthodoxy'."

John 3:16 and elsewhere holds me to the Methodist Church." [7]
Many, many years earlier, while still in the pastorate, North had
reviewed a book which summed up this theological position—
convincingly for him, though he sharply criticized the author on
other grounds. It was *Systematic Theology: A Complete Body of
Wesleyan Arminian Divinity* by Thomas O. Summers, professor of
systematic theology at Vanderbilt University. North termed it—

a scheme of theology . . . originating as a distinct system in the views
of Arminius upon human freedom and the doctrines of grace . . .
rebuking, modifying, and at times conquering the prevalent ultra-
Calvinism. Its strong appeal to the tribunal of human consciousness
against the metaphysical subtleties which damned men by logic
whom God would save by mercy, won . . . a large support from the
class of thinkers who . . . were beginning to throw off the chains of
scholasticism. . . . It was in Wesleyanism that Arminianism became
practical, vital, regnant; and the living energy of Methodism . . . is
at once a magnificent protest against metaphysical misinterpretation
of the divine character, and a mighty demonstration of the Scriptural
integrity of its own Arminian creed.[8]

For this young preacher it was no shallow humanism—as is so
often alleged against the social gospel—or Arminians—or modern
Methodists. Frank Mason North possessed a strong consciousness
of man's sin and God's judgment. "Our relation to the Judge in
that day will be determined by our relation to the Redeemer
now" (August 1, 1880). But always, in his theology, there is the
open alternative, the invitation to choose. There is no damnation
without the hope of salvation, no judgment without an offer of
grace. Nor is this ever a mere bargaining point between God and
man. Always Jesus Christ stands as a Mediator, a Saviour, a
personal Friend. North would never tolerate any mechanical,
substitutionary theory of atonement, any more than he would
accept an automatic salvation by works. Frequently he emphasized
"the difference between a warm love and personal devotion to

---

[7] "Why I Am a Methodist," esp. p. 74.
[8] "Wesleyan Arminian Divinity" ("By An Arminian Divine"), *Christian Union,*
May 9, 1889.

Jesus and the severe and chilling legality that induces obedience to a law" (March 1, 1874).

Frank Mason North believed firmly and totally in justification by faith. A college paper composed in his sophomore year expressed the view that "the experience of past centuries unites with that of our own in bearing witness to the truth, that a man is far more willing to be saved by works than by faith. . . . It hurts our pride to think of *being* saved." [9] During the first year of his ministry he preached on the great verse in Galatians 2:16: "by the faith of Christ, and not by the works of the law." A mere moralist, he warned, is both dangerous and in danger, for "morality is not religion." "Religion," he concluded, "is the relation of man's soul to a person not to a law, and hence reaches not only to his actions but to his heart" (November 30, 1873). Two years later he stated bluntly: "As faith is the entrance to heaven, so is unbelief the gate to hell" (November 7, 1875). This faith, for North, meant always an intimate sense of the Living Lord. If Jesus is merely historical or merely an ideal, he asserted, then the gospel is a failure, not the power of God unto salvation. "The Resurrection of Christ is the keystone of the Gospel. . . . We need to feel that Christ is this morning an actual being—a personality as truly as you and I are, that he thinks, feels, perceives" (April 21, 1878).

What, then, constitutes salvation by faith? At the end of his first year of preaching North told his hearers that it was *not* education, intellect, or wealth; not sacraments or ecclesiastical organization; not ritualism or moralism or intellectualism or aestheticism in the church; not even "union with the Church" or a "well-regulated life." It consists of a personal union with Christ. But when he insisted in the same sermon that salvation was *entirely* dependent on Christ, he meant *necessarily* but not *solely*. He meant that Christ's role was essential but not automatic. Each individual has his responsibility for accepting and following the Master. In fact, North once asserted flatly: "He could not save us without our consent, but He could die for us and by that death prove to us the Father's love" (July 25, 1875).

<hr>

[9] "The High-Church Party," unpublished manuscript, September 23, 1869.

This theme runs constantly through the young preacher's theology as well as through his later administrative work in the city: "We are labourers together with God" (I Cor. 3:9). It is important, he reminded the congregation in his first parish, "to know relations between His power and our effort" (November 30, 1873). "Society is one vast co-operative association," he told them a few months later, but "the *plan* and the *power* are Divine" (April 26, 1874). In an even earlier sermon on the bread of life, he emphasized the fact that the Jews had to gather the manna for themselves—and had to do it every day—even though it came as a gift from God (May 25, 1873). Likewise also in the New Testament Christ stands at the door and knocks; he does not compel. "To you who are waiting for some irresistible influence to carry you into the Kingdom," North warned, "it will never come" (November 21, 1875).

Thus did the young Methodist repeatedly affirm his opposition to any Calvinistic doctrine of predestination. "Men are fully responsible for their treatment of God's gracious offer," he quoted in a commentary on revision of the Presbyterian Creed, asserting "that his decree hinders no man from accepting that offer; and that no man is condemned except on the ground of his sin." [10]

Even in the intimate realm of prayer this element of human freedom appeared to North as absolutely essential. Clearly, in his judgment, if petition was to have any meaning or any reality other than self-hypnosis, it must reject the notion of completely foreordained order in the universe. "We are thankful," he said during his first year of preaching, "that not holding the uncomfortable doctrine of predestination we are not obliged to reconcile it with our belief in prayer." Some things must be considered open to the free working of a personal God rather than a mechanical providence. The general plan of salvation has been predetermined, yes; but *who* will accept it, no (November 16, 1873).

Although men are free, according to North's theology, to reject God's love, it seemed almost incredible to him that they should do so. The glory of the gospel, the appeal of Jesus Christ,

[10] "A Crisis and a Victory" (by "Grapho"), *Western Christian Advocate,* May 28, 1902, p. 7.

was throughout his long life a radiant reality. Preaching on the simple words from Mark 7:24 ("he could not be hid"), Frank Mason North poured forth his full fervor of assurance: "Walk if you choose in your own shadow. Hide yourselves—you cannot hide the Sun. Burrow into your rocky caves—the Sun is no less shining. Hurry into your idol temples and peer through the stained windows of your superstition—and yet—the Sun is risen" (May 11, 1879).

If Jesus Christ is a living, active, present companion for Frank Mason North, so, too, is the Holy Spirit. "When we think of the Holy Ghost as a mere pervading influence," he insisted, "as a manifestation—a mode of action—a Something impersonal and indefinite—we dishonor him as terribly as we dishonor Christ by making him nothing but a historical character—without Divinity" (October 31, 1875). But the Holy Spirit has a more positive role:

Educate the nation; and we shall have good government—multiply schools and colleges—improve our methods—use every effort to bring the race up to the higher grades of intelligence, increased intelligence will bring in its train greater self-respect—morality will follow—and as a result of intelligence and morality—good laws and great prosperity will come. Yes—this is true—may God speed the day— But in all these plans one element and that the greatest is entirely ignored— and that is the power of the Spirit of the Almighty God. Intelligence and morality do not constitute religion (March, 1873).

If Frank Mason North believed firmly in justification by faith, he was equally convinced that faith without works is dead. "Conversions which still leave men liars, cheats, covetous, worldly-minded are not counted in the Kingdom of God," he wrote in *The Christian City*. In fact, he went on to say: "The moment the processes of preparation are in themselves reckoned to be that manifestation of the Spirit which alone is 'revival,' the false note is struck, and ignorant presumption has destroyed what humble faith might have carried to a glorious completion." [11]

On the other hand, while the Holy Spirit may be prematurely or hypocritically claimed by some Christians, he can also be found

[11] September, 1899, p. 146.

at work in quite unexpected places, in quite unregenerate persons. "In many we find great kindness, generosities, a lofty ideal of integrity, adherence to truth, and abhorrence of that which is vile or mean. Whence are these virtues?" North had no hesitation in affirming his answer—though he was just barely twenty-four years old at the time. "They are to be ascribed to the Holy Spirit, granted to man through the atonement. Hence even these unconverted men who seem upright and good are not so of themselves naturally—but of the grace of God" (January 24, 1875). If this appears to be a rejection of "natural religion," it is at the same time an extension of the Holy Spirit and the atonement. In fact, six years later North deplored the separation of faith and reason and spoke of Christ as revealer of—and revealed by—the Bible *and* nature. "We need a Christian Revival of Natural Religion," he declared (April 11, 1881).

Still more surprisingly, from his very first year in the pulpit, he professed to find this wider activity of the Holy Spirit among non-Christian faiths. He did say, to be sure, that before Christ mankind (with the noteworthy exception of the Jews) had "no knowledge of the true God, no moral restraint upon passion and no legal, no respect for human life, no anticipation of the future" (December 20, 1874). But the year before, significantly in a sermon on prayer, he had traced the instinct toward God in natural religion, *supplemented* in revealed religion, through the Greeks and Egyptians, through the fire-worship of Persia, Juggernauts and throwing babies to the crocodiles in India, "revolving machines" in China, through Patagonia and Africa, and among the "Esquimaux." "In every heart," North concluded, "is manifest this instinct of worship," and it is "planted there by the hand of Him who hath made us" (October 12, 1873). On another occasion he illustrated the same point with the story of Paul's shipwreck on Melita (Malta), where "the barbarous people shewed us no little kindness" (Acts 28:2). This hospitality, according to North, shows "one of the traces of the Creator's hand upon the character even of unenlightened and unChristianized men." Furthermore, in spite of their ignorance and fear, their pagan generosity "finds its true basis and its real manifestation under the influence of God's revealed truth" (December 9, 1877).

258

Clearly this theological position reflects a Christology vastly more far-reaching than the simple, human "Jesus of Nazareth" emphasis usually attributed to the social gospel. In fact, at a time when most missionaries were denouncing the idolatry and superstition of other faiths, Frank Mason North—how little dreaming of his own future administrative role!—anticipated the concept of "the Christian Presence" in non-Christian nations. "Here the Christ ideal must be an unconscious one," he admitted, "for they have never heard of Him. But when He is preached He at once fixes upon Himself their demand for perfect character and meets it." In this fulfillment and this assurance—rather than through intolerant denunciation—heathen races will find in Christ "not only the perfection that condemns our sin, but the power that saves us from sin" (November 6, 1881). A decade later North expressed his conviction that "salvation means character, and that character means freedom of moral choice, and that thus, in some way, Christ is the Saviour of all who are saved, whether they have ever heard of him in this life or not, and that it is in the nature of God to deal with every soul both righteously and mercifully." [12]

At the same time, however, North frequently voiced the optimistic confidence in progress and the relationship of Christianity to Western civilization, for which the social gospel has been subsequently condemned. In one of his earliest sermons, for example, he declared dogmatically:

Now here is a wondrous fact—and facts are undeniable. Wherever Christianity has gone ignorance has given place to intelligence and superstition has yielded to the power of faith. . . . [And if one argues that civilization would have come to these lands anyway?] . . . Ah! but you forget that there is no civilization without Christianity. They must go together. . . . Every good seed has been warmed into life—every healthful influence has been quickened—and the result is manifested in the relative state of morals in the world now compared with ages ago—when Christ's influence was not felt (May 25, 1873).

Or again, nine years later: The spirit of Christ "has stirred the benevolence of men, has unlocked the hidden powers of the mind, lifted the burden from the wretched, opened the coffers

[12] "Methodism and 'Progressive Orthodoxy'."

of the rich, steadied the hand of the surgeon, and inspired the genius of the philosopher" (May 14, 1882).

This certainty of human progress is to be found in many realms. On the subject of missions, North asked rhetorically: Is the world growing worse? "Not a bit of it," he answered, there has been "not only a steady gain but a cumulative gain" (March 12, 1882). But this blithe optimism so characteristic of most social-gospel writers applies particularly to nationalism and democracy. The patriotic pride of Frank Mason North shines almost as brightly as his Christian faith. On Thanksgiving Days and the first Sunday of each July it becomes positively dazzling. In 1874 he declared: "It is sufficiently plain that there has been a steady though gradual progression from bad to good. . . . The tendency has never been from the freer forms to the more despotic."

Yet this open vista of the future applies not only to America but to the world, not only to national life but to individual character. Speaking on "What the Young Man of Today Should Be," North challenged youth exultantly: "The Christian is *in life*—he feels its currents. He sails the seas—as well as studies charts. His business now is not to illuminate missals but to enlighten men. Christian character now is . . . robust, aggressive, stirring . . . frank, brave, fresh in heart, earnest in action, a life in the sunlight." Then, after references to Dwight L. Moody, Henry Drummond, and the Y.M.C.A., he concluded confidently: "The day has already dawned when Christ shall sway the destinies of men by the conquest of the world's youth" (November 13, 1887).

In the certainty, in the language, in the very dream itself, there is a naïveté which provokes smiles—or tears—or both. The horrors of two world wars and other carnage, the growing awareness of man's inhumanity to man, the alleged irrelevance of religion to modern morality—all these have called into question the optimism of the nineteenth century. Frank Mason North was a man of his times and a man of God. He remained both of these—even as those times changed so dramatically from 1850 to 1935. And even as his colleagues recognized in his very life the watchword of progress, so his theological vision ever faced toward the future.

Within the first few months of his ministry North proclaimed his forward look: "That which kept them yesterday does not answer for today—that which keeps them today will not serve them tomorrow" (May 25, 1873). Twenty-five years later he wrote in an editorial: "The response of the human mind is not to the venerable, but to the true; not to the traditional, but to the Divine." [13] Frank Mason North was never bound by the venerable and the traditional; he was always open to the true and the Divine.

In fact, in his semi-centennial address for the New York East Annual Conference, marking fifty years in the Methodist ministry, North reaffirmed his unfaltering emphasis upon the essentials of belief: "The sufficiency of the word of God, the Fatherhood of God, the brotherhood of man, the call and capacity of Love to conquer the world, the abiding presence of the Holy Spirit in human hearts, the measure of spiritual achievement by conduct, the supremacy of a Divine Christ." But in the very next paragraph he stressed the necessity for "adjustment of the machinery of the craft [and] greater anxiety that the seamen should not neglect the stars nor fail to take daily observations by the Sun." [14]

In the progressive outlook of Frank Mason North there was never a conflict between science and religion—not between true science and true religion. "Science is good," he affirmed at the outset of his ministry, "when used to illustrate the truth of revelation" (May 25, 1873). Repeatedly he utilized his own knowledge of science—and continuous study of contemporary developments—to undergird his proclamation of eternal truth. As the solar spectrum brings to man illumination, heat, and transforming chemical power (e.g., the daguerreotype!), he said, so the gospel comes to man in darkness and brings light and life and change ("a divine alchemy") (May 25, 1873). Thus, scientific discoveries did not threaten North or his basic beliefs. Reporting an address at the Second Ecumenical Methodist Conference in 1891, he wrote: "The truth of evolution was in the paper assumed, and its effect upon the fundamental doctrines of the Christian faith—as God, sin, free will, the fall of man, immortality, and the

[13] *The Christian City*, November, 1898, p. 682.
[14] April 12, 1923 (unpublished manuscript), p. 5.

person of Christ—indicated. The writer's conclusions and intimations are unwelcome to many." [15] There was no indication whatever, here or elsewhere, that such "conclusions and intimations are unwelcome" to North himself.

What did offend the young cleric was any attempt to displace religion by science. In an early sermon on prayer (November 16, 1873) he spoke of the regularity of nature as not just a machine, but an activity of God in which he can "interfere." In particular, he explained, atmospheric laws (for example) are methods, not causes, of weather; and in general, it is God who is sovereign, not natural law (November 16, 1873).

Nevertheless, North could lash out at "brutalizing materialism in unlawful wedlock with pseudo-science" whenever he felt that "infidel science and neo-materialist philosophy" were seeking to obscure God. Whatever future scientific research might reveal, the young New York pastor was sublimely confident that it need not and would not jeopardize Christian truth. "Philosophy can hew no tomb which can hold the Son of God," he declared; "Science can roll no stone against the sepulchre large enough to keep Him prisoner" (May 11, 1879).

So also, in relation to the church and the pulpit, North was concerned to keep science and culture and the secular world in proper perspective. In a hard-hitting discussion of the ministry based on II Corinthians 4:5 ("We preach not ourselves, but Christ Jesus the Lord"), he condemned efforts to be "abreast of the times," to turn pulpits into "lecture platforms" or "stages for mountebanks." Clergymen are *not* primarily, he insisted, priests, ethical teachers, or social regulators. Worshipers come not to hear "a lecture on London" or "a tirade against ecclesiastical thumbscrews," but "the gospel—simple—pure—direct." Preachers are not hired to give "in a half hour all they know about science . . . theories of art and the influence of architecture . . . [or] wonderful displays of oratory." On the other hand—and here North displays his typical balance, his understanding of both sides of an issue—every effective minister must know not only the human heart, but also philosophy and science, "the world to

[15] *Christian Union*, October, 1891.

whom the message is sent." "There is no part of history or science or art," he conceded, "which has not a bearing more or less direct upon the Gospel which we preach" (June 11, 1876).

Preserving this precarious balance between timeless truth and timely relevance remains a central problem for preachers today. In 1881 Frank Mason North asserted: "No generation has seen the world and the church in such close proximity as ours" (September 11, 1881). One wonders not only what he would say today, but how he would have qualified that statement fifty years later within his own lifetime. Even earlier he had recognized the threats of conformity and compromise. "Would we save the world? We must meet it half way," he suggested. Then he answered himself emphatically: "Here is one of the most dangerous half-truths now in vogue. The seeds of destruction are in it." Activity and energy—what the modern age would call "involvement"—without purpose will be fatal, North said in the first of three sermons on Ezekiel's valley of dry bones (September 26, 1875).

Clearly, Frank Mason North believed in the separation of church and state. "The Church—as an organization—should be entirely distinct from the government of the state," he declared one Sunday evening (July 7, 1878). "But," he hastened to add, "individual Christians have a most important relation to civil order." One may legitimately question the consistency of the ecumenical statesman who, many years later, welcomed the association of political leaders in urban reform and church federation, or put himself and the Federal Council of Churches at the service of the government during World War I. Perhaps—as was charged of many churchmen at that time—sheer patriotism took precedence over principle. Perhaps—with many followers of the social gospel—he equated the cause of democracy with the will of God and thus saw no conflict. Perhaps he had changed his position nearly forty years after his youthful sermon.

This writer is inclined to believe that the explanation lies in North's own distinction between the church and individual Christians, and that—furthermore—the line of separation was never intended to be a rigid barrier. When war broke out, the focus of Federal Council concern was threefold: closer communion with

Christ in a time of peril, service to men in the armed forces, and support of morale and moral fiber in the nation. To these were added later the relief measures for war-torn areas and appeals for peace. Even the Council's endorsement of the League of Nations was presented in terms of general aims rather than detailed blueprint.

To the question as to whether North would approve of church lobbies, pressure movements, study conferences, and political resolutions, some clear answers emerge. Over against his sincere commitment to separation of church and state and his determination to keep the pulpit free from strictly secular affairs, can be put his conviction that the church is a bearer of education and morality and that these are essential ingredients for a functioning democracy. "I do not want a national church," he once said, "but I do want a national Christianity" (November 26, 1874). In other words, he did want to see the standards, the values, the attitudes of the gospel permeated throughout society. More specifically, however, he wrote in 1898: "It is a function of Christianity to stimulate the commonwealth to undertake that which belongs to the common weal. . . . It is neither socialism nor paternalism for the Christian body to demand of government just provision for the physical and social welfare of the people whom, in God's name, it governs." [16]

On one other issue of contemporary involvement North's early position is very explicit. In addition to working for good laws and voting (even in primaries) for good Christian men, the individual follower of Christ had one further obligation to civil order:

He must obey the laws even though they seem to him inexpedient—unless such obedience would be a violation of conscience. Then he must—until the law is changed—submit to the inconveniences and penalties of his enforced violation of law. Thus the most obedient citizen should be found in the Christian Church (July 7, 1878).

Despite North's commitment to social justice and human brotherhood, one may assume—from his restraining influence in the

[16] *The Christian City*, October, 1898, p. 650.

Methodist Federation for Social Service, for example—that this would still be his attitude toward so-called civil disobedience.

In any theological summary covering the social gospel period, one cannot omit the subject of biblical criticism. At a time when the derogatory label of "modernist" was freely applied—even to those who preached Christ crucified, salvation by faith, and the Second Coming—the literal interpretation of Scriptures proved often to be the decisive criterion. Frank Mason North appeared to be just as progressive as he was on such doctrines as evolution, but far more forthright in affirming his views. In his first year of preaching he referred to "the author of the Epistle to the Hebrews—whoever he may be—" although the King James Version still attributed that book to Paul (August 17, 1873).

Immediately when the English Revised Version (1881-85) first appeared in the United States, North took the occasion to preach on it, to correct "the misapprehensions of this whole matter and the false inferences that many . . . will draw from it" (May 29, 1881). He reminded his congregation that the new translation followed successive revisions of Wycliff, Tyndall, the Geneva Bible, the Douay, and others, and that "not one of the four most ancient mss. now in our possession was known to the King James translators." "It would be folly to assert that we have in it [the King James Version]," he declared, "more than the best translation that the Biblical Study of the originals could afford in the beginning of the 17th century." As for the new revision, North gave this assurance to allay the prevalent anxieties of many earnest Christians:

No great doctrine has been touched—nothing in any way essential to Salvation has been left out—the Bible as it has entered into the hearts of the masses for these centuries is the same Bible. . . . The scheme of salvation is untouched by the latest criticism. . . . [It should be received as] not a new Bible nor a rival of the old . . . [but as] an incentive to study . . . [and a] testimony to the power of God to preserve His truth. . . . We place this version side by side with the one so familiar and trust it.

This openness to biblical criticism involved no reservations in North's own reliance on scriptural authority. Obliquely refuting

265

some of Robert Green Ingersoll's atheistic lectures, he offered "Some Reasons for Believing in the Bible"—which he called not only a Good Book but God's Book. In this sermon (March 2, 1890) North avowed: "I accept it as a supernatural book—supernatural in the truth taught and supernatural in its origin." This did not, for him, nullify the freedom to examine its God-given text with historical and scientific methods, any more than it nullified the Christian's obligation to interpret its significance in modern and practical terms. What did distress him greatly were the attacks on distinguished churchmen because of the new biblical scholarship. These must have reached a peak in 1899, for three issues of *The Christian City* that year included references to this kind of denunciation.

The friends of the Bible will not need to be greatly troubled because such men as James M. Buckley, John J. Reed, Joseph Pullman, S. Parkes Cadman and Bradford P. Raymond discuss questions of origin, authorship, the canon and inspiration. These are not firebrand critics. . . . They are known as ardent defenders of the truth and as vigorous preachers of the evangelical type, differing in temperament and method, but one in love of the Christ and of the Word which declares Him . . . . From such men we want not less but more utterances concerning great truths.[17]

Two months later North deplored the use by certain evangelists of the slogan "Anti-Higher Criticism" as a rallying cry. "Telling of Christ is far better than telling about His critics," he commented curtly.[18] But in another two months the editor felt it necessary to deal with the opposition even more fully.

When men reject the doctrines of sin, of personal regeneration by the Holy Spirit, of atonement in Christ through faith and the resurrection of our Lord from the dead, they cease to be preachers of the Gospel. When men intelligently and with profound conviction hold these things to be the truth, and declare them with unction, authority and effect, they are not to be classed among the deniers of the faith once delivered to the saints because they are also giving earnest and even

[17] March-April, 1899.
[18] "Sidelights," *The Christian City*, June, 1899.

critical attention to the foundations in history and in literature of the records which contain the truth they hold. The time is not distant when the attempt to divorce the best scholarship from the most ardent evangelism will be condemned in the high court of Christian opinion.[19]

Here, as elsewhere, one of North's major concerns was that such internecine debate within Christian ranks inevitably threatened the true function of the church; namely, witness to Jesus Christ through deeds of compassion and regeneration. In an article on "New Areas for Service" he wrote: "Probably the real explanation for a certain lack of spiritual energy in the American churches during the past two decades is to be found, not in a criticism which is supposed to undermine the foundations of belief, but in an ecclesiastical complacency which ignores the wider ranges of the purpose of Christ in the Gospel." [20]

Probably the entire scope of North's theological perspective is best revealed in the following passage on the mission of Christ. It appeared in a speech before the Itinerants' Club in Buffalo, New York, May 4, 1894, and in various subsequent sermons. If this is popular preaching rather than systematic theology, it nevertheless indicates unmistakably both the ground and the goal of Frank Mason North's Christian faith.

If the mission of Jesus was the satisfaction of the outraged justice of God, then Calvary was the completion of his service, and the trend of the almighty design is not toward human need but toward divine perfection.

If the mission of Jesus . . . aimed to select from humanity some chosen spirits who, saved from the common lot of a degraded race, should be the basis of a new commonwealth of the skies . . . then men's interest and God's must be in the few and in the effective methods by which they are to be—as we call it—*saved.*

If the mission of Jesus . . . seeks to upbuild upon the earth an institution which shall represent him to men, conserve his truth, and stand as does a fortress the embodiment of war, or as a capitol the emblem of government, or as a schoolhouse the symbol of education,

[19] "Tent Work," *The Christian City,* August, 1899.
[20] *The Christian City,* March, 1906.

or as a cathedral the expression of the religious idea; if he concentrates his purpose upon the Church and invites men to rear it for what it expresses and for what it embodies, and to bring into it other men, that the Church may become more and more dominant and glorious as the one spiritual institution upon earth—then upon the Church, as such, of whatever name or description it may be, it behooves us to center our affection and our effort, and our mission to men will be defined by their relation to the Divine Institution.

If, however, the mission of Jesus be a mission to humanity; if he came to establish a Kingdom of God—that is, the reign of God in human hearts and so in human life and institutions; if that reign of God be not relegated to some far-distant, perfect future, but if it *is coming* constantly in this imperfect near-by present; if salvation mean not simply the "escape of a soul," not only an individual conversion, but the reclamation, the calling back, of all the wandering children of God whose redemption Christ has purchased by his death, and whose mastery of life he has made possible by his own eternal conquest; if the revelation of John be a disclosure of the triumph of the gospel upon the earth as well as of the victory of individual spirits in the skies; if the ideal of social righteousness expressed in the Old Testament Scriptures and reasserted in the New be not intended as an *ignis fatuus* to delude a race "bemired and benighted in the bog," but as the revelation of a realm where the instinct for justice shall become the law of life, and the struggle for peace shall be crowned with the victory of harmony complete—then must we who would represent Jesus in the world gird ourselves for a greater effort than the Christian Church, through all the heroic centuries, has yet asked his followers to undertake.[21]

[21] "The City and the Kingdom," pp. 298-300; cf. "The Institutional Church," *The Christian City*, March, 1908, pp. 118-19.

The Anniversary Hymn

O God of every waiting land,
We honor here a cherished name;
The touch of Thy almighty hand
His life has kindled to a flame;
It burns within a thousand shrines,
As down the century it shines.

Here in its radiance once again
The challenge of his faith we hear—
His sacrifice, his scorn of pain,
His mastery of doubt and fear,
His ardent zeal to tell abroad
The grace of Christ, the love of God.

O God, to whom a thousand years
Are but a day, grant us the power
That stirred his heart and quelled his fears;
That helped him at the crucial hour,
In pain and obloquy and loss,
To show the glory of the Cross.

For us his narrow stretch of shore
Has widened to a hundred lands;
The isles are waiting evermore,
Strange peoples plead with eager hands,
And ceaselessly the cry is heard
For Thee who art the living Word.

As now a restless age appears,
Help us to show the way to Thee;
Thy triumphs through a hundred years
Are pledges of fresh victory.
O Christ, Thy halting Church inspire
With life and love, with faith—with fire.

Centennial of the sailing of
Melville B. Cox to Africa
1932

14

"Down the Century It Shines"

My time, my powers I give to Thee;
My inmost soul 'tis Thine to move;
I wait for Thy eternity
I wait in peace, in praise, in love.

When Frank Mason North retired from full-time appointment at the age of seventy-three and became secretary counsel of the Board of Foreign Missions, he had enough new leisure to keep a record of his otherwise almost unabated activities. During the month of June, 1924, he listed the following meetings attended, in addition to continuing responsibilities in the Board:

Committee on Mercy and Relief
Commission on International Justice and Goodwill, Federal Council of Churches
Board of Managers, American Bible Society
Committee on Preservation of Sacred Places in the Holy Land (Mott, Macfarland, Haven, McDowell, etc.), Federal Council of Churches
Foreign Missions Conference of North America (North served as chairman in 1916 and again in 1925)
Board of Trustees, Nanking University (2-8 p.m.)
Committee on Reference and Counsel, International Missionary Council (2 days)
Commission on World Peace, Methodist General Conference
Nexus, a joint committee of the Federal Council and the World Alliance for International Friendship through the Churches (Robert E. Speer, chairman)

271

Executive Committee, West China Union University
Committee on Goodwill Between Christians and Jews, Federal
Council of Churches
Committee on Relations with Eastern Churches, Federal Council
of Churches (North presiding in the absence of Bishop Brent)
Special Committee on the Scope and Program of the International
Missionary Council and its Committee on Reference and Counsel
American Members of the International Missionary Council (to
request establishment of an office in the U.S.A.; Mott, chairman)
Committee on Policy, Federal Council of Churches
Commission on World Peace, Methodist General Conference[1]

Quite obviously, Frank Mason North remained far more active
than most men of his age. Within the Methodist Board missionaries and staff members still came to him with their problems,
and this may well have produced irritation and jealousy on the
part of his successors. Nevertheless, Ralph Diffendorfer and John
Edwards acknowledged graciously in their first annual report that
North's "daily counsel and unwearied labor have been a source of
strength and inspiration to your new Secretaries." [2]

In the "retired" relationship North was assigned a threefold
task: (1) to serve in an "advisory capacity in all matters of policy
and administration," (2) to represent the Board on international
and interdenominational missionary organizations, and (3) to
prepare a comprehensive history of the first hundred years of
Methodist Episcopal foreign missions. From the first role "he
gradually withdrew as he knew Diff didn't like it." [3] However,
as late as 1929 he sent to Diffendorfer a memorandum on the
"Aim of Mission" which had been drafted largely by John R. Mott
and adopted by the General Conference of 1928. Should the stress
be placed on indigenous (and self-sufficient) churches or on
foreign missions, on "the science of building the church" or "the
art of saving a soul"? North asked, reaffirming his conviction that
"essentially Methodism in its method is missionary." [4]

As the list of committee meetings in June, 1924, proves, North

[1] Memorandum on Outside Activities, June, 1924 (Board of Missions files).
[2] Annual Report, Board of Foreign Missions, Methodist Episcopal Church, 1924, p. 8.
[3] Thomas Donohugh, letter to the author, July 21, 1958, p. 2.
[4] June 2, 1929 (#107, Board of Mission files).

272

carried the second burden faithfully. At the end of the 1924-28 quadrennium, preparing to step into a more nearly *emeritus* position, he drew up a record of the organizations from which he should withdraw.[5] The first category consisted of appointments made by the Methodist Board of Foreign Missions:

Board of Trustees, Yenching University (China)
Board of Founders, Nanking Theological Seminary (China)
Managing Committee, Ginling College (China)
Board of Governors, West China Union University
Board of Trustees, Shanghai American School (China)
Board of Directors, Union Theological Seminary (Philippines)
Joint Committee on Work in Syria
Newman Trust, School of Missions, Jerusalem
Board of Trustees, Clifton Springs Sanatarium
Cooperative Committee of Christian Education in Korea (reappointed by Dr. Diffendorfer to 1934)

In the next group were those boards and agencies which had themselves directly elected North, but from which he felt he should resign as he left the Methodist Board:

International Missionary Council
Committee of Reference and Counsel, Foreign Missions Conference of North America (and various sub-committees)
Executive Committee, Peking Union Medical College (China)
Board of Trustees, North China Union Language School
Committee on Christian Headquarters in Tokyo (Japan)
Christian Literature Society for Moslems
Joint Committee of Trustees, Isabella Thoburn College (India)
Cooperative Committee, Women's Christian College of Tokyo (Japan)
Permanent Committee on Christian Education in China

Five other organizations he retained on his active list, presumably because he had had long personal connection with them, antedating his service in the Board of Foreign Missions: the Federal Council of Churches, the American Bible Society (of which his son was by this time general secretary), the Evangelical Alliance, Near East Relief, and the American and Foreign Christian Union.

[5] Memorandum on Offices Held, August 6, 1928 (Board of Missions files).

Only then, in 1928, did North find time to begin in earnest on the third task, the historical research, and then the sheer bulk of material apparently staggered him. If an opening chapter was completed, the manuscript has been incorporated into the work of subsequent historians, but various notes survive along with a detailed general scheme for *"The Missionary Idea in Methodism:* a comprehensive study of missionary motive and expression in the movement called Methodism, involving the story of its origin, progress and results." [6] North's proposed outline included the following areas:

(1) the relation of the missionary movement to the Evangelical Revival of the 18th century;

(2) "essential beliefs and experiences . . . at the heart of it, with special emphasis upon the meaning for the individual of the experience of religion, and of the obligation to get the message of good will —the good news—to the last man in the world";

(3) a general interpretation of the movement developed in the 18th and 19th centuries;

(4) the place of the distinctive Methodist movement in the group of organized missionary units;

(5) treatment of each branch of Methodism—British and American, Methodist Episcopal Church, South, etc.—as units in the total missionary enterprise;

(6) a beginning with home missions.

The retired secretary had equally clear aims about the style of this major undertaking. The approach, he said, should be "not that of an annalist but that of a narrator . . . not only what [events] are but what they mean. . . . Individuals should be not figures but persons. . . . The weaving of the pattern should draw the attention away from the rattle of the loom."

"Here is the material for a great Epic," North continued, an epic in which "the inner life of missionaries belongs," yet which would deal also with the "desires of vast peoples . . . the problems of international diplomacy." Nor can it afford to neglect "missionary progress in the home church." Although North's proposed chronology has been revised, the general scheme has been followed

[6] Miscellaneous manuscripts (History of Methodist Missions).

in the first three volumes already published.[7] Even here, with comparatively little definite accomplishment, Frank Mason North has left his imprint—and his dream—on the life of Methodist missions for decades to come. This may be true simply because he gave himself so completely to any cause which he believed to be of God.

Here is my testimony. There were days when I shared in the fear sometimes expressed by others, that our church and its missionary agencies may be at work in too many fields. Recently I have studied the men, the measures, the motives, the methods by which Methodism has come to occupy the lands of the world. I am convinced that it is not of man's choosing but that it is God's will.[8]

Still another activity to which he devoted time and energy in his final years was teaching. From his "first" retirement in 1924 until his death in 1935, North lectured on "The Missionary Idea in Origin, Principle and Action" at Drew Theological Seminary, the school which his father had helped inaugurate in 1867, and where he himself had helped establish a College of Missions. In addition, North spent a great deal of time in the University library and "every now and then emerged from its alcoves and crypts with nuggets of Methodist biography, history, or psalmody of whose existence no one dreamed. This love of exploration possessed him up to the last week of his life, and among his papers he left notes of discoveries as yet unannounced."[9] Two years earlier his faculty colleagues had expressed their admiration and affection in these terms:

Though we love him truly for what he has done for us, his works; though we sincerely admire him for the choice and undying records of what he has written for us and for all men in his words; we, nevertheless, base our profoundest appreciation of his personality upon what we discern to be his character. What he is, far exceeds what he has ever said or can ever do.[10]

[7] Wade Crawford Barclay, ed., *History of Methodist Missions*, Vols. I, II, III (New York: Board of Missions and Church Extensions, 1949-57).

[8] "The Foreign Mission of the Methodist Episcopal Church," undated manuscript (Drew Library archives).

[9] "Resolution in Appreciation of Dr. Frank Mason North," *Drew Gateway*, April, 1936, pp. 2-4.

[10] *Drew Gateway*, January, 1934.

Certainly his close association with many facets of Drew University, while he lived close to the campus for twenty years, both demonstrated and contributed to his ever-youthful spirit.

One of the clearest proofs of this forward-looking perspective lay in his loyal though often critical support of the Methodist Federation for Social Service. Before North died, the Federation had already come under sharp attack for some of its radical stands. Bishop Welch, the first president (1907-12), resigned in the early 1930's because "our original idea was that the Federation should be a common meeting ground of varying ideas. . . . It became later a partisan organization. Clearly Ward was the formative man in that." [11] Harry F. Ward, with an integrity for which many of his critics fail to give him credit, confirmed this account. "In a sense Welch was quite right," he agreed, about the Federation abandoning an impartial, moderate role. "But here was the breakdown of the whole economic order. We were in a situation of catastrophe. It was a crisis. . . . We were saying what was wrong ethically, not technically, with the economic order" —and with war.[12]

Frank Mason North disagreed vigorously with many of the Federation's stands, but he did not withdraw. According to Ward, North was "always an easy man and a good man to work with . . . always open to new proposals, and his counsel was always wise." However, he was not very active at the time these controversial decisions were being made in the early 1930's, though he remained a member of the Executive Committee until his death. To charges of procommunism Ward declared: "We never discussed Soviet Russia in the Federation. That was not our purpose." But he adds this tribute to his senior colleague: "North would have decided purely on the ground of whether it was tactically wise or not. He wouldn't have let anything the Russian government has done or might do remove his sympathy with the Russian people as such."

As Ward understood, North in many such controversial issues

[11] Personal interview, January 21, 1958.
[12] Personal interview, January 23, 1958.

stood not on precedent but on principle. If he seemed a cautious moderate from some perspectives, Harry Ward, still appreciative of their association, characterized him as "not more conservative. I would label him a progressive liberal." [13] To Frederick B. Newell "he probably had the finest social concepts of any man in his age." [14] Lynn Harold Hough, long the dean of Drew Theological Seminary, recalled many conversations with North on the commuters' train from Madison, New Jersey. "He was a strict believer in the actual application of Christian principles," Hough observed, "and perhaps watched with some anxiety the more extreme utterances and actions of some fiery young social prophets. By his support of social positions he gave a certain dignity to a cause which was at that time more or less fighting its way." [15]

Of paramount importance, however, North's opposition to specific policies did not affect his attitude toward persons or toward long-range goals. For example, at one meeting of the Federal Council's Commission on the Church and Social Service, with which North and Ward had been associated from its beginning, the younger man had become disgusted with the conservatism of certain denominational groups and the hesitancy of some "elder statesmen." "After all, this isn't a kindergarten we are organizing," he exploded. Later he encountered Frank Mason North and apologized for his outburst. "Oh, no," North reassured him, "it was good for them. It was good for all of us. Don't you worry about that." [16]

Perhaps because of his paternal role, it was through the Federal Council of Churches that North found the most satisfying expression of his own social commitment. At his memorial service Worth M. Tippy, then executive secretary of the Department of the Church and Social Service, reminded the gathered friends—

that Dr. North was not only a founder of the Federal Council of Churches, but that he was the directing mind in the original organization of its social relations; and also that more than any other one

[13] *Ibid.*
[14] Personal interview, April 1, 1959.
[15] Letter to the author, April 23, 1957.
[16] Harry F. Ward, personal interview, January 23, 1958.

person he was responsible for its emphasis upon the welfare of the masses, its pressure upon industry to follow Christian ideals, its staunch defense of organized labor, and its demand for a more Christian social order.[17]

It was a fitting honor, therefore, that in his eighty-third year Frank Mason North should be invited to serve on the Revision Committee to draft a fresh statement of the Social Ideals of the Churches, and to present that report to the Federal Council in 1932. The new provisions sound, even today, startling and radical to many Christians: (1) Repeal of laws prohibiting the dispensing of birth control information by physicians. (2) Recognition that there may be conditions where divorce is "preferable to the enforced continuation of a relation which has no true basis in mutual respect and attention." (3) "Wider and fairer distribution of wealth." (4) Social insurance against unemployment, sickness, old age, and want (adopted nearly three months before the inauguration of President Franklin D. Roosevelt). (5) "Social control of the economic process." [18]

As the author of such a liberal Social Creed, how did Frank Mason North hold the friendship and trust of so many conservative businessmen? Arthur B. Moss, his close associate in the Board of Foreign Missions, answered simply: "By his own personal integrity and their love of him." [19] Worth Tippy offered substantially the same explanation in more formal language at the memorial service: "Dr. North definitely fused social and spiritual passion. He had technical knowledge of the field in which he worked. He had balance and courage, and he never swerved from his loyalty to Christ. He kept the faith to the end." [20] Barely two weeks after North's death his widow put into a letter her interpretation of her husband's life commitment: "In the Federal Council he found great satisfaction in three lines,—its illustration

[17] *Frank Mason North*, p. 18.
[18] "Social Ideals of the Churches" (New and revised ed., Federal Council of the Churches of Christ in America, 1933) ; cf. *New York Herald Tribune*, December 18, 1932.
[19] Personal interview, October 12, 1958.
[20] *Frank Mason North*, p. 24.

of the practical unity of the churches of Christ in its methods of ministry,—its social service,—and above all, its supreme allegiance to our Lord and Saviour, Jesus Christ." [21]

In this same letter to Worth Tippy Mrs. North dealt with another question which has long fascinated students of the social-gospel era:

You ask concerning his [North's] association with Dr. Gladden and Dr. Rauschenbusch, with the thought perhaps that their influence had led him to an interest in social service. That would not be true. Both they and Dr. Josiah Strong, whom he greatly loved, were his contemporaries or else younger than he, and not at all his tutors in the subject.[22]

Mrs. North was not entirely correct in chronological detail. Washington Gladden (1836-1918) was fourteen years older than North, active in social and ecumenical movements before North emerged from the "obscurity" of the pastorate. Although Gladden, who was working in New York when North entered the ministry, moved to the First Congregational Church, Columbus, Ohio, in 1882, the two men worked closely together on a number of interdenominational projects. Both were among the active organizers of the Open and Institutional Church League in 1894. At the 1905 Inter-Church Conference on Federation, which North as vice-chairman largely planned, Washington Gladden presided over one session and delivered a brief address on the possibilities for social justice coming out of this new federative movement. Moderator of the National Council of Congregational Churches of the United States, he served as the Congregational member of the Business Committee, where North represented the Methodist Episcopal Church. However, Gladden was *not* present at the inaugural meeting of the Federal Council of Churches in 1908.

On the whole, Frank Mason North made very few references to contemporary writers or church leaders, but occasional mention of them reveals his profound and genuine appreciation. For example, North praises Gladden's 1891 book, *Who Wrote the*

[21] Louise M. North, letter to Worth M. Tippy, January 4, 1936.
[22] *Ibid.*

Bible? for presenting "in concrete and condensed form much that is in the thought atmosphere of the present time."

He writes with his usual fearless freedom, and manages to escape the extreme conclusions of radical rationalists without at all making terms with the strict conservatives in biblical criticism. . . . Without endorsing all the author's conclusions, one can admire his strength, his spirit, and his style, and may concede that the consensus of the best thought of the Church agrees upon the results he adopts as probably and in the main correct.[23]

Twenty years later, in an article on "Preparation of Ministers for Social Work," North quotes from Gladden's lecture on "The Church and Modern Life" a sentence which applies very aptly to North himself: "We get our preparation for great work in the work itself." [24]

Josiah Strong (1847-1916) was a much closer friend and associate of North's than either Gladden or Rauschenbusch, in part because they were so nearly the same age. Strong, then pastor of Central Congregational Church in Cincinnati, assumed a leading place in the social-gospel movement with the publication of *Our Country* in 1885. With North and Gladden he helped found the Open and Institutional Church League in 1894. But his outstanding service came as secretary (1886-98) of the Evangelical Alliance, the pioneer ecumenical agency in America. After the publication of *The New Era: or the Coming Kingdom* (1893) and *The Twentieth-Century City* (1898) it became obvious that Strong's social vision had outstripped the somewhat staid Evangelical Alliance, and he resigned in 1898 to organize the American Institute of Social Service.

There were, of course, many Christian leaders of different denominations who involved themselves in the "complex tangle of social and religious needs presented by the modern city. Josiah Strong, Frank Mason North, and Charles Stelzle were perhaps the most widely read among the many who dealt with this situa-

---

[23] Review of Washington Gladden's *Who Wrote the Bible?* (North files).
[24] *Methodist Review*, September, 1911, p. 673.
[25] Hopkins, *The Rise of the Social Gospel*, pp. 249-50.

tion." [25] Similarly, Frederick B. Newell linked these social-gospel spokesmen in a common goal, however disparate their particular functions. "There was born into the world at the time of his [North's] secretaryship to this Society a new vision of the social implications of Christianity. This new idealism came under the leadership of such men as Dr. Walter Rauschenbusch and Dr. Josiah Strong. In this field he was a pioneer." [26]

Like Gladden, Josiah Strong took active part in the Inter-Church Conference on Federation in 1905 but not in the founding of the Federal Council of Churches in 1908. However, he did follow North as chairman of the Council's Commission on the Church and Social Service from 1912 to 1916, and he had already served the Commission as a member of the team (probably appointed by North) to investigate the Bethlehem Steel strike in 1910. Elias B. Sanford says, in his history of the Federal Council of Churches: "Few men in their day and generation, have done more than Josiah Strong, in aiding to bring the Kingdom of God into the thought of men. With prophetic vision, he uttered a message that profoundly influenced the life and ministry of the Church of Christ." [27] That he influenced the life and ministry of Frank Mason North can hardly be doubted.

Walter Rauschenbusch (1861-1918) added a new note of social justice to the pietistic conscience of his predecessors. "Characteristic themes of progress, skepticism of dogma, emphasis on the religious value of socialism and on the economic interpretation of ethics are frequent in his writings." [28] As a pastor in New York's "Hell's Kitchen" from 1886 to 1897, Rauschenbusch felt so acutely the tension between vast social forces and individual compassion that he "literally broke down during his New York pastorate" and "retreated" in 1897 to the Rochester Theological Seminary, where he taught German and later church history.

Arriving in New York in 1892, Frank Mason North must have been well acquainted with the ministry in "Hell's Kitchen." A life-long leader of the Methodist Federation for Social Ser-

[26] *Frank Mason North*, p. 57.

[27] *Origin and History of the Federal Council*, p. 335.

[28] Donovan E. Smucker, "Rauschenbusch After Fifty Years," *The Christian Century*, April 17, 1957, p. 489.

vice credits "the previous prophetic statements of Walter Rauschenbusch" (plus Lincoln Steffens and Upton Sinclair) with having "created an atmosphere where practical Methodists like Worth M. Tippy, Frank Mason North, Harry F. Ward, E. Robb Zaring, and Herbert Welch could organize an opportunity where churchmen could study, inquire and act for changes in our social order in harmony with the spirit of Jesus." [29] It is no mere coincidence, then, that the Federation should have been founded the same year that Rauschenbusch published his first powerful book, *Christianity and the Social Crisis* (1907). But the original draft of that theological milestone had been commenced in 1891, laid aside the next year, and deferred again in 1902, as the author "discovered that he had already moved beyond the positions taken in his first sketch." [30] Thus it is not at all unlikely that among the ideas playing upon his mind were the *Zion's Herald* series on "Socialism and Christianity" and other articles by Frank Mason North. This supposition finds support in "these classic words" from Rauschenbusch himself:

The Methodists are likely to play a very important part in the social awakening of the American churches. . . . They have rarely backed away from a fight when the issue was clearly drawn between Jehovah and Diabolus. . . . Their leaders are fully determined to form their battalions on this new line of battle, and when they march the ground will shake.[31]

From the establishment of the Federal Council of Churches in 1908 Rauschenbusch served on its Commission on the Church and Social Service, of which North was the first chairman.

Such evidences of frequent contact among church leaders in this social-gospel period do not at all imply any priority or single dominant influence. Each of these men came to their central theological convictions with different backgrounds in different places from different traditions. Nevertheless, no historian can escape the "climate of opinion" in both secular and religious

[29] Loyd F. Worley, address on the Fiftieth Anniversay of the Methodist Federation for Social Action, Washington, D. C., July 17, 1957.

[30] Robert D. Cross, Introduction to Walter Rauschenbusch, *Christianity and the Social Crisis* (Torchbook ed.; New York: Harper & Row, 1964), p. xiii.

[31] Quoted, editorial in *Christian Advocate*, April 19, 1928, p. 487.

circles, a climate to which Washington Gladden, Josiah Strong, Frank Mason North, Walter Rauschenbusch, and many, many others had contributed. Worth Tippy's aphorism that "Rauschenbusch was the prophet, North the leader. What a climax of accomplishment!" [32] was true in a sense; it was not the whole truth.

Although North retained his forward vision for eighty-five full years, the advance of age—and history—and the demands of his friends—did occasionally force him to look backward. In his semicentennial address at the New York East Annual Conference of 1923 the still-active minister did reminisce, for a moment, about his "first little church, thirty by forty [feet in size], salary six dollars a week and a donation. The seat of the mourners' bench had fallen apart." Within the next year, he recalled, there were a hundred and fifty conversions in that village and its surrounding countryside, "most of them at that mended mourners' bench." With quiet whimsical humor North confessed that the day after his first sermon the paper from the entire ceiling fell; "it was clearly a new brand of preaching for that church." But his ringing conclusion will never be forgotten by the Conference brethren who heard him, for it was truly North's own lifelong creed: "It is a dull task to build churches for building's sake. To build, that in what you build men may find God—though the dust of toil may rest upon you—is one of the high privileges of the Kingdom."

His second valedictory marked the twentieth anniversary of the Federal Council of Churches—though ironically it was one of the very few sessions North missed because of illness. The years have given the churches and the nation, he wrote, "a constantly deepening conviction in the minds of thoughtful men that it [the Council] is an essential element in the religious life of the country and, some would say, of the world." [33] Fittingly, North paid tribute to the ecumenical leaders, the pioneers of world conferences at Lausanne and Stockholm and Jerusalem, the men who held "convictions and hopes concerning the community of

[32] *Frank Mason North*, p. 24.
[33] Untitled appraisal of the Federal Council of Churches on its 20th anniversary, n.d. (North files).

Christian life and the bearing of organization upon the principles of liberty and the ideals of unity." But with typical humility and sensitivity he focused his concern on the "casual observer" in street or pew or school:

Almost instinctively his attitude will be friendly and favorable. For usually if there is anything this casual man dotes on it is the vision of Christian folk working together rather than pulling apart. He is apt to be vague as to the principles involved. Methods and objections give him no worry. He is often quite flippant when any question of what are essentials and what are not essentials, of what may be held in common and what must be held in severality, gives these well-meaning "workers together" trouble. He cannot in the least understand their debates and distinctions. But without doubt from this casualist's standpoint many a man is looking at the Federal Council with quickened interest and possibly with growing hope. . . .

The federative principle is as really in the nature of things as is the principle of unity—both are elemental and ineradicable. In the unity of the atom, we are told, is the interplay of the electrons; the plant grows by the coordinated forces of its spreading roots; the solar system is steadied by the inter-relation of its circling units; the community is a federation of persons, or, if you choose, of families.

In Macfarland's recorded version of this statement, North asserted: "Tested in the world conditions which now prevail, the reasonableness of the Council's basic principles can hardly be doubted. . . . The ruling ideas . . . of those who played a part in the development of the Federal Council may be found in the words most frequently heard in their conferences—words like 'Freedom,' 'Fellowship,' 'Service,' 'Cooperation,' 'Federation.' " [34] "Possibly," the former president challenged his younger associates, "we should now confer no less but actually do more."

Frank Mason North's summation of his missionary principles came not in a formal speech, but in his evaluation of the controversial Laymen's Inquiry of 1932.[35] Out of his own breadth of experience and depth of commitment, North called the report "significant, unique . . . unlike in origin and in method earlier

[34] Quoted by Macfarland, *Christian Unity in the Making*, p. 316.
[35] *Re-Thinking Missions: A Laymen's Inquiry After One Hundred Years* (New York: Harper & Brothers, 1932) .

group studies . . . worthy of appraisal. . . . An Episode, indeed. An Epoch? Not yet! It may be the beginning of an epoch." [36] He pointed out astutely that as the report itself criticized missionaries for placing too much emphasis on doctrine, so the missionaries and other critics were focusing their objections too largely on the opening chapters dealing with Hocking's philosophy of missions. "Jesus Christ is not ignored," he insisted; "he is there, the object of reverence and devotion. But he seems not to be the Christ of these statements. . . . Let these churches not hesitate once more with a new and burning enthusiasm to declare, 'Our message is Jesus Christ.' "

Then the writer addressed himself to seven specific issues, issues with which he had wrestled earnestly during his own tenure as corresponding secretary of the Board of Foreign Missions.

(1) The character and equipment of personnel. North, like many others, considered the "dispraisal" unjust because untrue in spots, and he capitalized his assertion that "THE MISSIONARIES OF OUR CHURCHES RANK NOT ONLY IN SACRIFICIAL DEVOTION BUT IN PERSONALITY, CHARACTER AND EQUIPMENT WITH ANY GROUP WITH WHOM THEY MAY REASONABLY BE COMPARED, EITHER AT HOME OR ABROAD."

(2) The difficult problem of government subsidies for mission institutions.

(3) Standards of education. "We ask for an Oriental spirit and method, but judge by Western standards. . . . Let the appraisal include what has been done [in an average period of forty to forty-five years] as well as what has not been done."

(4) Should we be silent on the relation of evangelism to institutional service?

(5) As to the relation of the gospel to non-Christian religions, North believed with many critics that the report urged "a sort of syncretism."

(6) The principle and process of devolution should be welcomed and hastened.

[36] "The Laymen's Foreign Missionary Inquiry: Report of the Commission of Appraisal—Episode or Epoch?" in *Record of Christian Work*, February, 1933, pp. 65-69.

(7) In movements toward cooperation and union "mission fields have outstripped the church at home," but the plea for unified administration of foreign missions needs very careful study.

In quite a different vein, Frank Mason North maintained his concern for foreign missions—and his capacity for righteous indignation. After listening in his local church to a sermon which lauded missions but gave no opportunity for action, he dashed off a letter to the treasurer of the Board of Foreign Missions pleading for "some simple process by which the stimulus of a good missionary sermon can be made effective in the increase of contributions to the work." "To point out to comfortable people on the shore the sad condition of a number of drowning people in the stream without indicating where there is a lifeboat or where to get a rope—is picturesque but futile," North mourned. And with droll humor he added: "But for the sweet restraint of my pew companion on Sunday morning, I should have delayed the closing services by making a half dozen regrettable remarks! Let me know of anything I *can* do." [37]

As previously noted, Frank Mason North had been restricted in physical activity during college and warned about his frail health when he entered the ministry. He must have enjoyed the irony of being invited, even at the age of forty-eight, to judge an essay contest on "How I Keep My Health." [38] On December 3, 1935, he celebrated his eighty-fifth birthday and looked forward to his golden wedding anniversary twenty days later. On December 12 he wrote his friend, George Sutherland: "I have been housed with a cold for three or four days—including Sunday last. I hope I am emerging." [39] Apparently he felt confident that he had "emerged," for the next day, after shoveling coal and perspiring heavily, he went out in the cold to attend a faculty meeting at Drew. The next day, Saturday, he returned to bed with pneumonia and died quietly on Tuesday afternoon, December 17, 1935.

At the funeral service on December 20 the honorary pallbearers

[37] Letter to George Sutherland, October 18, 1929 (Board of Missions files).
[38] *The Church Economist*, October, 1899, p. 326.
[39] December 12, 1935 (Board of Missions files).

represented such a cross-section of his manifold career that they deserve listing here: Arlo Ayres Brown, president of Drew University; Samuel M. Cavert, executive secretary of the Federal Council of Churches; Ralph Diffendorfer and John Edwards, corresponding secretaries of the Methodist Board of Foreign Missions; Frederick B. Newell, corresponding secretary of the New York City Society; Ralph Wellons of India, Frank Gamewell of China, William Shaw of Korea, missionaries of the Methodist Episcopal Church. There were no eulogies (except Bishop McDowell's lengthy prayer!), but the congregation sang, "Jesus, the Calm That Fills My Breast," and "Where Cross the Crowded Ways of Life." Exactly a month later a memorial service was held in the chapel at 150 Fifth Avenue, headquarters of the New York City Society and the Methodist Board of Foreign Missions.

It is not, therefore, appropriate for the present writer to eulogize or even to summarize the life of this Christian statesman. Frank Mason North has spoken for himself through these pages— spoken of a life and a message and a faith that are in many respects as timely today as fifty years ago. When Charles L. Boynton, principal of the Shanghai American School, sought the counsel of Robert E. Speer and Frank Mason North as two members of the New York Board of Trustees, North—with rare intimacy and fatherly frankness—shared his own experiences of disappointment, defeat, and even "enemies," simply advising Boynton to "fear God and fear no man." [40] To many readers it may seem incredible that this man could speak of disappointments, defeats, or enemies. Such activism, such prominence in the church, such universal esteem, all connote success by any popular standards. Such dedication to Christ's mission in the world, in manifold ways, should be conducive to genuine spiritual satisfaction. And there is no evidence to suggest that he reached his fourscore years and five with any fundamental regrets. "I wait in peace, in praise, in love."

On the other hand, Frank Mason North had borne keen personal sorrow—and borne it with very little outward sign. The death of his second son and his first wife in the same year,

[40] Charles L. Boynton, personal interview, Alhambra, Cal., July 6, 1963.

the fatal accident to his revered elder brother, the gradual wasting of his father and in 1920 of his sister Lila, the death of his eldest son at 38 from tuberculosis—all these brought the intimate experience of grief. We do not know whether North ever wanted to be a bishop, but the highest honor his church could bestow is not an unworthy goal, particularly if it comes within sight unsought. Nor does a sincere willingness to sacrifice position for principle, prestige for mission, necessarily lessen the inner struggle. If North was disappointed at apparent desertion by some of his closest associates at the height of wartime burdens and postwar fatigue, he was probably more hurt by insinuations that he had been responsible for their mistakes.

More crucially, however—and here we tread lightly in the field of speculation—North may have been discouraged by the fading of his fairest dreams. Even the most realistic of social-gospel spokesmen could not escape a sense of defeat at the outbreak of global war and the revelation of man's brutality. North himself had never been a pacifist, but he had declared at the outbreak of the Spanish-American conflict: "The truest patriots will be found among those who are most reluctant to admit the necessity or the propriety of war." [41] Still more deeply he felt the pain of national apathy when the world war ended, the tragedy of his country's refusal to join the League of Nations. At the centennial of Yale Divinity School in 1922 he voiced a strenuous protest "against certain conceptions of the place of America in the centuries and in the world—a conception which prefers self-content to service, that teaches our youth that a broken and blazing world does not greatly concern us." [42]

But isolationism was merely one symptom of a deeper malady, and North's frustrations were indicative of a deeper malaise. For the confident anticipation of a coming Kingdom had been shattered; the postwar world revealed a network of tensions and conflicts and cross-purposes. Even theology—perhaps one should say, particularly theology—was not exempt.

[41] Editorial, *The Christian City*, May, 1898, p. 467.
[42] Yale Divinity School Centennial Address, Center Church, New Haven, Conn., October 24, 1922.

What troubles one is that so few of the men who, as we say, think clearly, think alike. . . . On the one hand there has come a certain rigidity in familiar types of interpreters of the Gospel and of life which is, to say the least, awkward. On the other the stretch of the canvas to cover new facts and phases has developed an elastic liberalism which, frankly, does not always keep the rain out, to stand by my figure.[43]

"The world believes in rightness," North still insisted, but precisely for that reason Asia's condemnation of the "Christian" West for wholesale war was the more painful to accept. "The practicable is not always the wise," he had commented on a policy of missionary administration early in the twentieth century, but now in the postwar period the expedient seemed often to replace the honorable. Such somber notes were rare and usually private; the stirring verses of his final hymns still summoned Christian men to forward vision and to social action. But his triumphant faith had put down deeper roots through storm and stress.

> How poor a life where pathos tells no story,
>   Whose pathways reach no shrine,
> Which, free from suffering, misses too the glory
>   Of sympathies Divine!

One could choose encomiums for Frank Mason North from hundreds of sources. These few are selected more for their diversity—and their clues to his diversity—than for factual detail or panegyric style. But here are glimpses of the man as his contemporaries at different periods saw him.

Editorial "ramblings" in the *Central Christian Advocate* (February 24, 1909) :

Dr. North knows the city as a surgeon knows the body; few men understand the "city brethren" more thoroughly and more sanely—scholar, thinker, lover of literature, art, at home with Browning and Dante and Moquin and Macdowell when the household is asleep, he is by day, through its longest hours, the patient, constructive, stout-

[43] *Ibid.*

hearted head of our attempt to meet the city hydra and not be stung and baffled by her hydra heads.

William V. Kelley in 1924, comparing North to a Corliss engine, the forerunner of modern automation, which had been on display at the Philadelphia World's Fair of 1876:

Stable amid the ebb and flow of conflicting opinions and demands, unperturbed in the *sturm und drang* of tempestuous times, under alternations of success and failure, exultation and disappointment, approval and criticism; his very temperament making for steadiness, calm judgment and rational consistency; a laborious servant of Christ and His Church, diligent, devoted, forever "on the job." [44]

Lynn Harold Hough, dean of the Drew Theological Seminary, at the time of North's death: "In Dr. North's presence you always sensed a personality of large dignity and quiet distinction. All of this was made human by a subtle and flashing sense of humor." [45]

Robert E. Speer, noted Presbyterian counterpart of North in the ecumenical movement and in missionary administration:

For his wisdom in counsel, his serenity of spirit, the clarity and strength of his convictions, his firm sense of duty, his warmth of friendship, his wide expanse of vision, his discernment of things that are afar off, his courtesy and graciousness, his steadfast, gentle patience, his flawless honor and truth, the fulness and maturity of his manhood, and the charm and strength of his character.[46]

Reinhold Niebuhr, whose influential theology in the past forty years was deeply rooted in his own early industrial ministry and in the social gospel: "In regard to the late Frank Mason North, I knew him only as a younger man would know one of the truly great men of the Federal Council. . . . I can only express my sincere admiration for one of the most responsible and creative leaders of the social gospel movement." [47]

[44] "A Corliss Engine," *Christian Advocate*, June 5, 1924, p. 716.
[45] Quoted in *Madison Eagle*, December 20, 1935.
[46] *Frank Mason North*, p. 15.
[47] Letter to the author, June 4, 1965.

Harry F. Ward, in a personal reminiscence (January 23, 1958) : "North is not an easy man to find out what made him tick. As nearly as I can figure it out, the key is in that hymn of his. He was interested in *people*. He cared about institutions only as they serve people." Frank Mason North spent his life serving institutions: churches, federations, city societies, mission boards. Yet never once did he waver from that fundamental purpose which Ward only half understood: that above the noise of selfish strife, in haunts of wretchedness and need, and among the restless throngs, famished souls of every race and class and creed might hear the Voice and catch the vision of divine tears. The real secret *is* in "that hymn of his," but it is not only people. It is expressed more sharply in the last line of North's last published poem: "The love of Christ, His life, His power."

Frederick B. Newell, in personal letters to Mrs. North and to their son Eric (December 18, 1935) :

Never have I seen in any man more of the dignity and charm, more of the gentle spirit of Christ, more of the deep humility which is the one essential trait of greatness, and more of the profound love of all mankind. . . .

So many times I have picked up these literary treasures and wondered how he had time to express so graciously and carefully the spirit of Christian missions which abounds through them all. . . . Our eyes are taken off the "crossings of the crowded ways" by the insistent demand of our material problems. This is something your father never allowed to come into his life. . . . To live to those years and at the end have a spirit undimmed, a poise and calmness undisturbed, a vision of social justice undiminished, and the likeness of Christ permeating one's being in ever increasing beauty—that is something which comes to our world only occasionally in many generations.

291

The Christmas Conference, 1784

Eternal God, beneath Thy hand
Stretch far the coasts of every land;
The boundless plain, the hidden mine,
The streams, the forests,—all are Thine.
At Thy command the mountains rise;
Thou art the Lord of earth and skies.

Thine are the men of zeal and worth
Who search Thy ways through all Thy earth,
Who face the storm, who brave the sea,
In light and darkness, seeking Thee,
Who flash the message through the air,
That God, our God, is everywhere.

Come we some stalwart souls to praise,
Who found Thee in the far-off days,
Who saw in continents Thy will,
Thy truth in prairie, lake, and hill,
But knew that only in man's heart
The everlasting life Thou art.

Here now these rugged spirits meet
From lonely trail, from city's street,
From Southern heat, from Western breeze,
From kin and comrades overseas;
Their throbbing purposes we feel,
As bowed with them our spirits kneel.

Within their counsels can there be
A world-wide Church's destiny?
Will here they make a valid plan
To search the world for every man?
They did their part! God grant that we
May now fulfil their prophecy!

Today as yesterday the same,
Breathe Thou on us the sacred flame;
The paths our valiant fathers trod,
Help us to find, O Changeless God;
Reveal in us anew this hour
The love of Christ, His life, His power.

Methodist Sesquicentennial
1933

INDEX

295